# THE MAN IN THE BOWLER HAT

# THE MAN IN THE BOWLER HAT

His History and Iconography

by Fred Miller Robinson

The University of North Carolina Press

Chapel Hill and London

Publication of this work was made possible in part through a grant from the Division of Research Programs of the National Endowment for the Humanities, an independent federal agency whose mission is to award grants to support education, scholarship, media programming, libraries, and museums, in order to bring the results of cultural activities to a broad, general public.

97     96     95     94     93     5     4     3     2     1

For Claire, love forever

# CONTENTS

# PREFACE

This book* began with a simple question: why did Samuel Beckett specify that the four major characters of *Waiting for Godot* wear bowler hats? It took me almost all of the book to address the question, and by the time I did (and not entirely to my satisfaction), it was hardly a climactic revelation. Too much else had been turned up, as one question led to another. Granted that Beckett was influenced by Chaplin and Laurel and Hardy, why were these comics wearing bowler hats? Granted that Chaplin and Laurel were trained in music hall, why did all these music-hall comedians wear bowler hats? And so on. I followed the traces of the bowler, as though a wind were blowing it just beyond my reach, into Victorian social history, into the hectic and overcast days of the Industrial Revolution. This is a route I recommend to any Modernist who cares to discover—at an earlier age than mine, I would hope—that the Modern Age did not commence with Cubism or the Great War, much less with Henry Adams's belated alarm over dynamos, the deaths of Yeats's tubercular friends, or Conrad's and Eliot's estuary anxieties.

Nor did the Modern Age begin with the bowler hat. But the bowler was one of its significant accessories, for modern life as for modern dress. From precisely the middle of the nineteenth century it floated like an emblem through the then-incredible changes that industrialism was engendering—but as an emblem of many things, a sign of the times. It became clear to me very early on that I was studying modern life by tracing the meanings of this sign. And more, I was gaining a perspective on modern life that was fair to people's real experience of it.

*Actually, an article ("The History and Significance of the Bowler Hat: Chaplin, Laurel and Hardy, Beckett, Magritte and Kundera," *TriQuarterly* 66 [Spring/Summer 1986]: 173–200) began with this question, and this book grew out of that article.

At the time I was studying Chaplin I rediscovered, in René Magritte's paintings, a figure familiar to me through advertisements and magazine cartoons from the 1950s: the bowler-hatted man. A larger question suggested itself: what did this stiff, formal suit of clothes with his furled umbrella have to do with the vivid and disheveled bowler-hatted comedians? Why bowler hats on both? Here was a machine hat, designed like a bolt cap, on a machine body, the stereotyped modern man, the herd creature we were always in danger of becoming. Yet at the same time here were countless comics, with all the energy of grace and humor and chaos-making, continuously and creatively expressing themselves. The focus of my study became the question of the relation between these figures, a relation, finally, of two visions of modern life. Roughly speaking, one was of people who had lost their selves in the midst of painful change; one was of people who had gained theirs. The former vision was already trite by the end of the nineteenth century but has persisted long enough to be so embedded in modern culture that critics of every political stripe can draw on its stale rhetoric, reviling the soullessness of the age of machines. (Magritte, as I hope to show, does not share this perspective.) The latter vision, in which modern life is seen more positively for what it has brought to the lives of innumerable people, was tainted early on with the rhetoric of Progress and has fallen into disrepute. I have not so much tried to revive it as to re-articulate it in the interests of a richer account. What led to my re-articulating it was a submersion in the particularities of life that the weight of any common object, but especially an item of fashion, can effect.

As more and more bowler-hatted figures turned up in my study, they seemed to express something finely textured and true about *la vie moderne*. Gamekeepers, squires, street vendors, omnibus drivers, counterjumpers, bankers, union men, women on horseback and in cabaret acts, detectives and hanging judges, dictators and bums—all of these seemed more important in their relations than in their variety, however elusive those relations and seemingly random that variety. Perhaps inside the impossibly reserved bowler-hatted man that Magritte painted so obsessively (and knew he resembled) there lurked someone with an overly animated face, the ability to doff and spin his bowler as though it were alive, and a song and dance about his life. And inside him were both a costermonger with bad teeth and shiny trousers, living on his wits, *and* a dandy on the town, living on his. And inside the dandy was a woman on a bicycle, liberated from her crinoline. And so on, each figure animating and informing the other, until the aspirations and limitations of each described a composite modern experience, an experience that had centrally to do with the need—together with the opportunity to realize that need—to step outside traditional boundaries and into the mainstream, not the margins, of social life. In the Modern Age, to break from traditional constraints was to step into the center of something rapid and ongoing, with its own pressures to conform. Modern life was *continuously* novel, which gave it the weight of continuity and the lightness of fashion, both of which qualities are expressed in the semantics of the bowler hat, in the way we can make sense of it as we "read" it.

To supply these semantics, I will proceed through these chapters in a rough chronology, beginning with the bowler's origins, then tracing its fortunes, in England and France and eventually Germany and America, to the present day. Of course bowler hats, like any significant item of fashion, turn up everywhere, and I have a great deal of material (mostly visual; there is very little written on the bowler) that has not found its way into these chapters. I did not want this book to be a compendium or a sort of visual concordance. Nor did I want it to be, strictly, a book of fashion, though that is an honorable genre, difficult to do well. I have wanted this book to be a cultural study of modern life as seen through a sign of its times.

*Waiting for Godot*, it is generally agreed, is a quintessentially modern play. What Beckett's bowler-hat props signal to us is that—however abstract the play's landscape, metaphysical its range, and theological its implications—the experience it describes has a social history, rooted in how mostly ordinary people thought about and presented themselves in very specific and resonant circumstances. (Beckett knew this better than anybody.) The lives of these people, and the representations of them, have been where the bowler hat has taken me, and I am grateful.

# ACKNOWLEDGMENTS

am grateful to my wife, Dr. Claire Nelson, for her insights into sculpture and painting, and for her unflagging support; to professors John J. Clayton of the University of Massachusetts, Amherst, and Willy Shumann of Smith College; and to Suzi Attwood, whose astonishing ability to find articles, postcards, paintings, advertisements, illustrations, and cartoons with bowler hats in them has saved me at least a year of work.

# THE MAN IN THE BOWLER HAT

*It is in the very*
*substance of objects . . .*
*that the true history*
*of men is to be found.*
Roland Barthes,
"The Diseases of Costume"

# INTRODUCTION

## SABINA'S BOWLER

One of the central images in Milan Kundera's novel *The Unbearable Lightness of Being* (1984)—honored in Fred Marcellino's cover design for the Harper & Row edition—is Sabina's old bowler hat. It belonged to her grandfather, "the mayor of a small Bohemian town during the nineteenth century," and is also a "memento" of her father, the sole inheritance from him that she had claimed.[1] This "hard masculine hat" bears the weight of paternal generations, and of public life: Sabina has a photograph of her behatted grandfather on a raised platform with other small-town dignitaries, perhaps "officiating," as she thinks, "at some ceremony, unveiling a monument to a fellow dignitary who had also once worn a bowler hat at public ceremonies" (65). In this way the bowler becomes, for Sabina and for her lover Tomas, an emblem of the nineteenth century, a time "without airplanes and cars" (88), and of the history of a region that would become Czechoslovakia, a history that, especially after the Russian occupation, seems to disappear into public photographs. It has the poignant weight of a respectability and a continuity that has faded into time.

When Sabina and Tomas move (separately) to Zurich after the

cruelty of the Russian invasion that ended the Prague Spring in 1968, she greets him at her hotel, as she has before, wearing only underwear and the bowler:

> She stood there, staring at him, mute and motionless. Tomas did the same. Suddenly he realized how touched he was. He removed the bowler from her head and placed it on the bedside table. Then they made love without saying a word. (28)

Later, in a chapter devoted to Sabina's bowler, Kundera returns to this moment, explaining that both Sabina and Tomas were touched because the hat was now, to them as émigrés, "a recapitulation of time, a hymn to their common past, a sentimental summary of an unsentimental story that was disappearing in the distance" (88). For them, as Czechs who had left their homeland, the bowler was no longer "a prop for [Sabina's] love games with Tomas"; it was "a monument to time past" (87) and receding. In the "lightness" of their exile, the bowler touches them with the familial (paternal, regional, national) pressure of its history. It signifies the ethnic and emotional bond between them. By wearing it as an item of erotic costume, Sabina tries to free it from the weight of its associations, as she has tried to free herself from the pain of Czechoslovakia's history, only to don the power of these associations, this history. Both she and Tomas are aroused by the power of the contrast between her sexual freedom and femininity and the masculine respectability of the hat, between the private and the public. The bowler is at once a "jaunty or sexy" prop (87) and a moving reminder of the past. The contrast at first strikes them as a "joke," but then "suddenly the comic became veiled by excitement. . . . It signified violence against Sabina, against her dignity as a woman," a ridiculing and humiliating of her (86–87). The fact that the significations of the bowler can shift provides for both joking contrasts and mysterious, touching relations: for Tomas, the relation between the "lightness" of Sabina's free life and the weight of their common past, the mix of desire and memory.

Sabina has chosen a life of exile, moving from city to city, lover to lover: "Her drama was a drama not of heaviness but of lightness. What fell to her lot was not the burden but the unbearable lightness of being" (122), unbearable because full of emptiness. This is part of her appeal to Tomas, for whom she represents the "pole" of lightness, as his wife Tereza represents the pole of weight (28). Unlike Sabina, Tomas makes each of his major life decisions in favor of the weight of responsibility to his homeland and to Tereza, and loses everything but these two, ending his and Tereza's life on an obscure farm in the Czech countryside, "a life based on repetition" (298).

Sabina thinks Tomas and his wife died "under the sign of weight. She wants to die under the sign of lightness" and so wants her ashes thrown to the wind (273). Which sign, or pole, is to be more valued? At the outset of his novel, Kundera poses a question about the ambiguity of oppositions in general and of the opposition of weight/lightness in particular. When things recur, they have the weight of responsibility, of judgment—and of possible fulfillment, since "the heavier the burden, the closer our lives come to the earth, the more real and truthful they become." Lightness, on the other hand, frees us from the earth and makes us soar, our movements "as free as they are insignificant." Kundera asks, "What then shall we choose? Weight or lightness?" Parmenides, in ancient times, concluded that "lightness is positive, weight negative" (5). Yet we cannot be so certain; we must struggle with this most ambiguous of oppositions (6).

Although the bowler hat is able to recover the historical past for Sabina and Tomas, history itself is "as light as individual life . . . as whatever will no longer exist tomorrow" (223). The source of the ambiguity of weight/lightness lies in the truth that things pass on in a constant renewal and yet accumulate a remembered history. "Being" is at once unbearably light and unbearably a burden. The bowler hat is a central sign of this necessary ambiguity, a continuous image of the discontinuous, of the weight of a time past that cannot be repeated. Though imbued with the official life of another century, it floats free of it—a shell, a prop, a bit of costume—to be donned in other circumstances, as Sabina dons it with her underwear. When Tereza sees it on Sabina's wig stand, she recognizes it only as "the kind of hat Chaplin wore" (64). She had seen it on the screen, not in family photographs, and so it seems "lighter" to her, jaunty and comic; she asks to take pictures of Sabina nude with it on.

The bowler, then, is rich with its various and (seemingly) contradictory meanings; its iconographic vocabulary is complex. In the most important passage in the novel for our purposes, Kundera addresses this complexity:

> The bowler hat was a motif in the musical composition that was Sabina's life. It returned again and again, each time with a different meaning, and all the meanings flowed through the bowler hat like water through a riverbed. . . . The bowler hat was a bed through which each time Sabina saw another river flow, another *semantic* river: each time the same object would give rise to a new meaning, though all former meanings would resonate (like an echo, like a parade of echoes) together with the new one. (88)

To Franz, another of Sabina's lovers, the bowler hat seems merely "terribly out of place" (85) on her: "What made him feel uncomfortable was its very lack of meaning." Between him and Sabina no "semantic susurrus" flowed (88). But for Tomas and Sabina, the bowler is at once comic, erotic, violent, monumental, sad, nostalgic—ultimately, as mysterious and ambiguous as any vocabulary. And it is so because they have shared a history, as lovers, as members of families, as countrymen.

## THE BOWLER AND MODERN TIMES

**K**undera's reflections articulate the method and purpose of this book. The bowler hat will have its history recovered—or as much of it as I can muster—for the first time. Then it can be a fully resonant object, its "semantic susurrus" can flow through it and through us. This history is both social and iconographic, each of those aspects feeding into the other. We will see that, as new meanings, new ways of reading the bowler hat, arise, its former meanings will resonate with the new. It will accumulate its semantics, but not always in a steady increment: one reading or signification will disappear and resurface, though none will drop out altogether. Kundera's weight/lightness opposition will serve us as well. For the bowler will always have its heavy and light aspects: from its history as a sign of the middle classes to its status as an object of design, an interesting shape seeming to levitate from its contexts. And yet of course it cannot escape those contexts; the burden of its associations will be felt again, and then be lifted before it can be fixed.

In this way the bowler hat is a sign of modern times—that is to say, the times of the emerging and expanding modern middle classes ("modern" and "middle class" have a metonymical relationship in this argument, as they have had in the past 150 years or so). On the one hand, what is "modern" is what is new, and continually renewing itself, like fashion. It was "modern" to take a train to a suburb for a Sunday outing, to ride a bicycle, to mix with other classes in a music hall—and to sport a bowler while doing all these things, and many others. This has been the main sense of "modern" and "modernity" since the full effect of the Industrial Revolution altered everybody's life, introducing change as something rapid and constant. So, on the other hand, the "modern" has its history as well, a history of the middle classes principally, a continuity in the midst of change, a continuity *of* change. These were—and still are—"modern *times*" because the modern middle classes have established themselves. The modern is not merely empty or transient or, as Kundera would say, "light"—in the way that a season's fashions are light (they will not "exist tomorrow"). It is also heavy with an articulated worldview, substantial in its persistence and consistency.

To study the history and the iconography of the bowler hat is to be aware of the
importance of the depth of modernity, its accumulated life and developing consciousness. This is important because it has been under attack, or denied, for so
long: the "modern," like the "bourgeois," has from the middle of the nineteenth
century to the present been vilified, from many different social and political angles, as standardized, mechanized, materialistic, anonymous, empty, and so on.
It has been denied any culture or community (*Gemeinschaft*). The "lightness" of
the modern has been taken as a synecdoche for the modern as a whole: it passes,
while something *else* of more value remains, or struggles to remain, or is mourned
with nostalgia. But the modern has not passed; it has remained, like the bowler
hat that became one of its signal features.

Only the bowler, among all articles of dress from 1850 (the year of its origin)
on, could serve as the "motif" of *The Unbearable Lightness of Being* as well as the
motif of Sabina's life. Only the bowler could be the bed of a semantic river. Only
the bowler has a history complex enough to require such a semantics. As Kundera suggests, it is a memento and emblem of the nineteenth century, worn all
over Europe and America in the latter decades. It comes to us as such in countless advertisements (representing the Gay Nineties or the vaguely "Victorian")
and in photographs of men walking city streets, gathering in crowds (fig. 1), presiding like Sabina's grandfather at official functions, riding on omnibuses and in
automobiles, posing in shooting parties, or mingling at the horse races, and in
photographs of women as well, on horseback or posed for sportive outings. And
the bowler is indeed the hat worn by Chaplin, and Laurel and Hardy, and many
other comedians of music hall and vaudeville and cinema—the most familiar hat
of a comic tradition that, as we shall see, has its roots in the aspirations of the
nineteenth-century lower middle classes. And the bowler is, as Sabina uses it, a
costume prop in our own century, worn to clash with lingerie (as in cabaret theater), with bohemian outfits, with hobo dress—worn by dogs and children—
transferably light but still weighty enough with respectability to be available for
all manner of contrasts.

The semantics of the bowler also go beyond Kundera's uses, beyond Tomas
and Sabina's vocabulary. It is also the symbol of England, the country of its origin, whose imperial power and influence in the nineteenth century would scatter
the bowler over the Western world and Japan, then recover the hat for itself in
this century, in which it often signifies "British." But above all the bowler signifies "modern" or "middle-class" and has done so for so long that all the various

*Fig. 1. Labor demonstration, Boston, c. 1900 (author's collection)*

aspects and fortunes of the middle classes have come to resonate in its hard shell. Sport, leisure, urbanity, suburbanity, finance, respectability, conformity, democracy, aspiration, comedy, capitalism, republicanism, Jews—these constitute the fundamental semantics of the bowler, the middle class, and the "modern" life that the middle class came to define and, in the main, enjoy. Each makes its historical entrance, replacing, qualifying, or altering the others, sometimes dropping out and returning, but always evolving. No other single item of fashion in this period has evolved a semantics complex enough to be regarded as a "sign" of its times.

## THE VESTIMENTARY SIGN

In his essay "The Diseases of Costume" Roland Barthes argues that "in all the great periods of theater, costume had a powerful semantic value; it was not there only to be seen, it was also there to be *read*, it communicated ideas, information, or sentiments."[2] Barthes offers "an ethic of costume" for the theater by insisting on the relation between costume and "what Brecht calls its social *gestus*, the external, material expression of the social conflicts to which it bears witness" (41). Hence "the costume is nothing more than the second term of a relation which must constantly link the work's meaning to its 'exteriority'" (42). Like Kundera, Barthes thinks of costume as a semantic site, linking immediate dramatic uses (Sabina's or Macheath's or Didi's wearing a bowler, e.g.) with a social background. An item of costume is to be *read*, and the "intellectual or cognitive cell of the costume, its basic element, is the sign," or, more specifically, "the vestimentary sign" (46). With as much consistency as I can sustain without being theoretically constrained, I will follow Barthes's suggestion and regard the bowler hat as a semantic sign in which can be read a complex social *gestus*.

By "sign" Barthes means something less conventionally determined than "symbol" in comparison to the richness of what it stands for.[3] A sign is more evolutionary than static; it gathers and modulates rather than codifies its meaning.[4] The bowler hat is a good example of a sign in this sense because what it represents changes over time, retaining older associations while adding to and modifying them. It can be the hat that Sabina's grandfather wore *and* that Chaplin wore *and* that Sabina wore with her lingerie, and so on, each wearing altering how we read the hat and each reading adding to its meaning. The bowler can be conventionally symbolic—as, for example, when it stands for the British—but usually it expresses unfixed and multiple relations to what it signifies; it floats more freely through the history, the weight, of its references.

# THE MAN IN THE OPEN AIR

Elie Nadelman's bronze statue *The Man in the Open Air* (c. 1915; fig. 2), which stands placidly but provocatively near the center of the sculpture garden of the Museum of Modern Art in New York City, has been called a "modern dandy,"[5] and that may be how the Man first strikes us. Clearly his open air is that of the boulevard, and we can see in him some of the qualities that Baudelaire attributed to the dandy: "his lightness of step, his social aplomb, the simplicity in his air of authority . . . his bodily attitudes which are always relaxed but betray an inner energy . . . [his] air of coldness which comes from an unshakeable determination not to be moved."[6] The Man in the Open Air's suave urbanity—the almost insouciant stance, the attenuation of his legs and feet—belongs to the city life we think well of, as we think well of New York City in the confines of the sculpture garden, the high walls of which muffle the midtown roar outside.

The reference to Baudelaire is not a casual one. Nadelman drew horses after Constantin Guys (195), whose sketches Baudelaire celebrated in his essay "The Painter of Modern Life"; he carved a head of Baudelaire;[7] and he reflected Baudelaire's influence when he said, "To interpret the charm of life, often at its most fragile and shifting—by inflexible and solid physical laws—here is the definition of art."[8] This definition owes a good deal to Baudelaire's idea of modernity as articulated in "The Painter of Modern Life": "By 'modernity' I mean the ephemeral, the fugitive, the contingent, the half of art whose other half is the eternal and the immutable."[9] Like Seurat, whom he admired and who influenced him (168), Nadelman wanted to create figures at once recognizably contemporary and archetypically solid, in order to "extract," as Baudelaire felt Guys did, "from fashion whatever element it may contain of poetry within history, to distil the eternal from the transitory."[10] (The tension inherent in this motive is what makes so much of modernism mock-heroic.) For our purposes, the signal aspect of the Man in the Open Air is that, aside from his string tie (a way of pointing out that what seems to be his skin is not), his modernity is solely indicated by his bowler hat. Without these two items of dress, the Man would be a nude without genitals,

*Fig. 2. Elie Nadelman, The Man in the Open Air, c. 1915 (Collection, The Museum of Modern Art, New York. Gift of William S. Paley [by exchange].)*

an abstract allusion to classicism, "iconographically referring to the persona of Hermes—Adonis—Narkissos" (201).

So his bowler hat becomes a sign of the modern. The more we consider what it is about him that suggests this—that is, the effect the bowler has on the figure as a whole—the more complicated the idea of the modern becomes, and the more tense and mysterious the statue. If the Man in the Open Air is the culmination of Nadelman's "turn toward the essence of contemporaneity" (201), with what is he contemporary? If he is a man of his time, what time is that? What times are modern times?

The bowler, a hat which enjoyed the zenith of its popularity in Nadelman's formative years (roughly, 1890–1910), provides us with answers to these questions that take us in two related directions. We may describe them in Kundera's terms, as "lightness" and "weight." To apprehend the convergence of these two directions is to grasp the nature of modern times. So many semantic rivers flow through the bowler that what it signifies (whether "modern" or "middle-class") necessarily has a multiple and evolutionary meaning. The "modern" includes within it, or can be used as a synonym for, the "contemporary" (as Kirstein uses it, for example) in the sense that it means the continuously up-to-date; it means, in effect, "fashion," the realm of the style of the ongoing. At the same time the "modern" has its history and its collective memories, even if they are memories of speedy change. It is a period with its own continuities and iconography—the period of the Industrial Revolution and its various shocks, in which we are still living and wearing bowler hats for costume. Like Seurat's bathers (see Chapter 2) Nadelman's Man alludes not only to an artistic tradition (specifically, classical sculpture) but also to recent social history—in Nadelman's case, a history with the weight of over sixty years.

Elie Nadelman was a Polish Jew who arrived in New York City in 1914, escaping the Great War. He finished *The Man in the Open Air* about a year later, and no doubt sculpted some of the tension of his own emigration into it. The statue carries with it, in its bowler, some of the recent social history of Europe; but it first strikes the observer as being the stylish, lightweight, even comic figure of someone capable of making himself new—a dandy with a "lightness of step." A ballet dancer from the waist down—his "gloved skin," as Kirstein notes, is like a leotard (201)—he could, we imagine, let loose his absurdly tenuous hold on the filiform tree and spring into the air, away from the past and into what may not exist tomorrow.

In this way the Man is the ultimate figure of fashion. There seems to be no distinction between his exterior and interior self because there is no demarcation between his dress and his actual skin. It is as though dress had become essence for him, and vice versa. What is stylish about him has made him stylized, just as his bowler is almost a bowl. His dress fits him like a glove, and he is dashingly at home in it, on display, at large, in the open air.

The statue's bowler hat caps this style, is a "vestimentary sign" of it. In the first place, it seems merely a disc pulled down over his head (Nadelman developed it "from the sketch of an egg-head sliced by a single curve" [201]). Yet it is clearly a hat, for the bowl is too high for the shape of his head. Beyond this, the bowler signifies precisely the modern industrial period (c. 1850–1950) when public spectacle became more important, as public sites in the cities opened up, and when dress became standardized and ready-made enough to create "fashion" as a rapidly and continually changing phenomenon. "Fashion" was one aspect of everything being on the move. The bowler had been, in the nineteenth century, the male (and sometimes female) headgear of motion and mobility, unfixed as to region, occupation, class, or gender. It was as fashionable among costermongers as among gentry, among cabdrivers as among bankers. This mobility is concomitant with the dispersion and expansion of the middle classes, the standard-bearers of the modern. With the exception of its constant use among horsemen and horsewomen, the bowler has, for the reasons noted above, always tended to be an item of costume as well as dress (see Postscript).

In this light(ness), Nadelman's statue seems relatively unburdened of social and historical references; the Man seems someone heady with his own migrancy. Modernity, in its chronic casting off of the past, yearns for a stylization of life, the spirit of the dandy or flâneur, to which Nadelman inclined in his own life (28, 161, 170, 228, 244). One extension of this tendency is for a person to become a mannequin: anonymous, empty of social affect, uni-form, made to be dressed— a display object, the player on the stage of the technological city.[11]

Nadelman was attracted to this dummy ideal. He had a technical interest in "mass-produced statuary" and "wished to promulgate idols of adaptable homogenized blandness, composed from interchangeable parts" (30–31). The Man in the Open Air is a more sporty and individualized example of this type: his body is as smooth and sexless as a mannequin's; his expression is unreadable; his eyes are blind. But like Magritte's mannequin-like bowler-hatted men (see Chapter 5), he is too solidly conceived and too self-possessed to be merely a satiric figure. His stylization is a source of his own pleasure, and of ours in him. There is something comic in him that rescues his identity, which is a way of saying that something contradicts his lightness.

Around the time of *The Man in the Open Air* Nadelman sculpted a Chaplinesque bronze figure thumbing its nose. His love of music hall, variety shows, and revues in Germany at the turn of the century, as well as of American vaudeville later on (161, 219), would naturally have led him to see Chaplin films in New York in 1914, when Chaplin's popularity was rising. What he might have seen in Chaplin, and sculpted in the Man, was a comic contradiction[12] between rootless aspiration and rooted social conditions. To the extent that the statue's bowler is Chaplinesque, it at once expresses his sportive insouciance and grounds him in a bourgeois life which that very "lightness" is attempting to transcend. Chaplin's tramp was regarded as a timelessly romantic character, yet his costume had its sources in the slums of South London, and his aspirations can be regarded as class-bound and class-defined (see Chapter 3). In Nadelman's figure, this contradiction is most immediately expressed in its simultaneous attenuation/solidity, nonchalance/gravity, rakishness/anonymity. Less apparent is the wit in what Kirstein notes in the presence of the tree trunk: such support is traditional for marble copies of metal sculpture, but bronze does not require it (201), so the superfluous allusion suggests the lightness and weight of the sculpture (it needs/does not need an exterior armature). Contributing to this effect is the fact that the "branch" of the trunk "outrageously pierces, rather than sustains, the right arm" (201).

But it is primarily the bowler hat that both lifts the Man from, and anchors him in, a social and historical reality. The very desire for a contemporaneity abstracted from historical processes is itself, of course, historically specific, just as Sabina's desire for a life of lightness is an expression of the heavy national and cultural tragedy from which she has emerged a survivor. Modernity has the weight of its own ironic history. So in signifying modern mobility, both actual and social, the bowler signifies as well the continuity of that mobility. Its design has been hard-headedly functional from the start, and so it expresses, with its unchanging shape (relative to other styles) the unchanging aspects of the middle classes, on which the forces of change had the greatest impact and with which those forces were identified. These aspects are practicality, detachment and objectivity, sobriety, the official and unofficial life of crowds in public urban sites, and so on—in a word, the "weight" of modern, industrial, middle-class history.

It is the unique quality of the bowler—among items of dress—to be at once stylishly sportive and regimentally sober, light and heavy. With it on, the Man in the Open Air can be something of a boulevardier, left hand behind him as though he were making a formal bow, or as if he were jauntily presenting himself to us. And at the same time, he can be encased in the reserve of the respectable, his left hand withholding something from us—a secret, perhaps. This regimental formality gives the Man a vaguely military quality from the waist up: "at ease" stance, broad chest, "tree" as rifle, hat as helmet. The relation of the bowler to helmets has been frequently remarked—often ironically, at the expense of the "armies" of middle-class clerks, and so on. Indeed, as we shall discover in Chapter 1, it was designed as hard-hat protection against tree branches, for gamekeepers on horseback. Later, this utility made it perfect headgear against the grit of industrial cities, at the same time that its streamlined snugness made it useful for riding in the vehicles that supplanted horses.

By the time Nadelman carved *The Man in the Open Air*, the bowler hat had already enough of the weight of its history to make it seem as "traditional" as the classicism of the statue's simplified and solid volumes.[13] But if the bowler anchors this figure in continuities, it also gives it the alacrity of the contemporary. It is no coincidence that Nadelman also sculpted the head of Mercury, "god of roads and travellers," as if he were "a modern boy with a bowler hat" (193, 258n). Indeed, the Man's hat "echoes the type worn by a Pheidian 'Hermes'" (201): headgear for speed, lightness, motion. Nadelman, "saturated in history" yet determined to imagine contemporary man (31), found the perfect hat for this project, a project to signify the "modern" as something solid and unvarying, distilled (in Baudelaire's terms) from "fashion"—the "modern" as the continuously progressive. Like Sabina's bowler, Nadelman's has both the weight and lightness of modern history, a history to which we now turn.

# ORIGINS

## THE IRON HAT

t is more than appropriate, it is significant, that the bowler, which came to be dubbed early on the "iron hat," made its appearance at the pinnacle of the Iron Age. The hat was designed by the hatters James and George Lock of Mr Lock of St. James Street in 1850, one year before the Great Exhibition of the Works of Industry of All Nations in London's Hyde Park, which celebrated the triumphs, most especially Britain's, of the industrial system and heralded the era of industrial society. Like the Crystal Palace, which housed the exhibition, the iron hat was designed with the marriage of style and function in mind: a style of simplicity and symmetry, a function of effective protection against the elements and the necessary standardization of material. If the hat was a good deal less spectacular than the palace, it would easily outlast it (the Crystal Palace was taken down and reerected at Sydenham in 1853, and then destroyed by fire in 1936) and become a better symbol of the democratization that it was hoped the Great Exhibition, and the Machine Age, would usher in, as well as of the *Weltkultur* of which a German visitor felt the palace to be a sanctuary. The new middle classes of the Industrial Revolution would never see their homes or their workplaces transformed into mini-palaces, but they would be able to clap a bowler on their heads as a "badge of office" for a reasonable price. The bowler was a good hat for riding the iron horses;

it simply *went* with the railroads, which were, of course, a democratic mode of transport. In the photography of the nineteenth century, the bowler hat would increasingly take its place in a composition involving iron and steel, trails of smoke and puffs of steam.

Indeed, William Coke II, for whom the bowler was designed, rode not by coach but by a new railway—from his country estate in Norfolk to No. 6 St. James Street—to be fitted for the hat he had commissioned from Lock's. Frank Whitbourn, whose history of Lock's[1] is our primary source for the origin of the bowler, gives a vivid account of Mr. Coke's fitting:

> Yes, certainly it was very snug. But was it hard enough? He would see. He put it on the floor and trod on it. Nobody had ever done that in No. 6 before. But Mr Lock, as we have seen, was incapable of surprise; he withstood the shock. And so did the hat. Mr Coke repeated his experiment. The hat yielded not so much as a quarter size. It remained round, domed, undented. Mr Coke replaced it on his head. It would do. (123)

This trodding has for us an odd symbolism, pointing as it does to the sheer material integrity of the hat, to its functionalism in a hard and masculine environment, and to the practical hard-headedness of its wearers (since, as Alison Lurie notes, "traditionally whatever is worn on the head . . . is a sign of the mind beneath it," an idea put more gracefully and directly by George "Beau" Brummell when he wrote, "We can distinguish by the taste of the hat, the mode of the wearer's mind"[2]).

Mr. Coke, later the Earl of Leicester, had a less symbolic function in mind. He had been equipping his gamekeepers with a high round hat, also designed by Lock's, called a thanet, but found that it became entangled in branches as the mounted gamekeepers rode on their business through the estate. Like his grandfather, Thomas Coke, William was an experimentalist in matters of headgear as well as agriculture. (Thomas grew "hat barley," so-called by his tenants because it was so thick a hat thrown on its surface would rest there,[3] a test of productive grain borne out in *Punch* cartoons of the time.) He felt that the new hat should be, like the thanet, round and hard, so that objects falling from trees would glance off it more easily. But he also felt it should be shorter, "so closely fitting the head that it would remain *in situ* no matter which way up its wearer happened momentarily to be. A gamekeeper's life, when he was in pursuit of poachers, could be eventful" (122). On the latter score, Whitbourn is understating the case: there was a war against poachers on country estates in mid-century, as agricultural laborers came closer and closer to starving.

So the bowler was, from the outset, a riding hat (Americans called it a "derby" because of its popularity, in the late nineteenth century, with the crowd at the Derby horse race at Epsom Downs, near London), which it remains to this day, in however ritual and vestigial a way. It was not even the first round riding hat, the prototype of which the original Mr. Lock had introduced in the late 1780s (122). Domed crowns—"a natural concession to the shape of the head"—had long been an option in headgear, from as early as the fifteenth century. Since, however, a domed crown suggested a bald head, feathers and other ornaments adorned it, or its height was increased, or it was "worn at a rakish angle."[4] With the progress of the Industrial Revolution, these qualms seem to have disappeared; round hats were conformed more and more to the shape of the head, and their brims were narrowed—no doubt to harmonize with changes in dress. Hats are, after all, stressed words in the grammar of costume.

So the Messrs. Lock did not invent so much as modify the round hat. Their new hat had a lower crown and was more snug, a quality achieved by the "conformateur," a strange machine resembling a torture device that, when applied to a customer's head, pricked a card to record its shape and size. It was also harder, mainly because of the invention in 1846 of a machine for making felt, a machine that made possible the creation of many new styles.[5] "Felt" is wool and other animal fibers matted together by heat, moisture, and mechanical pressure. This matting process produces "non-directional" fibers, that is, ones that point in all directions and can be cut any which way without unraveling.[6] The felt used in bowlers is then shellacked, a process involving enough mercury to make some hatters mad. The bowler hat is usually called in the trade a "round-crown hard felt."[7]

The Locks sent their design across the Thames to the hatmakers Thomas and William Bowler, who had a factory in Southwark and were Lock's chief suppliers (122–23). William Bowler produced the prototype, which bears his family's conveniently descriptive name to this day, although Lock's has always insisted on calling it a "Coke" hat. "On the south side of the river, the thing was naturally called a Bowler, because Mr Bowler had made it. In St. James's Street it was equally naturally called a Coke, since Mr Coke had bespoken it" (123). No doubt the commercial rather than the aristocratic appellation won out because of the hat's bowl shape.

Calling it a "Coke" may have been a mistake, since it has long been confused with the "billycock" hat. Indeed, Frank Whitbourn titled his chapter on the bowler "Disposes of a Controversy" in order to clear up what had become, and what even after Whitbourn's disposal (in 1971) has continued to be, a confusion in

terms. In a book as recent as Sarah Levitt's *Victorians Unbuttoned* (1986), it is
said that the bowler was nicknamed billycock *because* it was commissioned by
William Coke,[8] a mistake repeated in reference books like *The Dictionary of
Eponyms* (1985), which lumps the bowler and the billycock together as a hat re-
quested of a hatter named Beaulieu by "Billy" Coke.[9] According to Whitbourn,
a controversy over the bowler's origins and name arose on the centenary of the
bowler in 1950, with arguments in newspapers and on radio and television.
Whitbourn resolves the controversy by clearly distinguishing between the Coke
and the billycock. The latter was the name for two kinds of hats: a cocked hat
worn by upper-class sporting gangs called "bullies" (hence bully-cock) and a
hard Cornish miner's hat, confined to local use, manufactured by a hatmaker
named William Cock for the protection of men working underground (121). So
the practical, protective nature of round, hard hats was always a factor in their
design and use; Whitbourn points out that the bowler was later adopted by ship-
yard foremen as a shield against rivets and bolts (126). The machine parts of the
Age of Iron were to glance off the iron hat, the manufacture and fitting of which
were done by machines.

But the bowler was a more than functional hat; it was stylish. Whitbourn rightly calls it at once "protective and progressive" (127), "progressive" pointing to
its use as a general sporting hat for more vigorous and informal times. This quality of being both practical and stylish would make the bowler increasingly popular among many classes in the nineteenth century. It was probably the most democratic of all hats, and perhaps the most persistently worn, the most lasting, hat
of all time. As Whitbourn proudly notes, "It did not occur to any of the parties of
this arrangement that the artifact they were proposing would one day be in production at the rate of sixty or seventy thousand hats a year" (122). It was a hat,
as they say, "for the times," and those times were to be lengthy.

## THE COUNTRY HAT AND THE CITY HAT

Like much of England at mid-century, the bowler moved from
the country to the city; and like English fashion and manners, as distinct from
English politics, it moved down the social scale. No one, to my knowledge, has
yet traced its early fashion fortunes, and we must proceed with piecemeal information. The key lies in the bowler's being at once a hat as hard and functional as
the industrial environment in which it was worn and a sportive hat for the leisure

activities that were on the increase in this environment. If it was a practical hat, we should understand "practical" as having as much to do with Victorian ease and adaptability as with Victorian utility and respectability.

The bowler did not remain solely on the harassed heads of Mr. Coke's gamekeepers for very long, although it is mainly as an occupational hat for horsemen—gamekeepers, hunters, cabmen, et al.—that it appears in *Punch* cartoons during the 1850s (the ugly, low-crowned, plate-brimmed round hats worn by cabmen probably predate the bowler). Country gentlemen themselves would soon wear it for riding and lounging, and continue to do so throughout the century. An 1855 photograph of the sons of the Earl of Suffolk by Nevil Story-Maskelyne (fig. 3) shows the two of them outdoors, the younger son languidly seated, wearing a rather large bowler. His elder brother wears a cloth cap, and both men are dressed carelessly in country tweeds, perhaps ready for or recovering from a sport of some kind, probably riding, since the elder brother was a writer on the subject. Most fashion histories refer to the bowler's early use as an informal hat of the sporting squirearchy. It spread from riding to other sports, as for example "summer informal dress" on a group of cricket players in 1864 and on some members of the Highstead Torquay boarding-school football team in 1864–65.[10] Later it would be worn by aristocracy, gentry, servants, and farmers alike as they posed outside manors or in shooting parties (fig. 4).[11] It would lose its country (or "county") associations slowly.

But the bowler would soon—probably in the 1860s, a decade of great railway expansion—make its move to the cities, with which it would become identified. In this, of course, it followed the fortunes of the nineteenth century; but more particularly, it would follow the general direction described in James Laver's influential theory about the stages of men's dress in the last few centuries:

> A particular combination of coat, waistcoat and trousers begins as sportswear, in the country; then it passes to town, as informal wear, and after being made "smarter," i.e. tighter, it becomes formal town wear. From this it becomes evening dress . . . and finally it becomes servants' wear, perpetually out of date.[12]

The bowler, being a remarkably transportable and adaptable accessory, would spread more rapidly, and along more parallel tracks, than this theory accounts for, being worn by laborers and servants long before it became a classic item of City of London wear. Nevertheless, the development from sportswear to informal and thence to formal city wear does roughly describe the shape of its dress history.

*Fig. 3. Sons of the Earl of Suffolk, c. 1855, photographed by Nevil Story-Maskelyne*
*(from Anthony J. Lambert,* Victorian and Edwardian Country-House Life
*[New York: Holmes & Meier, 1981])*

*Fig. 4. Shooting party, 1866, photographed by Frederick Thurston
(Luton Museum and Art Gallery)*

In the cities the bowler became an item of informal walking dress among the middle classes, and so played a part in their gentrification. With the effects of closure, the reduced significance of land in the national economy, and the reform of the franchise, many of the gentry had moved to the cities, where they began their complex negotiations with the *bonne bourgeoisie* of business managers and manufacturers, negotiations involving the preservation of a social elite achieved through a persistent but always delicate assimilation. The assimilation of landowners and businessmen, which produced the "public" schools, also produced the specifically Victorian ideal of the "gentleman," an ideal that would spread throughout the middle classes. "Gentlemen" would define and influence male dress for a long time. We find them sporting top hats and, increasingly, bowlers on the street and in the clubs. But who and what were they?

The Victorian concept of "gentleman" was a complex one, but it is useful to approach it through Bertrand Russell's blunt suggestion that it "was invented by the aristocracy to keep the middle classes in order"[13]—that is, it imposed on them a style of emulation that helped to maintain a social elite. The very indefiniteness of what constituted a gentleman "in effect gave the arbiters of high society an unpredictable discretionary power to bind and to loose."[14] A gentleman was no longer simply someone of gentle birth, who owned a landed estate, but someone who could aspire to gentility through forms of emulation—in particular, an attention to manners, deportment and dress, a cultivation of style and leisure—to which the middle classes would add their own moral qualities, "embodied in a fairly strict code of what was 'done' and 'not done.'"[15] Gentility was a middle-class substitute for aristocracy. It had not so much to do with social mobility as with social acceptance; as one historian of Victorian Britain has explained, "Nobility and gentry had commanded you to defer to their rank. Gentlemen persuaded you to defer to their quality."[16]

If this was a great burden to the urban middle classes, especially the lower ones—creating, for example, a cult of respectability that made merchants and their well-liveried servants clenched with the effort—it was a burden that nevertheless allowed them to pursue a style influential beyond their numbers, a style we have come to think of as "Victorian." James Laver claims that "if the typical Englishman of the eighteenth century is the country gentleman, the squire; the typical Englishman of the nineteenth century is the solid citizen who has a 'counting house' in the City and who lives in the parlieus of Bayswater or South Kensington, the prosperous merchant."[17] (We are, of course, dealing here with emblems of dominance; in demographic terms, the typical Englishman of all centuries is of the laboring classes.) The squire is a gentleman by birth; the Victorian solid citizen is a "gentleman" by virtue of cultivating gentility to accommodate a prosperity achieved through capital rather than through land.

## BOWLERS AND TOPPERS

In mid-Victorian times this "gentleman" wore a top hat more often than a bowler, though the latter was, like him who wore it, on the increase. A comparison between the two hats is instructive. The "topper," also an English invention, had been worn since the mid-eighteenth century as aristocratic headgear. Like the bowler, it was hard, black, and shellacked (originally made of beaver, it became a silk hat when the American beaver market declined). Like the bowler, it was "passed down the market" and had become common street wear from the 1820s,[18] while at the same time remaining de rigueur wear for the upper classes. Like the bowler, it afforded good protection against the elements peculiar to industrial life: "the steady downpour of grit, smoke and soot."[19]

Unlike the bowler, however, the topper had aspects that would keep it relatively class-bound. Its height alone made it an obvious sign of the "upper" classes and hence a sign of power—becoming almost parodic when worn, say, by a laborer as a hand-me-down with his Sunday best. A remark by a writer in *The Cornhill Magazine* in 1880 bears out J. C. Flügel's claim that hats are phallic symbols[20]: "Nothing better illustrates the absence of the need of rapid movement in our modern form of civilisation than the huge erection of the hat."[21] While it is certainly true, at least in the nineteenth century, that the higher the caste the taller and harder the hat, the association of class with virility should be seen as another desire to reify the distinctions between social classes. Just as the "height" of the upper classes was often noted in relation to the smallness of the masses ("little men") without consideration of the effects of nutrition, so slippages in class—the effects of democracy—were identified with impotence without reference to birthrates. To say that the bowler's being relatively short and hard is a sign of the virility of the rising (!) middle class, is to accede to this nonsense. What can be said without assent to a cultural mythology is that the bowler was a sign of the power of democracy in the latter half of the nineteenth century—an idea that recognizes the symbolism of dress without reifying it in human behavior and physique.

The top hat was also more expensive than the bowler, and so had to be passed down to rather than purchased by the lower orders. And it was deucedly uncomfortable. Ralph Nevill, professional snob and mourner of times past, said of the topper, "The artistic eye has denounced it as being unsightly and scientists have accused it of promoting baldness. On the other hand, it has found defenders to declare that it is the most healthy head-covering ever worn, on account of the cooling atmosphere which it produces above the head in summer and the warm one in the winter."[22] But given all the inventions for ventilating it and the various methods of reducing its weight, it is clear that, as Sarah Levitt notes, the top hat was heavy and sweaty, a "nuisance in crowded omnibuses and railway carriages" and "unmanageable when removed."[23] If it conferred the height and dignity of social standing to its wearer, it did so at some cost in comfort and convenience, a cost that only the upper classes, and those of the lower classes who wished to ape them on Sundays, were willing to pay.

The bowler, by contrast, was cheaper, more stable and snug, and cool or warm as the weather required. It was more progressively stylish—that is, more adaptable to the conditions that industrial life imposed. You could wear it on horseback, on trains, and in omnibuses. Indeed, later in the century it would become official headgear for streetcar conductors, who found its stability useful among jolting crowds.[24] The qualities it shared with the topper made it dignified enough to be worn by gentlemen (though with different clothes, as we shall see), but its peculiar qualities made it casual enough to be more sportively democratic. Nevill, in 1913, regarded the preference of comfort over dignity to be "that inartistic spirit which seems to be inseparable from modern civilisation,"[25] a spirit which had displaced top hats with bowlers and boaters, and there can be no question that the bowler was indeed a "modern" hat, in the Victorian sense of that word. If the spirit of the Victorian era can be summed up as being at once obsessed with regulation and possessed with nervous restlessness—both related aspects of industrial progressivism, of modernism—then the bowler is its most appropriate emblem.

# UTILITARIAN DRESS

Any hat is an exclamatory word in the syntax of dress. As part of country wear, the bowler was worn with lounge suits or jackets, versions of the earlier "sack" coat. Generally made of rough tweed, this loungewear was the prototype of the twentieth-century business suit or sports ensemble. It was made up of a short jacket (rather than a frock coat), trousers (rather than knee breeches and hose), a turned-down shirt collar, and a waistcoat. The lounge suit appeared, along with the bowler, in the 1850s, "as casual undress for country holidays when Edward VII [then Prince of Wales] would wear them out of town" (fig. 5). Exemplifying Laver's theory, it gradually "crept into town, notably among the artists who found the short jacket more convenient to work in than the frock coat, and consequently it spread among the literati and sophisticated."[26] Just so, the "need for a democratic alternative to the top hat had long been felt by artists and intellectuals."[27] The democratizing tendency of this dress would not stop there, as it became popular among the laboring classes: "They wanted to wear suits, even if shoddy, and the short jacket and trousers were the modern version of the hip-length jacket and kneebreeches that they had been wearing since the seventeenth century."[28]

Although frock coats, toppers, and stiff collars would remain formal wear through the nineteenth century[29]—becoming even more de rigueur as their exclusiveness was threatened—their use was largely ceremonial, and by the 1890s it was vital only among the "upper strata."[30] The lounge suit, however, became the dress of convenience for work and play in modern times. The bowler looked

*Fig. 5. Edward and Alexandra,*
*Prince and Princess of Wales,*
*at Sandringham, 1863 (from*
*J. B. Priestley,* The Edwardians
*[London: Heinemann, 1970])*

a bit absurd with a frock coat, which required a tall hat to match its "line." It matched up well, though, with dress that aspired to comfort and was appropriate to a more kinetic style of life. If the top hat, according to our *Cornhill* essayist, illustrated the modern "absence of the need of rapid movement" among certain classes, the "lounge suit and bowler" (a common fashion phrase) illustrated that need among those who worked in the city, rode the railway (and, later, bicycles and automobiles), regulated their increasingly hectic lives by clock time, and pursued leisure as vigorously as they worked. In C. W. Nichols's painting, *On the Beach: A Family on Margate Sands* (1867), the father wears a curled-brim bowler with an informal but stylish lounge jacket. Doubtless he and his family rode to Margate on one of the railways that were making seaside resorts available to the middle and working classes (indeed, that were *creating* such resorts for them) for short jaunts during the new break in the workweek.

The marriage of utility and comfort in nineteenth-century men's dress expresses, of course, middle-class taste as the middle class came into prominence (though not necessarily into power) by its sheer numbers. The middle class dominated the style of the century by its emergence as those who designed the machines and manned the desks and counted the money (the very contact with which signified them as middle-class) and filled the houses and crowded the streets. If, as Edmund Burke wrote to the Duke of Richmond in the previous century, the English noblemen, as "the incarnation of tradition," were "the great oaks that shade a country and perpetuate their benefits from generation to generation," while the commoners crept "along the ground, bellying into melons that are exquisite for size and flavour, but like annual plants perish with their season,"[31] then the bourgeoisie could be said to be those who walked under the shade, watered the trees, and sold the melons. The aristocracy, which maintained its privileges and power, was not so much usurped as visually displaced. It continued to rule, and deference to it—one of the constant and signal facts of English life—found, and finds to this day (as we shall have occasion to note), partial expression in alarmed reactions to middle-class tastes and habits by the middle class itself.

The reaction to the trends in men's dress was, and continues to be, harsh. Laver notes, with more objectivity than most other commentators, that "between 1800 and 1850 a new class emerged, and the dominant flavour was no longer aristocratic but genteel," which gentility had its origins in the God-fearing and king-beheading Puritans. The Victorians "built the black towns, invented black clothes, put on black looks when there was a suspicion that anyone else was enjoying himself, and did their best to imitate the lives and manners of the black Calvinists who had been extinct for two hundred years."[32] In 1865, an anonymous writer in *The Cornhill Magazine* lamented that, even as the English had put most Puritan customs behind them "as a yoke too grievous to be borne," they "have preserved in dress a certain affectation of gravity and monotony in colour, as being still the mark of a well-regulated mind." The result, according to the writer, was the decline of individualism, gaiety, and distinctiveness in costume, motivated by the Puritan desire "that one man should be made to look as plain, sad, and depressed as another."[33] Ralph Nevill, too, blames Puritanism for a "deadly monotony of costume": "Apparently the main object of modern, so-called civilisation, is to assimilate everyone to workers in a factory—their life strictly regulated by rule, their garb all cut on a similar pattern, while everything original or unconventional is sternly repressed."[34] Much later Pearl Binder echoed this criticism when, attacking the "dull anonymity" of men's dress in the 1950s, she pointed disapprovingly to its roots. "The sartorial decline of Western man, which coincided with and was conditioned by the Industrial Revolution," she complained, "accompanies the machines wherever they go. . . . All over the world men of every race and colour have tried to adopt the garb of the machine-owning conqueror, of the successful modern merchant."[35]

Monotonous, uniform, anonymous, mechanistic: such rhetoric has not, of course, been confined to men's dress, but has pervaded every reaction against modern (i.e., urban, industrial) life, from Baudelaire's "fourmillante cité" (ant-seething city), to Eliot's dead crowds flowing over London Bridge, and on to the present day. It is a rhetoric so familiar as to require interrogation, and in this study we will have many occasions to examine it, since the bowler hat is so often clapped on those anonymous, uniform men. For now it is worth noting that a key to the attitude behind this vocabulary of lament lies in the fear that people (in this case, men) *will look like one another.* The alarm is fundamentally over the blurring of class boundaries, the insidious effects of "the growing power of Democracy," which has resulted in masculine dress being "pretty much the same for millionaire as for shopman" in the "sartorial assimilation of all classes."[36] Whereas pre-"modern" class boundaries were so nicely marked by styles in dress "appropriate and distinctive of . . . calling and condition,"[37] the Machine Age has produced its black-clad, mechanized, *replicatable* men, all middle-class and all the inheritors of the Puritan penchant, not so much for repression, one guesses, as for a revolutionary disruption of a social order keyed to monarchy and aristocracy. In this way, the sheer popularity of the increasing convenience, comfort, and utility of men's dress as it developed in the nineteenth century is transformed into a dull orthodoxy in a society in which "the maid desires to be taken for her mistress, the cook for the housekeeper, the valet for his master."[38] The bowler hat easily became the sign of this orthodoxy, or conformity. By 1909, the trade magazine *Tailor and Cutter* cried out that "the Bowler hat is an abomination to the individualist."[39]

While the topper and frock coat (and all the variations thereof) were more exclusive and class-bound than the bowler and lounge suit ensemble, the former were clearly the precursors of the latter in this lamented fashion trend. Even Nevill, who admires the top hat, describes "a long row of men in top-hats and frock coats leaning against the railings of Rotten Row [a fashionable bridle path in Hyde Park]" in the 1880s as looking like "a flock of birds which had settled on a telegraph wire."[40] But the bowler and lounge suit would accelerate the middle-class triumph of uniformity over particularity, class slippage over class hierarchy, industrial and democratic dullness over what we are asked to assume was a feudal gaiety and color, at least for the aristocracy. There is no question that the "unwavering sobriety" of Victorian male dress represented "a unique phase in the history of fashion."[41] The eighteenth-century attention to the "cut" of clothes was replaced by an attention to their "fit,"[42] a distinction that would displace invention with convention and gradually move fashion away from the aristocrat's tailor and dressmaker and hatter to the middle-class shop, and eventually to ready-made clothes.

Yet the subject can be addressed in terms that don't assume or presume alarm at the spread of the middle class (in both directions) at the expense of the maintenance of distinctions of calling and condition. Dress is a sign of ideas and attitudes that can be regarded from within as well as from without. Victorian men did not aspire to dullness and anonymity; they aspired "to comfort and manliness"[43]—"manliness" as it was understood in an increasingly commercial world, which depended "for its survival on a degree of professional integrity, 'the preservation of order and the sanctity of contracts,'" a world that relied on the virtues of dependability, earnestness, and the lack of frivolity and ostentation.[44] Walkley and Foster quote a passage from *Tailor and Cutter* in 1871 that gives us a strong flavor of the times:

> Carelessness and a want of neatness in personage, invariably indicate an entire lack of that methodical exactness so essential to the accomplishment of all pursuits in life, while on the other hand, a display of order and taste is a pledge that these excellent qualities extend to business transactions and manners.[45]

It is, of course, chilling to think that *all* life pursuits were, or should be, characterized by "methodical exactness," and one can hear in the background, and sympathize with, the chorus of outcries against the creeping effects of bourgeois commercialism, of a style of life become a method of life. But method has its own style, sobriety and regularity have their own integrity, and a tendency to comfort, utility and informality has the virtue of eroding feudal distinctions in favor of a relative democratization of work and prosperity. If Victorian men dressed more alike, it was at least partially because more of them were engaged in productive and undemeaning work on the one hand and increased leisure on the other. They wanted useful and adaptable and affordable clothes, and the bowler and lounge suit would triumph for that very reason.

# MODERN GENTLEMEN

In the city, the bowler hat would continue to cross class boundaries as notions of gentility changed. The middle-class citizen in the bowler could be a prosperous merchant, or a less prosperous member of the new administrative and professional classes, or a dandy, or a gent—each concerned, in various ways, with gentility. T. H. Pear describes the Victorian gentleman as someone who bridged the gap between the trade and upper classes, who, wishing to be inconspicuously genteel, dressed like a banker.[46]

We can imagine him as an urban-becoming-suburban London man, working in but no longer living in the City, hence a man who finds himself in the streets a fair amount of the time. He requires clothes that will allow him to cope with "an endless roar of traffic, under an opaque sky and a steady drift of smuts, sending up, according to season, fountains of mud or whirlwinds of dust, straw, and paper"[47]—that is, black and comfortably fitted clothes, and hard headgear. He not only travels the streets, he enjoys the outdoor leisures that burgeoned within the cities. R. H. Mottram imagines him as "in the main, as he always was before or since, an outdoor man, a dim urbanized attempt at a country gentleman, who accepts invitations to shooting parties, attends races and steeple-chases, fishes solemnly at Richmond, sees the Thames regatta rowed at Hammersmith, and cricket played at Lord's (one bowler is worn, and one cap, in a field otherwise surmounted by toppers)."[48] "Fishes solemnly" is rather good: such gentility was always marked by a sensible propriety in all things.

This is one version of our type. Another and less sober one is the dandy, or exquisite, who affects the style of a man of leisure. The original of the dandy, or at least of the English dandy, is thought to be George Brummell (1778–1840), who more than any other single figure of the time altered men's fashion. Brummell eschewed the more colorful and ostentatious eighteenth-century dress of the upper classes in favor of black and white, sober, elegantly well-fitted clothes. He

> established the trouser sooner and more firmly than more undirected public taste was ever likely to have done, and thus performed a great and unintentional service for the new, poor, but obligatorily respectable clerk population of London and the towns. It was a great step toward comparatively sensible if not rational dress in an age still thoroughly horsy, in which fashion otherwise clung to Wellington boots and the correspondingly uncomfortable and useless knee-tight garments.[49]

In other words, despite Brummell's coded and finicky attention to the precise fit and usage of menswear, the net and unintentional effect of his influence was democratic. It eventually spread to town clerks and tradesmen. Brummell preferred broadcloth and linen to velvet and lace, insisted that looser drapery was better than tighter dress (his "first principle of costume"), and believed that simplicity and inconspicuousness were the hallmarks of good taste.[50] It is worth noting that when he said "the severest mortification a gentleman could incur, was to attract observation in the street by his outward appearance,"[51] he pointed to a displacement of men's elegance to the outdoors, to the arena of city life. Such a displacement entailed a redefinition of elegance, one that would inevitably appeal to the variety of men in that arena (clerks among them), for whom simplicity and in-conspicuousness were an attractively available aesthetic, even if their "line" was less than elegant, their cloth not so fine. Those who have railed at the widespread and dark sobriety of men's fashion usually avoid mentioning Brummell, perhaps because they prefer to imagine a decline in elegance under a vaguely Puritan in-fluence rather than a redefinition of it under the influence of an exquisitely prop-er man of Society who devoted himself to a life of pleasure.[52]

Dandies would have disdained the democratic if they gave it any thought at all. But like Brummell, they wished to be gentlemen-about-town, to seem as re-fined and moneyed as a close attention to dress could make them. They were, of course, middle-class, and were much satirized in the comic papers. Mottram lo-cates the London variety of the dandy around "Clubland," the West End "semi-residential associations" in which the rich mingled with the middle class, intel-lectuals, and even criminals.[53] This mix would have appealed to Baudelaire, who, in writing about the work of Constantin Guys in 1859–60, described the French dandy, much influenced by his English counterpart, as emerging in the period of transition between the initial totter of the aristocracy and the rising and, for Baudelaire, lamentably leveling "tide of democracy." Before this tide makes work and money an obsession, the dandy, who is "socially, politically and financially ill at ease," can strike his heroic and déclassé poses as an aspiring aristocrat (and we can glimpse him in sketches by Guys, as a top-hatted man in frock coat and trousers).[54]

A lower-middle-class version of the dandy is the even flashier "gent" (perhaps so-called because he "was rather less than a gentleman"[55]), a type also satirized in *Punch* in the 1840s and 1850s. Albert Smith, who wrote *The Natural History of the Gent* in 1847, described him as evidence of "that constant, wearing strug-gle to appear something more than we in reality are, which now characterizes everybody, both in their public and private phases."[56] The gent, a showy devil from the lower orders,

> earned his living in shops and offices, warehouses and counting houses. He was one of the new breed of wage earners, whose small salaries were yet suf-ficient to provide some luxuries in life, and whose education, though basic, encouraged him to dream of rising beyond his humble position.[57]

Another type of gent is the "swell" or "lion," who will, as we shall see in the next chapter, make his comic appearance on the music-hall stage. It was inevitable that these various aspiring "gentlemen" be made the butts of comedy. Men aspiring beyond their conditions could be laughed at satirically by those interested in keeping the conditions intact and sympathetically by those with similar aspirations.

The point of describing these types of gentlemen is to establish what they have in common and why bowler hats came increasingly to be worn by them as the century entered its latter stages. They were indeed a "new breed" of modern middle-class men who wished at once to imitate the manners and dress of their "betters" (substituting gentility for breeding) and to blur the boundaries of class—a desire, as we have seen, always accompanied by the wringing of hands and the sharpening of satiric quills by those who feared bankers resembling gentry, valets their masters, and clerics everybody else. The bowler hat—at once sporty and staid, fashionable and sensible, novel but not unusual, like the rest of middle-class dress—was adaptable as a sign in some contrast to the situations in which it was worn. It conferred dignity upon the undignified; it made the dignified seem casual. It brought a certain sobriety to leisure activities and a sportiness to more dressy occasions. It expressed a gentility that had become active and energetic while remaining solidly respectable. It was the appropriate emblem of the contrasts of modern life—that is, the life of the anxiously aspiring and leisure-seeking middle class.

# THE WATCHERS OF MODERN LIFE

## FASHION AND TYPE

n roughly the last quarter of the nineteenth century, the bowler hat had already borne enough of the history of its cultural symptoms to have become something of an icon, though a nascent and variable one. A man in a bowler hat in the 1860s would be simply *this* man (a squire on a hunt, a cabdriver) wearing *that* hat (useful enough under conditions of speed). But later on, a man in a bowler hat became a bowler-hatted man. A fashion item—novel, unstable, in the motion of its social history—became part of an image approaching a type. This had much to do, of course, with the sheer popularity of the hat: it was ubiquitous headgear in the late nineteenth and early twentieth centuries. Yet the durability of the bowler had also to do with the durability of the aspiring middle classes. They had staked out their territory in the cities and suburbs; and if this was a landscape of anxiety, it was constant enough to evolve its vindications and pleasures, to become the center of "modern life." If this life was in flux—as it was, almost by definition—it seemed to be durably in flux, and the staid bowler, floating along on the hydra head of this life, was an appropriately unvarying sign of it.

The German sociologist Georg Simmel, who lived during this period, wrote a long and probing essay entitled "Fashion" (1904), in which he argued, among other things, that fashion embodies the conflicts between social adaptation and individual differentiation. It satisfies at once the need for imitation and for personal style, for uniformity and peculiarity. Simmel's argument is a general one, but it is also rooted in the nature of what he calls "these latter days," in which

> fashion exercises such a powerful influence on our consciousness that the great, permanent, unquestionable convictions are continually losing strength, as a consequence of which the transitory and vacillating elements of life acquire more room for the display of their activity. The break with the past, which, for more than a century, civilized mankind has been laboring unceasingly to bring about, makes the consciousness turn more and more to the present.[1]

This "accentuation of the present" makes fashion salient because fashion "always occupies the dividing-line between the past and the future, and consequently conveys a stronger feeling of the present . . . than most other phenomena" (303). Simmel is, in his way, describing *la vie moderne*. But the present, like the middle class for whom the present was so anxious and hopeful, is not merely transitory, fragmented, weightless. It is also, like fashion, a constant. When Simmel says, "The fact that change itself does not change . . . endows each of the objects [of fashion] which it affects with a psychological appearance of duration" (319), he points to the aspect of fashion that gives its ephemeral nature a solidity, a "balancing of destruction and upbuilding" (306). What is built up is the joining of a "set" (310), the "embodiment of a joint spirit" (305) in which even unimportant individuals can feel raised and supported.

It is these unimportant individuals to whom we will now turn. They are, in this period, the bowler-hatted men of the lower middle class. And the bowlers that they wear are at once the signs of the creation and continuation of their novel class and of its nervous lack of definition in the systems of class. They represent a "joint spirit" uncertain of itself. The type of this class is not of the *bonne bourgeoisie* of owners and financiers, negotiating his relations with the aristocracy, but of the *petite bourgeoisie*, marking his social territory as distinct from the lower orders of servants and laborers and negotiating his style of life within this territory. For purposes of dramatic clarity, let us personify this type, designating him as an office clerk and describing him first as a man at leisure, then as a *badaud*, or a man who merely watches things, and finally as a suburban nobody.

# LITTLE PEOPLE AT LARGE

iana deMarly, in her book *Working Dress*, describes the following situation:

> The journeyman engineer Thomas Wright reported in 1867 on the new privilege of Saturday afternoons off work. At 1 p.m. the men would be waiting at the gates of the factory with their shop jackets or their slops rolled up under their arms. At the bell they dashed home for dinner, then spent the afternoon at the public bath houses to wash and change from dirty clothes into the clean ones for next week, donning a fresh pair of moleskin or corduroy trousers, and a clean shirt. They combined with this the top part of their Sunday suit, the black waistcoat and jacket, for Saturday night out at the pub or music hall.[2]

We will have occasion to return to this outfit in our discussion of Charlie Chaplin's costume. Wright does not include the bowler that more than likely would have accompanied it: the most common best hat of the minimally but significantly leisured working man, *l'ouvrier endimanché* (the worker in his Sunday best). As Hugh Cunningham points out apropos of Thomas Hughes's *Tom Brown's School-Days* (1857), "It was the life-style of the gentry which was held up for admiration, a life-style which could reconcile the middle class's urge for social acceptance and its wish not simply to ape the aristocracy"[3]—a reconciliation partly achieved by the donning of a hat identified with but not limited to the upper orders.

Of course Cunningham is describing the middle-class male, not a factory worker, but it is precisely the blurring of these boundaries that created the social landscape of the new class, the *petite bourgeoisie*, a "fragile urban liberal community of local bourgeois, shopkeepers and small employers, and radical artisans,"[4] which emerged after 1848, two years before the bowler was designed. In the very year that Lock's came up with this design, the Factory Act of 1850 guaranteed workers in textile factories a Saturday half-holiday (made up by an extra half hour's work on weekdays), and this minor benison of leisure soon spread to other factories. In 1867, "factory" was defined as including most industrial enterprises, the result being an eventual regularization of the working week and the organization of leisure. By the mid-1860s, real wages had increased and the creation of new leisure facilities was in full swing.[5] Thomas Wright's factory workers had something to do after 1 P.M. on Saturdays, and a few extra pence with which to do it. The pubs and music halls, of course, beckoned—as we shall see in the next chapter—but so did a world of street entertainments, circuses, games, races, seaside resorts, and so on, a world available and reachable because of increased public transport (railroads, omnibuses) and increasing distances between residences and work. Within this world were to be seen, more and more as the century progressed, men in shoddy but clean coats, waistcoats, and bowlers, pursuing their very limited leisure in urban crowds.

The same phenomenon occurred in France. A *petite bourgeoisie* emerged that was distinct from the feudal estates, emancipated from the strict work ethic and respectability of the *bonne bourgeoisie*, and close to the laboring classes in residence, conditions of work, and styles of life.[6] Much of what made the members of this *petite bourgeoisie* thrive had to do with their ability to imitate their betters and to require and appropriate a popular culture of leisure and festivity, in full swing by the 1880s,[7] which put them in touch with a working-class ethos. They were capable, that is, of being both respectable and vulgar, enjoying a public, city life at once of leisure and of the streets. And it is here that we find them: in the streets, at the fairs and parks and velodromes, in the nightclubs and dance halls—commonly wearing bowler hats also worn by those above and below them on the social scale, the boss who gave them their paychecks and the costermongers from whom they bought goods with their hard-earned spare change.

These are the little people (*tres petits gens*), the department store clerks (*commis de magasins*), the draper's assistants (*calicots*)—or members of the *nouvelles couches sociales* (new social strata).[8] They have some money to spend, mobility, and a desire to be entertained, often in a gratifyingly rowdy manner. They are, after all, not people *of* leisure, and so they have to take their leisure in a spirit of uncertain imitation. The art historian T. J. Clark, in his study of Paris in the art of Manet and his followers, regards these little people as the "heroes and heroines" of a "myth of modernity," the myth being the "view that modernity was no longer characterized by a system of classification and control but, rather, by mixture, transgression, and ambiguity in the general conduct of life" (258). I am not sure when modernity was ever "characterized by a system of classification and control," and I will soon discuss in some detail Clark's own anxiety about the transgressions of this system. It is enough to say now that what Clark points to is how novel the presence of the *petite bourgeoisie* is: that is what makes it so "modern," that is why its emergence is for Clark "one of the main circumstances of modernist art" (202) and modern life.

In order to discuss this circumstance, and to regard critically Clark's attitude toward it, let us return to the type of this new class—as he is painted by Georges

Seurat. Clark pays passing attention to two of Seurat's paintings that feature bowler-hatted men, *Bathing at Asnières* (*Une baignade à Asnières*, 1883–84; fig. 6) and *Seated Person: Study for Bathing at Asnières* (*Personnage assis, étude pour Une baignade à Asnières*, 1883; fig. 7). In these we may begin to observe the conflation of social history and iconography in the depiction of the bowler hat.

In both paintings people are at their leisure on an outing, either relaxing by or bathing in the Seine. Asnières is an industrial district on the northwest edge of Paris; in the background are the factories of the suburb of Clichy. Perhaps it is a Sunday outing, and the railroad, or an omnibus, has brought the people here. They may be working-class or lower-middle-class; the point of their dress is to make this distinction uncertain. They are in any case idling on a riverbank near the Pont de Courbevoie, "a public park much frequented by the Parisian lower middle class in their leisure moments,"[9] opposite the Island of Grande Jatte, where one could find a more fashionable crowd (two of whom are being ferried over in the distance). Clark points out that the Seine at this point had been made a smelly sewer by the waste from the factories in the background; we may assume, as he does, that the site is unfashionable (202).

In the study (also known as *Banks of the Seine at Suresnes*), the bowler of the overdressed, respectably middle-class man is the center of the composition. It signals that the man is indeed a *personnage* in a triple sense: as someone important, as someone mediocre, and as a character in a *rôle scénique*. He is aware of the role he plays sitting by the water, his acting out of leisure in unleisurely attire, heavy and out of place. He takes his grave and central place in the mixed idyll, the line of his back and head forming a rough triangle with the pastoral shore and the line of distant factories. If he were sitting straight up, rather than curved intently toward the Seine, he would bifurcate and dominate, or interrupt, the composition; as it is, he is very much part of it. At the same time he directs us away from the natural scene toward the industrial landscape, his black and "iron" hat an appropriate pointer to the factories. His heavy clothing and his face, shadowed by the bowler, are blurred, as if insubstantial. Yet if his displacement has a comic aspect, he is clearly part of the urban world that helps compose the idyll as a whole. He is a city man intent on experiencing the *banlieue* as a nature outing, and one imagines him content to have the factories there, an urban anchorage for his meditation.

Seurat makes his bowler-hatted man stand out in his respectability, but the relative density and darkness with which he is painted are balanced by the trees in the upper left-hand corner. And in the central triangulation, he completes the contrast of landscape and factory, he is *another* bridge between them. If the

*Fig. 6. Georges Seurat,* Bathing at Asnières, *1883–84*
*(The National Gallery, London)*

painting is mildly comic, then irony (the contrast between the *personnage* and the
traditional riverbank idyll) is only one aspect of its comedy; the other is the making of a new relation, the sometimes undiscovered rightness of things as they are
rather than as they should be (a landscape without a factory, a factory without a
landscape, a *petit bourgeois* perched appropriately and reassuringly behind his
counter).

It is interesting to see what Seurat did with this study (one of many) in the
actual *Baignade*. Unlike the dollhouse figures of his later *La Grande Jatte*
(1884–86), the people enjoying the Seine in the *Baignade* seem truly relaxed
and involved. Seurat has replaced the *personnage assis* with a boy seated on the
bank in bathing trunks, and put a bourgeois, with his bowler hat on, in the fore-
ground and off to the side, reclining and watching what two of the boys and a dog
seem to be watching. One of the boys, who might be calling across the river
through his hands, seems to suggest that the others are not so much meditating
on the natural scene as they are intent on something human outside the picture
frame; their *rôles scéniques* are social. The central boy's clothes, in a heap behind
him, are the same as the reclining bourgeois's clothes, except that his hat is
straw, perhaps befitting his youth. The sharp contrast between the black and
white of these clothes and the oranges, greens, and blues of the scene heightens

37
The
Watchers
of Modern
Life

*Fig. 7. Georges Seurat,* Seated Person: Study for Bathing at Asnières, *1883
(The Cleveland Museum of Art, Bequest of Leonard C. Hanna, Jr., 58.51.)*

their displaced formality. Whether kept on or shed, the clothes are out of place; indeed, the heap of them is very much like the reclining figure, in line, color, and formal arrangement, even to the placement of the hats (though the hat on the heap is amusingly upside down). This comic parallel suggests that the bowler-hatted man is like a pile of clothes, and he is—and that he is as bodilessly relaxed as the heap. So there is this air of mildly comic relaxation, of faintly vulgar dishevelment. Our eyes are drawn immediately to the ugly head of the boy, who seems profoundly, even stupidly, relaxed. The bowler-hatted man, just as relaxed and just as awkward-seeming, may be the boy's father. If he were to shed his attire, Seurat seems to suggest, he might well look like an older version of the boy, who looks like a peasant being idle.

As Clark notes, everything—the figures most especially—is *composed*. This is true both compositionally and behaviorally, the one reflecting and defining the other: the idlers compose the scene and are composed by and in it. They unself-consciously observe the water (or what is across the water) in such a way as to suggest, paradoxically, the playing of a conscious role, as city people getting in touch with nature. That is, the comedy cuts both ways: they are at once displaced and profoundly *in* place. Theirs is much more an idyll than that of the *personnage assis*. That is why, I think, Seurat displaced the bowler from the center, and clapped it—still black as coal—on a more relaxed figure, and why he undressed his central figure. They are more embedded in the reality of the scene. They are having *their* idyll, *their* bathing. The point is not that they and their site are unfashionable, but that they are making their own fashion, in view of, and perhaps in the effluence of, smokestack factories that may be considered their proper environment, and to which no one's gaze is drawn.

Seurat's bowler (there is another one in the distance) is here the sign of many things. It is the city hat of the *cohue hebdomadaire*,[10] the once-a-week vulgar press of people from Paris. Its stiff respectability brings with it the world of the bourgeoisie, who are reluctant to remove it, even on a weekend. But the bowler carries its gentry connotations as well, its country sportiness. It bespeaks its wearer, in both paintings, as someone more considerable than the common man he would seem without it, and someone more vulgar than a person used to leisure. But the *Baignade* softens this tension, casts less doubt on the triangulation of elements, lets these people be without failing to observe them as they are.

Clark is not sure what to do with the *Baignade*. It is, for him, an example of a modernist painter's trying to make articulate how people behave in moments of "performing idleness" and to "conceive [these moments] as part of the wider business of laying claim to bourgeoisie" (201), but he cannot account for such business in his brief description of the painting itself or discover much to suggest that "the idyll is awkward as well as dignified" (201). Awkward in relation to what? Seurat's attitude puzzles Clark because the painter gives such dignity and weight to a scene with possibly comic, or in any case unfashionable and vulgar, elements. About *Personnage assis*, he says that Seurat "seems . . . to be feeling for a way to characterize" the situation (157), and he can discover no clearer characterization in the *Baignade* itself. He notes in general that modernist art is at once fascinated by and distant from the *petite bourgeoisie* and its entertainments (202), but he has difficulty analyzing the nature of this ambivalence. At one point he says, "It is presumably one thing to avoid irony and another to attain to blankness, and often in modernist painting it is not clear which description is the appropriate one" (160). But whose lack of clarity is this?

For Clark, as for many social historians, the *embourgeoisement* of public life in the industrial age is a fall from some grace that he can only make vague suggestions about. His is an attitude worth spending some time on because it underlies the creation and reification of the anonymous and mechanical, the "blank," Man in the Bowler Hat. Clark's argument about the social background of modern art is that monopoly capitalism in the nineteenth century had extended to invading and restructuring "whole areas of free time, private life, leisure, and personal expression," marking "a new phase of commodity production—the marketing, the making-into-commodities, of whole areas of social practice which had once been referred to casually as everyday life" (9). Everyday life was now "colonized" in the cities by imperial capital, the most spectacular instance of this being the Hausmannization of Paris, beginning in the 1860s, which remade the city into one place, one "image" to be publicly consumed by those—the bourgeois—who could appropriate and lay claim to it as a "spectacle" (36). From this destabilization of old patterns and the organization of the city "round separate unities of work, residence, and distraction" (235) emerged the *calicots* and *rentiers*, the creatures of the lower middle class, interested in individualism and respectability, in being well-dressed and having—horrors!—opinions (236–37). They took possession of the city as spectacle, in which they could mark out their public identity as a "class," their private lives having atrophied in a "hypertrophy of official diversions" (9).

This is a rough summary, but enough to outline an anxiety that has very much to do with a central aspect of modern life: the blurring and transforming of traditional class boundaries. "Class," Clark affirms, "is a name, I take it, for that complex and determinate place we are given in the social body; it is the name for everything which signifies that a certain history lives us, lends us our individuality" (146). It follows from this comforting idea that the disruptions of class by social mobility deprive us of our personal identities. It is easy, then, to imagine the lower middle class, the emergence of which is central—as Clark persuasively argues—to modern life, as anonymous people: those odd new animals, those "unfixed and inauthentic creatures" (Clark's words), the crowd, the herd, the "clerks, shop assistants, and the like—who were the products, offensively brand-new and ambitious, of the same economic changes ["the growth of large-scale industry and commerce"], and whose instability had nothing to do with the loss of bygone status but, rather, with the inability of the social system to decide what their situation, high or low, might be in the new order of things" (7). Clark is alarmed by the "offensively brand-new" because it eludes, at least temporarily, the decision-making—the demarcations of class and status—of a social system.

This attitude Clark shares with the more reactionary and snobbish commentators in whose company he feels uncomfortable. As he rightly notes, the attitude of other writers critical of Parisians in the countryside was *"They* are all bourgeois, whereas my irony is not"* (153), but the same may be said of Clark's attitude: they are all bourgeois (including the commentators), whereas *my* argument is not. Clark is quick to point out that his Marxism is not "vulgar"—that is, strictly concerned with the brute "stuff of economic life" as the only basis of "social formation" (6)—and we may assume that his distaste for the vulgar carries over into his distress over people of the *nouvelles couches sociales*, with their habits of imitating their betters and losing their "individuality" in the process.

"It is characteristic of our modern times," writes the historian Eugen Weber in his *France, Fin de Siècle*, "that, while privileged and unprivileged subsist, the number of the former grows, that of the latter shrinks apace."[11] This introduces another vantage from which to view much of the social material that Clark covers. Weber is speaking specifically of the effect of bicycles during the Belle Epoque: "the humbler bicycle did more for human comfort—and for modernity" (209) than cars and airplanes because more people, including eventually the working classes, could afford them. (The bicycle was an emblem of progress, mobility, and democratization. Needless to say, the bowler hat became as common a headgear with bicyclists, both men and women, as it was with horsemen and horsewomen and with drivers of early automobiles. The snug, hard bowler had always lent itself to conditions of speed, from the pursuits of Coke's gamekeepers to the various accelerations of modern life—including film montage, as we shall see.)

But the larger issue concerns Weber's willingness to understand the transformations of the modern as an access to small but significant privileges, and not merely an access to anxiety and uncertainty. The principal aid to this understanding is his ability to identify and sympathize with the little people, from peasants to *rentiers* and countinghouse clerks, in their arrangements with modern public life. Weber sententiously deflects the detractors of industrial capitalist civilization—whether bohemians, snobs, reactionary aristocrats, decadents, or Marxists—by noting simply that "the horrors and vulgarities of modernity are felt most keenly by those who, enjoying its comforts, can treat them with contempt" (193).

Take the subject of the destabilization of "social identities," the blurring and crossing of physical and class boundaries that both Clark and Weber would agree are crucial to *la vie moderne*. Clark argues that there was an acting out of "class" in the spectacle of the public realm because the *calicot* had been "allotted no stable place in the established system of social identities; and it was this that led to his peculiar, excessive insistence on class—on class as a matter of forms and proprieties" (237). That last phrase is the telling one. On these margins, class was no longer part of an "established system" and a personal history, no longer a feudal *given* (the implied source of the "authentic" for Clark). Class had to be formed and claimed in the relative lack of "lines of demarcation" (47). The *cali-*

*cot* had to define his class in a system of public signs, fashions, and representations, in a culture of the "popular" produced for his consumption.

Weber describes this culture from another angle. He notes of Paris in the 1890s what Clark remarks of earlier decades:

> Social barriers were breaking down, altered patterns of life were showing the first signs of standardization, human relations became more complicated as they broadened, accelerated change picked away at stabilities. . . . As exclusive society gave way to the mass public, fashion replaced style, distinction replaced originality. . . . "Cultural" activities became an avenue or badge of social promotion. The cult of "culture," so characteristic of modern times, would not have occurred when the upper classes either had it or did not need it, and the lower did not have it (they had their own) and did not care. (151)

Although Weber attends to the negative aspects of these changes, in his last sentence he succinctly provides the full social background so missing in Clark: the modern culture of spectacle, if seen against the more feudal past (when cultures were strictly class-specific), is progressive. Weber notes elsewhere—indeed, it is a theme of his book—that "the mechanisms of modern life," from railroads to bicycles to electricity to manufactured and standardized goods, regarded as so beneficial to progress, were already, by the end of the century, "being traduced" as hellish and destructive (77). Modern life had engendered a widescale attack on itself, which was to become, in our century, the very stuff of modernism. Where Clark, like so many other commentators on modernism, recovers and reaffirms this attack by purging it of its grosser elements (the Goncourt brothers' petulant snobbery, for example), Weber recovers the benefits and advancements of modern life, viewing them, not from a nostalgia for "established systems" and old neighborhoods, but from a more acute awareness of the reactionary aspect of "old wisdom and hoary certainties" (76). He can say, straightforwardly, "While the experience of progress was not an unqualified success, it involved far more than its detractors were (or are) willing to allow" (78), because he is attentive to what was happening in the lives of "ordinary people" from what might be imagined as their own point of view.

What Weber says about the lives of ordinary people in France in the 1880s and 1890s could be said of the English folk in the same period, although England had a more entrenched and influential aristocracy. While for most peasants and laborers life did not change significantly and free time meant unemployment (191), for increasing numbers of the working and middle classes there was greater employment security, a rise in real wages (67), an "availability of goods and services" that turned "the exceptional into the banal" (79), a liberating spread of literacy (78), medical advances and educational opportunities, and, of course, relatively cheap public transport that allowed them to enjoy increased leisure time, to "act out a certain urban ideal where the social order was less rigid, relations were easier, mobility was greater" (179). The new members of the middle class were "aspiring to imitate their betters and share their fun" (190) in a spirit of "democratic homogenization" (231) that would be called anomie and anonymity by those who were (and are) threatened by it.

Clark describes as follows the entertainments produced to fill in the "blank in the life of the lodger":

> It began with the *feuilleton*, the chromolithograph, and the democratization of sport, and soon proceeded to a tropical diversity of forms: drugstores, news agents and tobacconists, football, museums, movies, cheap romantic fiction, lantern-slide lectures on popular science, records, bicycles, the funny pages, condensed books, sweepstakes, swimming pools, *Action Française*. (235)

(This last item in the list is a cheap shot, because while it is true that the lower middle class was given to a sometimes toxic nationalism and supported anti-Semitic organizations,[12] Action Française was the creation of reactionary royalists like Charles Maurras, and militarism and anti-Semitism were supported largely by "those whom the world of modern industry and politics, with its orientation towards individualism and progress, had left behind: aristocrats and notables; clerical conservatives; threatened artisans" [36], and others rallying around various returns to tradition. Weber notes that Jews were identified "with the discomforts of modernity" [131], a subject to which we will turn in Chapter 5.)

Clark's is a familiar list, very much in the tradition of disparaging the vulgarity and mediocrity of the bourgeois. Weber, however, says of the various forms of the entertainment industry that they were "vulgar in the best sense of the term—that is, accessible and attractive to ordinary people—which means they have been dismissed as too vulgar for serious attention" (176).

With this background in mind, we may return to Seurat's bowler-hatted men. Clark would say, taking his "diagnosis" from writers who made fun of these folk, that the blurring of the landscape between town and country is echoed in "a blurring at the edges of the bourgeoisie" (201). In this uncertain landscape, they can enact the uncertainties of their social identities. They are striving to be middle-class by participating in this idyll at Asnières; their activity is an instrument of "class formation" (237); they are taking part in a spectacle to be consumed in a manner that will mark them as distinct from the working class: through their dress, through their self-conscious relaxation and gazing, their very *posing*. Since their class is not stable, not clearly encoded in their individual lives, their "'inside' *cannot* be read from the 'outside'" (255)—they themselves become objects, not self-contained but self-denying, expressionless: creatures of fashion, of modernity. And "what is visible in modern life . . . is not character but class" (258), or "class" as they conceive it, a series of cultural choices that don't inhere in their characters. This is Clark's subtle and muted and carefully *not ironic* critique of the *petite bourgeoisie*, and it amounts, in its implications, to an execration. These bourgeois are, for him, anonymous, unreadable, *incompetent* in their acting and posing as people of leisure.

Take the subject of their dress. Clark only notes it in passing, but elsewhere in his book he remarks on fashion in general. Fashion "is the strongest sign of the [bourgeois] order to come" (169) in Manet's art, for example; fashion is one of the major signs or representations of class when class cannot be assumed. That is why "fashions are still assumed a bit awkwardly and seem not to belong to their wearers" (169). Though he doesn't state the case so bluntly, Clark would agree with Elizabeth Wilson that fashion—that is, "dress in which the key feature is rapid and continual changing of styles"—*is* bourgeois, *is* "modernist irony,"[13] the irony being the discrepancy between what is creative and coherent, and what is wasteful, purposeless, ephemeral. Clark says that the face of the barmaid in Manet's *Bar at the Folies-Bergère* is "the face of fashion": disguised, hidden, expressionless, directed outward, illegible as to class (253)—that is, very much like the idlers in the *Baignade*.

Clark realizes that Seurat is depicting his figures seriously, giving them dignity and composure. To his credit, he does not impose irony on the *Baignade* (though he contrives it in the form of a joke about a possible source in Poussin). Instead, he says that in serious paintings like Seurat's there is "the play of ease and unease, restraint and spontaneity, pleasure and ennui, nature and artifice, fashion and recreation"—a "dialectic" of dignity and absurdity appropriate to these clumsy and novel performances of idleness (201). But is there a synthesis, a vision, in this dialectic, or are we simply left with Clark's uncertainty masked as Seurat's? Why *did* Seurat spend so much time on these bathers—so many studies and at least a year in the painting of the final, monumental canvas?

We can better answer this if we take a different attitude toward the scene depicted. Consider Weber's remarks on dress. His emphasis is on its democratization and homogeneity: "educational and material opportunities would slowly whittle down" the differences between "dress and bearing . . . between classes, between regions, between rural and urban populations" (79). While it was probably not true that, as many complained, masters and servants could not be told apart, "the true change was that differences long taken for granted were perceived as surmountable" and norms of dress and bearing "became more alike, tending toward the superficial similarities of the later twentieth century" (81). Mass production created "ready-made clothes, cheaper and more accessible linen, more and better underwear," opportunities to change "patterns of consumption, aspiration and propriety" caused by education, "domestic service, military service, greater exigencies of the upper class from the lower, greater expectations of the lower classes themselves, and so on" (80). The new department stores "established that clerks could behave and dress like gentlefolk" (81).

That is what Seurat's bowler-hatted men seem to be doing at the riverbank at Asnières. Are they anxiously acting out relaxation and leisure or are they simply enjoying a pleasurable and "truly democratic aesthetic experience"?[14] Is their self-absorbed separation from each other a sign of their posing, their lack of community and collectivity, or an expression of their shared absorption in their private relaxation—or, as Simmel would say, in their "joint spirit"? Is their dressing to imitate their betters and disguise their origins a sign of their anxiety or their liberation? Are they publicly expressionless or rapt with a privacy their kind had not hitherto been able to enjoy? Did Seurat labor over depicting them in order to express a dialectic between their situation (leisure) and themselves (urban working folk) or in order to resolve these tensions by allowing a democratic experience to have all the monumentality and ease and harmony and composure of a traditional painting of the traditionally and truly leisured classes—that is, to describe the timeless in the modern as well as the modern in the timeless? Is Seurat's gaze, finally, as hidden and private as theirs? (Simmel notes that the externality of fashion is "a sort of mask," a way for people to protect and reserve "their innermost soul" through obedience to public standards.[15])

Although it is clear that I lean toward the latter in each of these questions, perhaps it is well to leave them unanswered, as a way of balancing the account. "Experience, our own and that of others," says Weber with candor rare in a historian, "is like the yellow pages: we find what we look for" (235), and I have been looking for ways of uncovering what I take to be the fundamental motive behind all the denigrations and execrations and dismissals of *la vie moderne* and of those who most benefited, materially and otherwise, from the changes that marked it: fear of a lack of differentiation in class. This fear characteristically takes the form of contempt for a mixed crowd. Of such a crowd in Seurat's *La Grande Jatte*,

Clark says, "the bodies and dresses are like replicas of themselves, not quite the real thing" (267), and we are to imagine that the real thing would be a crowd of one class, which could then experience its own traditional collectivity and, presumably, relax and interact. It may be true that Seurat's distanced treatment of these figures implies a critique of how stiffly they negotiate their outing, but Clark's word "real" is troubling: it fills up Seurat's (amused?) objectivity with an essentialism in regard to class that is perhaps more British than French.

Similarly, Clark concludes his important book with a passage from Mallarmé's essay "The Impressionists and Edouard Manet," declaring that its "optimism about art and democracy" is "wrong" (267). In this passage, Mallarmé (hardly, one should add, a complacent extoller of progress) describes the "energetic modern worker[s]" found in Impressionism, a "multitude" of people "hitherto ignored" which "demands to see with its own eyes." Mallarmé honors this crowd as "radical and democratic" and hopes that artists, "new and impersonal men placed directly in communion with the sentiment of their time," will allow nature to reveal itself through the depiction of this multitude (268). It is a remarkably direct political statement, and Clark finds its optimism wrong because such a multitude was *not* radical, nor was the art that depicted it ("Impressionism became very quickly the house style of the haute bourgeoisie"), neither proving "directly useful to the masses as they take over the state" (267).

But Mallarmé is not calling for such a takeover; he confines his political agenda to a hope for universal suffrage. Are such hopes as he expresses wrong, even as predictions, because a revolution has not occurred? It is precisely the "masses" that Clark's argument necessarily avoids, given his subject, but Weber, in his *petite histoire*, does not avoid them; he recognizes the small and insignificant advancements they made. He quotes the Vicomte d'Avenel at the turn of the century:

> Never . . . has the French people been as well off as it is now, and never has it felt more sorry for itself. "Its grievances have grown along with its well-being; as its circumstances improved, they were judged to deteriorate. The character of this century, favored above all others, is to be displeased with itself." It was a fair assessment of a moment's mood, which would become the pervasive spirit of the new century. (77)

It is a spirit, as I have tried to make clear, that Clark and many others of various political and social orientations share. It was to deny a private life, a private *consciousness*, to the crowds of people swarming the urban streets of the nineteenth century. And it was to make of the bowler hats on the heads of so many men in

these crowds symbols of what was left when this denial had been effected: anonymity, conformity, uniformity, standardization, impersonality—in a phrase, all
the stale hells of modernity. To understand what the bowler signifies, a fuller account has to be made, an account its varied history can provide.

## GAWKERS IN CROWDS

Urban crowds in the decades before and after the turn of the
century were a sea of bowler hats. Toppers, boaters, and caps abounded as well,
but the bowler crossed more class lines. Some had low crowns and a wider brim,
while some had very high crowns; most had the curled brims increasingly fashionable in the latter decades; some were fawn-colored or brown or gray—and
they were everywhere. In London they were worn by men doing road repairs,
newshawkers, milkmen, knife grinders, rabbit sellers, and Sherbet and Water
vendors—all manner of working folk who seemed to wear their bowlers as
badges of the city street. Shabby workers sitting on benches outside pubs, pints
in hand, set their bowlers beside them like pets. The men buying from vendors
wore bowlers, men in shoddy black suits with tight shoulders and baggy pants,
the types that Chaplin remembered when he contrived his costume. At times
these men are difficult to distinguish from the workers and vendors; buyers and
sellers blend together, as if intentionally marking out a new class or as if eager
to blur the idea of class in a democracy of the street. More fashionable men,
with stiffer and cleaner collars and a better cut of clothes (larger coats, narrower
trousers), mingle with the others, or more likely with their top-hatted ilk near the
banks of the City, or in carriages (later four-wheeled gigs), or posed in various
public ceremonies. And of course, bowler-hatted cab and open omnibus drivers
guide clusters of bowler-hatted middle-class men through the thronged streets.
At political and labor rallies, in England and America, bowlers bob on the heads
of laborers in their Sunday best as if they were crowd hats, passed out for purposes of solidarity (see fig. 1).

In the many city fairs—which were dying out by the turn of the century but en-
dured longer in Paris than in London[16]—people of all classes, the men a swarm
of bowlers and toppers, gathered under electric lights and fireworks to gamble for
cakes (in the Paris gingerbread fair) and watch various sports. The "Parisian
common man," wrote the visiting Englishman Richard Whiteing, "descends to

his thoroughfare as the millionaire expects to descend to his breakfast-room or his study, with all the appointments fresh from the broom, and shining in their brightness of metal and glass. So, whatever the gloom of the domestic prospect, his street helps him to feel good."[17]

The bowler, then, is the most ubiquitous hat of the "huge multitude [that] has come out to see itself. That is the spectacle; just that and nothing more"; they "glide past like so many figures of the new-fashioned scheme for painless locomotion."[18] Two recurring themes are struck in these passages from Whiteing: that the crowd regards itself as the essential spectacle and that its mobility is a crucial feature of this spectacle. The crowd watches its own mobility, and that mobility is modern: movement into and through a public space not clearly marked out along class boundaries. In this space entertainment is provided cheaply or free. This was a bloodless revolution of sorts for people whose lives had been bounded by domestic and work places, and it was regarded as such at the time, either in celebration or dismay. The dismay comes from the fact that the crowds were gathering without any sense of collective identity apart from being a spectacle. Lacking this identity (and how could they have it, being mixed?), the crowds were often seen as alarmingly anonymous. "Nameless mob! chaos!" cried out Victor Hugo in a poem in 1880.[19] This supposed anonymity is better understood as a response to the crowd's relative likeness of dress and attention, despite its being mixed, than as a reading of its lack of humanity. Hugo goes on to say, "Those one has never seen, those no one knows." It is the suddenly public appearance of those who had before been hidden in their proper squalor, and those who could not be known (or named) because their class was uncertain, that makes the crowd seem chaotic.

In his study of Baudelaire, Walter Benjamin spends a good deal of time on these crowds. He quotes Friedrich Engels's description of the London street scene from *The Condition of the Working-Class in England in 1844* (1848):

One realizes for the first time that these Londoners have been forced to sacrifice the best qualities of their human nature, to bring to pass all the marvels of civilization which crowd their city. . . . The very turmoil of the streets has something repulsive, something against which human nature rebels. The hundreds and thousands of all classes and ranks crowding past each other, are they not all human beings with the same qualities and powers. . . . They crowd by one another as though they had nothing in common, nothing to do with one another. . . . It occurs to no man to honour another with so much as a glance. The brutal indifference, the unfeeling isolation of each in his private interest, becomes the more repellent and offensive, the more these individuals are crowded together, within a limited space.[20]

This description is of course historically early for our purposes, and is of slum crowds, before the leisure industries opened up public spaces. But the attitude is prophetic and firmly in place; it will be echoed later on, and to this day, in the many and various attacks on modern urban and industrial civilization. The *implied* crowds against which these are measured and found "repulsive" are composed, presumably, of the same class and could therefore behave communally. *These* crowds have only their humanity in common, and Engels has to remind himself of their humanity.

Benjamin responds to Engels as follows:

> Next to Engels' clear description, it sounds obscure when Baudelaire writes: "The pleasure of being in a crowd is a mysterious expression of the enjoyment of the multiplication of numbers." But this statement becomes clear if one imagines it not only spoken from a person's viewpoint but also from the viewpoint of a commodity. To be sure, insofar as a person, as labour power, is a commodity, there is no need for him to identify himself as such. The more conscious he becomes of his mode of existence, the mode imposed upon him by the system of production, the more he proletarianizes himself, the more he will be gripped by the chill of the commodity economy and the less he will feel like empathizing with commodities. But things have not reached that point with the class of the petty bourgeoisie to which Baudelaire belonged.[21]

The class bias of this version of Marxism is remarkable. There is, in the first place, nothing obscure about Baudelaire's statement: the crowd enjoys itself as a crowd. But Benjamin can only understand this pleasure as something experienced by people who have not yet recognized their own conditions, who indeed have ceased to be human and have instead become such commodities that they don't even realize it. When they do, they will have become the proletarians they were meant to be, and presumably will gather only in communal protest. It is telling that Engels's "all classes and ranks" have become, for Benjamin, the lower middle class—a synecdoche that permits him his dehumanization of the crowd as commodities. He too has to remind himself that they are human.

T. J. Clark is disturbed by the vulgar crowd's lack of private life, Engels and Benjamin by its lack of public consciousness—but all find it hidden, unreadable. This may have as much to do with the nature of its activity as it does with the dress and demeanor of its people. They strolled, they gathered, they *watched*—each keeping to himself but intent on what others are intent on, like Seurat's bathers. Their watching was a kind of spectator sport, and the sport was the spectacle itself. Such people were called, in France, *badauds* (gapers, gawkers): those so absorbed by what they see that they forget themselves. Benjamin quotes Victor Fournel: "The individuality of the *badaud* disappears. . . . Under the influence of the spectacle which presents itself to him, the *badaud* becomes an impersonal creature; he is no longer a human being, he is part of the public, of the crowd."[22] We are on familiar ground here. Whereas the flâneur was an artistic connoisseur of the city, an observer of its various delights for whom "the joy of watching is triumphant,"[23] the *badaud* simply gawks. Whereas the flâneur is an individualist who observes the crowds, the *badaud* simply loses himself in them, observing something else:

> He was not part of any celebrating community; his pleasure was devoid of the emotional transport and collective uplift that idealistic contemporaries sought in fetes. His activity entailed no human bonds, and it brought no fraternal ties. The badaud escaped the isolation of his room and found contact with a larger social world than workplace or neighborhood, but he remained uninvolved, alone, even among other badauds.[24]

This is the darker version of Whiteing's common man descending from his domestic gloom to a street that made him feel good. It is interesting to note how these cultural stereotypes assume a reality for commentators, as though they had been based on interviews rather than contrived by people with social biases of their own. It is also interesting to speculate how much various writers, Baudelaire included, projected flâneurs as idealized versions of themselves, and *badauds* as vulgar, stupefied herd creatures quite apart from themselves and their own presumed class.

In any case, the *badauds*, as Charles Rearick points out and illustrates, were the uncommitted watchers of modern life. They might watch the Seine flow, or the fishermen fish in it, or construction underway, or street acrobats, or fireworks, or just other people. Their gaze is level and uninvolved. Photographs show many of them with bowlers or caps. Some shoddy, some more fashionable, they gather around a street dentist or a street performer (fig. 8). The latter spectacle is disapproved of by Whiteing, who, observing Parisian onlookers at a wrestling booth, is repelled by the difference between the effort of the performer and the ease of the watchers, who are "open-mouthed"[25]—that is, *badauds*. (But who among us

*Fig. 8. A street dentist at work, Paris, c. 1900 (Musée Carnavalet, Paris)*

would not take pleasure watching skilled performers? Are we required to exert ourselves as well in order to reclaim our humanity?)

A photograph of sightseers on London Bridge near the City (fig. 9) shows a group of what might be called English *badauds* watching the shipping below them. Almost all the men wear bowlers; they are probably City men, of a higher caste than our other creatures of the crowd. The row of bowlers might be out of a painting by Magritte. Or some such scene might have inspired T. S. Eliot to describe, in *The Waste Land* (1922), his version of Baudelaire's "fourmillante cité":

> Unreal City,
> Under the brown fog of a winter dawn,
> A crowd flowed over London Bridge, so many,
> I had not thought death had undone so many.
> Sighs, short and infrequent, were exhaled.[26]

*Fig. 9. Sightseers on London Bridge, c. 1905, photographed by A. Woodley
(B. T. Batsford, Ltd.)*

Eliot's crowd is probably, after all, clerks on their way to the City—no doubt in bowlers (Eliot's preferred headgear) by this time—and the allusions to the *Inferno* in the last line quoted are to the base herd who were neither faithful to nor rebelled against God but to themselves alone were true; and also to the thick-thronged souls in Limbo. Perhaps these are versions of the uncommitted *badauds*, neither sinning nor graced. Perhaps they turn up later in the poem as "the loitering heirs of City directors" who have departed, having "left no addresses": unlocatable people, multiplying and swarming, faceless, unreal. Perhaps Eliot saw himself in them as Baudelaire saw himself in the hideous ghostly men in the city poem ("The Seven Old Men") to which Eliot refers in his notes. In any case, the bowler-hatted Men of the crowd are taking on their image of anonymity and anomie. As representations of Clark's *petite bourgeoisie*, they appear "in many ways to have no class to speak of, to be excluded from the bourgeoisie and the proletariat and yet to thrive on their lack of belonging. They were the *shifters* of class society, the connoisseurs of its edges and waste lands."[27]

**S**eurat's *La Parade* (1887; fig. 10) is a strange and chilling painting, an image of entertainment and festivity frozen in a kind of shared anomie, a wasteland of the circus spirit. It includes one of the earliest images, in art, of the bowler-hatted man as a figure of anonymity, a *badaud*. Indeed, he is reduced to a silhouette, facing away from us, a cutout facing a trio of bowler-hatted musicians, whose blurred faces are no less anonymous. The close relation between crowd and performers, which we shall see is essential to the music hall, is firmly established, not only by the bowlers but by matched profiles, the bizarre shape of the trombonist's hat echoed in a lady's, and so on. What *is* the relation?

A *parade*, in French, is a "free performance which is given on the show-front of a fairground booth to draw the crowd," sometimes concluding with a march to the circus proper.[28] It is a spectacle designed to attract, a display or pastiche of the circus itself, a come-on. Seurat's painting depicts the *parade* of the Cowi Circus, set up in the Place de la Nation.[29] The onlookers, at the bottom, may be mostly observing, or they may be in a line, which in any case is queuing on the far right, on stairs leading, one guesses, to the box office.[30] But in the picture frame this curve leads nowhere, like the diagonal below the trombonist. Instead, the space is foreshortened, flattened, in a series of friezes (gaslamps above, performers in the middle, heads of spectators below), a series of repeated forms imprisoned in a stark system of verticals and horizontals. The gaslamps cast a blurring haze of green, pink, orange, and blue over the scene—a very modern, street light, luridly eye-catching. The whole spectacle is a *parade*, or parry (as in fencing)[31] against the atmosphere, indeed the idea, of festivity. As Roger Fry notes: "These figures have nothing left of the life of the Boulevard Clichy. A magician's wand has made out of momentary poses an eternal monument. That moment of hurried life, of bustle and eagerness, of excitement, anticipation and noise has become transformed into something of more than Egyptian, more than hieratic, solemnity and stillness."[32] Seurat's is a come-on of an odd sort. Something is being exchanged, but what?

T. J. Clark does not mention this painting, but it is easy to imagine how he—and for that matter, Benjamin—might regard it. Clark uses *parades* as a metaphor for Paris in the 1860s, for the illusions and exhibitions it offered to its watchers and strollers (66–67). He would see Seurat's flatness as an uneasy commentary on the life of spectacle. Real and communal festivity, festivity *in depth*, has been replaced by the forms and representations of fun, the crowd merely possessing a commodity that reflects and so helps to define them as leisured and middle-class. *La Parade*, in this view, is truly a pastiche, an imitation of something else more real.

The presence of bowlers would support this reading, as signs of the *embourgeoisement* of entertainment. Bowler-hatted street musicians were not uncommon, in London as well as Paris (see fig. 11). Their hats were signs at once of their uncertain class as musicians/workers/vagrants, of the respectable formality of their performance, and of the life of the street. In *La Parade* they are, like the bowler-hatted man who observes them, replicatable figures: isolated, absorbed, utterly staid (the atmosphere is haziest around the musicians, whose expressions, like everyone else's, are closed off). What is here to entice a crowd except a replication of itself?

Seurat may or may not have read Arthur Rimbaud's prose poem "Parade," published, in a series later called *Illuminations*, a year before the painting was completed. But "Parade" casts an interesting light on the painting, stressing as it does the relationship between the performers and us, the readers. Rimbaud's threatening, performing rogues "are sent snaring in the town," their success at doing so a matter of "leur experience de vos consciences" (their experience of your consciousnesses)[33] This last word is better translated as "consciousnesses" rather than "consciences," because Rimbaud's performers attract us by acting out a burlesque of ourselves. Several of them "have exploited your worlds," those of the onlookers/readers; their costumes are "like something out of a bad dream." And indeed, Seurat's *parade* evokes what circuses and sideshows have always evoked: the fear and thrill of the Other that is only ourself, the "spectacle of actuality"[34] rendered as grotesque.

Why, then, bowler hats, which seem the opposite of grotesque? It is the anonymity that they confer that is troubling. They belong in the geometry of the sedate, the very quality that contrasts with festivity. They contribute to the "strange fixity and stillness"[35] of the scene; they are clearly *in place*, shapes repeated in the patches on the poster, the numbers behind the trombonist, the lights to the right. They are part of Seurat's by-now-familiar monumentalizing of the contemporary.

Seurat is primarily an iconotect: in the paintings I have examined he builds images of the modern, memorializing what by definition is passing. Who knows who the bowler-hatted silhouette *is*? He sees himself replicated in the spectacle, his own insubstantiality, like the *parade* itself, given a timeless weight. He may be a nobody, but the nobody has arrived and is multiplying. Whatever the spectacle is, it is for him, it literally *respects* him, and so he is respectable—neither

*Fig. 10. Georges Seurat,* La Parade, *1887 (The Metropolitan Museum of Art, New York, Bequest of Stephen C. Clark, 1960 [61.101.17]; photograph © The Metropolitan Museum of Art, all rights reserved)*

*Fig. 11. "Promenade Concert," London, 1884 (Greenwich Library, London)*

festive, nor gay, nor noticeably leisurely, but respectable. We don't know what is under his hat except that he is rapt in his watching, and that what he watches in some way mirrors him.

## NOBODIES AT HOME

Whiteing describes the Parisian common man, smiling on the promenades, as seeming to say "Please don't follow me home."[36] But that is what we should do now, lest he remain the cutout figure of the Man in the Bowler Hat, staring *badaud*-like at his image in the *parade*, lest he remain a nobody. To do this we will need to shift to London of the same period, around 1891. George and Weedon Grossmith's popular *Diary of a Nobody* (1892), originally serialized in *Punch*, is a record of a year in the life of the Pooter family, members of "the poorer middle classes" in a typical and "impecuniously respectable" London suburb.[37] The Grossmiths' comic intention is twofold: to amuse us at the expense of the Pooters, as typical nobodies, "little people," and to involve us enough in their peculiar lives to make them somebodies. We both condescend to and sympathize with them. We certainly have no trouble discovering the humanity of these members of the *nouvelles couches sociales*.

The Pooters live in a terrace house in the suburbs, close enough to the railway that takes Mr. Pooter to work in the City to have its noise crack their garden wall. They fuss over their "Home Sweet Home," they worry over finances, they are cowed by their help and by errand boys (Mr. Pooter paints the washstand in the servant's bedroom), they are cowed by their betters in the City, they gingerly discuss modern opinions with their friends, they work very hard at achieving a mediocre respectability. At a time when the lower middle class was economically vulnerable,[38] Mr. Pooter is lucky to be promoted to senior clerk at a commercial firm with a raise of one hundred pounds a year. They are, for all intents and purposes, content.

If the Pooters have a significant problem, it is with their son Willie, a more "modern" character who, according to his father, is "not falling in with our views."[39] Willie has been freed by his family's respectability to have a certain amount of contempt for it. He has no interest in his work at a bank and is fired. He takes on airs, using his second name, "Lupin," goes in for cigars and billiards, and is very concerned with fashion. Weedon Grossmith's two illustrations of him show him in a curled and short-brimmed bowler and clothes stylish

*Fig. 12. Bowler-hatted Lupin refuses to walk with his unfashionably attired father, illustration by Weedon Grossmith (from George and Weedon Grossmith,* Diary of a Nobody *[London: J. W. Arrowsmith, 1924])*

enough to have been put together at some cost (ironically, he loses his intended to a Mr. Murray Posh, who manufactures three-shilling hats). Pooter seems to re-sist bowlers, but his friends wear them for long walks through the suburbs. They are depicted, in the illustrations, as comically awkward doing so, but Willie wears his with panache. He finds fault with his father's wearing ordinary, not dress, boots, and refuses to walk along the Parade at Broadstairs with his father because Pooter is wearing a "new straw helmet" (fig. 12). The illustration of this is the funniest and most telling in the book: Pooter looks shabby and morose, and Lupin looks like a prototype of the City man as he regards his more clearly lower-middle-class father with disdain.

Near the end of *Diary of a Nobody*, Pooter records the visit of a Mr. Hardfur Huttle, a writer for American newspapers full of "unorthodox" views, who holds forth, rather rudely, on the nature of the middle class:

> "Do you know 'happy medium' are two words which mean 'miserable medi-ocrity.' I say, go first class or third; marry a duchess or her kitchenmaid. The happy medium means respectability, and respectability means insipidness. . . . A man who loves champagne, and, finding a pint too little, fears to face a whole bottle and has recourse to an imperial pint, will never build a Brooklyn Bridge or an Eiffel Tower. No, he is . . . a happy medium, and will

spend the rest of his days in a suburban villa with a stucco-column portico, resembling a four-poster bedstead."

We all laughed. (148)

Of course Huttle has described the Pooters' home and life perfectly, and their laughter signals their self-consciousness about themselves—points, in effect, to a hallmark of their uneasy existence, one that has produced a son almost disabled with self-consciousness. Pooter later reflects on how alike Mr. Huttle and Lupin are, with their "dangerous" ideas and love of extremes. "I believe *I* am happy," he writes, "because I am not ambitious. Somehow I feel that Lupin, since he has been with Mr. Perkupp [in whose office Pooter has gotten a job for his], has become content to settle down and follow the footsteps of his father" (150–51). This comforting thought is dashed when Lupin is discharged for having ideas about revolutionizing the business and proclaims, echoing Mr. Huttle, "The Perkupp's firm? The stagnant dummies have been standing still for years, and now are moving back. I want to go *on*" (157).

The bowler hats in *Diary of a Nobody* are signs of a fashion that has on the one hand become poky and staid, and on the other become "modern" and flashy. If Pooter and his friends are awkward but reasonably content with their lot, Lupin is anxiously looking forward, infected by the very ideas, and eager to improve on the very fashions, that his father's generation has cautiously nurtured. As a sign of the modern, the bowler represents a constancy of ongoingness.

Lupin, following a theatrical bent, belongs to the Holloway Comedians, a suburban musical group, and hangs out at music halls. In this he introduces for us an important site of the bowler-hatted crowd, a place where it can be entertained by versions of itself, usually comic—as we shall see in the next chapter. Lupin is dressed for the part. He doesn't want anyone to follow him home.

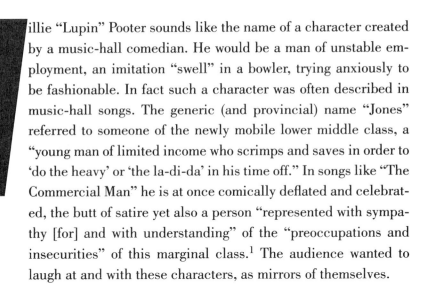

# MUSIC HALL AND SILENT FILM

## TEMPLES OF MODERNITY

Willie "Lupin" Pooter sounds like the name of a character created by a music-hall comedian. He would be a man of unstable employment, an imitation "swell" in a bowler, trying anxiously to be fashionable. In fact such a character was often described in music-hall songs. The generic (and provincial) name "Jones" referred to someone of the newly mobile lower middle class, a "young man of limited income who scrimps and saves in order to 'do the heavy' or 'the la-di-da' in his time off." In songs like "The Commercial Man" he is at once comically deflated and celebrated, the butt of satire yet also a person "represented with sympathy [for] and with understanding" of the "preoccupations and insecurities" of this marginal class.[1] The audience wanted to laugh at and with these characters, as mirrors of themselves.

It is pertinent that Lupin Pooter, in George and Weedon Grossmith's *Diary of a Nobody* (see Chapter 2), wants to go to the halls *and* be a performer, a suburban comedian. The relation of performers and spectators is frequently noted in descriptions of the music halls and their French equivalents, the café-concerts. The audience came not only to see aspects of itself onstage, but also to see *itself* perform, in the theater of its own intermingling and display. Strictly working-class in the days of the singing saloons earlier in the century, the audience of the more commercialized music halls from the late 1840s and 1850s on became increasingly "middle-class" in the sense of being an unstable mixture of laborers in their Sunday best, and—as the halls grew in popularity—more prosperous members of the middle class, and even aristocrats. No wonder the audience watched itself, and no wonder it was aware of dressing up, like performers. And although, by the 1890s, in London, certain halls catered to certain audiences, everyone pretty much saw the same show.

The workers wore bowlers, the clerks wore bowlers, and the performers, of whatever social origin, wore bowlers. Max Beerbohm described the audience as "that sea of billicocks" (that is, bowlers) during the more vulgar heyday of the halls, before they declined into "variety" and "refinement" by the end of the century.[2] That image, borne out in paintings and (later) photographs of the interiors, expresses the democratization of the halls. The blur of stereotypical headgear represented a blurring of class boundaries. (Did men keep their bowlers on inside because, if they misplaced them, they wouldn't know whose was whose?) The sea of bowlers lasted longer than Beerbohm would admit; he, like so many others, enjoyed aspects of the halls that could be located in the past—or, rather, he located in the past all aspects of the halls that he enjoyed. Modern life would go on as modern life—that is what Seurat saw so objectively—but it was an important aspect of modern life, as Weber points out, that this continuity amid change was always to be resisted: that modern life would necessarily be seen as a degeneration of some healthier and more vigorous time, often within the period of modernity. In 1912, W. R. Titterton wrote that the music hall had been "almost the one democratic institution left in modern England," and although he himself was a snob and lamenter of some vague "nobler age when we had a lower-middle-class of settled stately habits and public interests," Titterton was moved to remark that "the attack on the Halls is only a symbol of the undemocratization of life."[3]

Perhaps this characteristic note of lament simply expresses an embarrassed uneasiness about the very enjoyments the halls—and modern life in general—offered, as though one could appreciate a liberating swim in the sea of bowlers only by being aware of losing a foothold in a more firm social order. The middle-class Jules Lemaître remarked, apropos of a café-concert, "It is like a great bath of stupidity which one takes. . . . One feels born within oneself an imbecile which amuses itself in the same fashion as the others."[4] And Beerbohm, at the Tivoli music hall, notes with stylish ambivalence,

We came simply that we might bask in the glow of our own superiority—superiority not only to the guffawing clowns and jades around us, but also to the cloistered pedacules who, no more exquisite than we in erudition, were not in touch with modern life and would have been scared, like so many owls, in that garish temple of modernity, a Music Hall, wherein we, on the other hand, were able to sit without blinking. Were we, after all, so very absurd? It was one of our aims to be absurd.[5]

So Beerbohm, like everyone else, watches himself watching. His absurdity is like Lemaître's imbecility, a feeling of participating in a spectacle with people not one's kind, overcoming and affirming one's class at the same time. It's an amusement easily converted into lament.

The music hall, then, "functioned as a laboratory of social style and self-definition."[6] The spectacle was the urban, mixed crowd displaying itself, experiencing what one writer in 1871 nicely called "the power of being 'at large,'"[7] a power he attributed to factory workers acting like would-be gentlemen, but which could be attributed to everyone involved in popular entertainments. The performers themselves were mirrors for most of the audience, parodically distorting or realistically reflecting them, or both at once. The performers were often of working-class origin and played working-class types, like costermongers or cockney "swells." They wore bowlers with checkered lounge suits, or bowlers with velveteen coats and wildly flared trousers, or battered bowlers with umbrellas and red nose, like George Robey, who sang a patter song called "The Subbubs," in which he and his wife are portrayed in a suburban yard, starting a new life.[8]

The dress of the comedian-singers, along with the songs they sang, in effect deconstructed the images that the audience had made of themselves. A common member of the audience—say, Thomas Wright's factory worker in his Sunday suit—had put on a protective coloration that allowed him to blend in with lower-middle-class folk, who were dressed to imitate their betters (or, to put it more kindly, to join the urban crowd with a minimum of self-consciousness). The comedian exposed this by exaggerating the swell-ness of his outfit (as, say, Champagne Charlie) or making it ludicrously misshapen, while giving patter or singing songs that described the joys and trials of the working class, or of suburbanites. The audience responded raucously, shouting back, giving the "bird,"[9] or sometimes climbing onstage to lead a song themselves. And all this drama is "encouraged by a physical surround of huge mirrors"![10]

The comedy of this mirroring defined and exploited the precarious *embourgeoisement* of the audience. Lupin Pooter could laugh at himself as a Subbub, just as his family laughed at a description of their own mediocrity, in order at once to recognize himself and to distance himself from that recognition. Workers dressed in their best, even as dandies, could watch drunken swells and *lions comique* parade their simulacra of fashion. People with hard lives could listen to Harry Freeman, in a gray bowler, sing of being robbed and beaten, of his home being broken up, of his time in prison, and then conclude, "If *you* don't trouble trouble / Trouble doesn't trouble you."[11] Men with the physiognomies of the working class under their curled bowlers and low-crowned toppers could listen to a red-nosed comedian glory in his very commonness:

> His is the true bread-and-butter stuff, the divine surprises of every day— the fun of getting drunk, of going on the spree, of backing a winner, of meeting a fairy; the dangers of falling in love, of getting married, of coming home late, of having a mother-in-law, of meeting the broker's man; the fun of fires, fights, christenings and funerals; the fun of being a policeman, a porter, a plasterer, or a publican; the fun of losing one's job, the grotesque folly of being an exceptional person.[12]

This fine passage points to the nature of the humor, which was engendered by the contrast between the difficult and unexceptional troubles of marginal people and the world of gentility to which they now had some minor access. Or, put another way, the contrast between being-at-home and being-at-large, between private and public selves, between reality and fashion. Trouble becomes fun in the luxury of being expressed in a spectacle of fashion, and fun comes from trouble, from the realities of the spectators' and performers' lives.

It is characteristic of paintings of the music halls and café-concerts that the space between the audience and performers is crowded, in order to insist on the intimate relation of the two, and marked by anxiety. Trouble and fun are worrisomely blended in this crowding. In Walter Richard Sickert's *Bonnet et Claque* (c. 1890; fig. 13), which depicts Ada Lundberg singing "It All Comes from Sticking to a Soldier" at the Marylebone Music Hall, the intimacy between the jaded singer and the bowler-hatted men absorbed in her song is disturbing. In effect, the men *become* her: their skin is chalky and their mouths gape, like hers. They are so intent on her words that they could be singing them, and perhaps they are. Or they could be hired applauders (one meaning of "claque") and the whole scene an artificial event. Sickert seems to want to throw its reality/artificiality into question. Whether professionally or genuinely involved, the men are like ghosts or cadavers, feeding off the singer as though, having died, they look to her for life, although she hardly seems lifelike. There is energy in this exchange, a sort of communal life (or "joint spirit") that is nevertheless paradoxically moribund. And that seems to be Sickert's vision—that the shared festivity is qualified by the very neediness of the sharing, as though performer and audience were singing of misery, and so relieving themselves of it even as they expressed it, a white, working-class blues: this is where "it all comes from."

The bowler hats in *Bonnet et Claque*, blending into the men's suits or trapped in vertical lines, are signs, in the first place, of a respectability that everything else in the painting questions or qualifies. As in Seurat's *Parade*—which shares with Sickert's painting a foreshortened space, an aura of frozen festivity, and blurred faces—the bowlers are in contrast to the environment. And yet they are also a sign of the trouble that their respectability resists expressing: the anonymity of these men, which they are attempting to overcome in the shared performance. What is this claque of *badauds*? Are they working-class men glad for the chance to express a part of themselves that their dress covers up? Are they middle-class men getting in touch with the more vivid vulgarity of the lower orders? Or are they generic modern men trying to contrive some lost sense of community? All we can know for sure, from the painting itself, is that an intense interchange is taking place that makes of festivity and entertainment something private and troubled, and that makes of reserve and privacy something shared and festive—in any case, spectacular.

In Seurat's *Café concert* (c. 1887) we see, from close behind, silhouettes of heads with bowler hats on framing a singer they are watching. The bowlers, shadowy and fixed and grave, define the audience. These men *watch*, encased in an anonymous reserve. Their watching seems more important than anything else going on. Whatever attitudes can be projected onto them—amusement, engagement, bewilderment, alarm, contempt, apathy—the watchers of modern life reserve the right to remain inward while being at large. Their bowlers precisely balance and express this doubleness.

As I've said, the contrasts between reserve and expression, reality and fashion, trouble and fun, could be expressed sympathetically or satirically, or both at once. In terms of dress, the performers could reveal the fashions worn by the audience as a sham, a cover, an inept simulacrum. Pretensions could be exposed or deflated. Dress could be exaggerated (oversized coats and shoes, wildly checkered suits, ill-fitting hats) to the point of parody. On the other hand, the reality of the costermonger's or the toff's or the suburbanite's life could be transformed, in a public spectacle, into the fun of fashion. Trouble was given a style, and ceased, momentarily, to be troubling: "The coster turns, toys with his hat, in one quick movement the billycock has struck ten attitudes";[13] Little Tich, with his enormous shoes, can dance. The keeping up of appearances on a meager income could be "indulged" as well as "mocked" as a "small-scale social heroics"[14] be-

*Fig. 13. Walter Richard Sickert,* Bonnet et Claque, *c. 1890 (from Richard Shone,* Walter Sickert *[Oxford: Phaidon, 1988])*

cause the pretensions of the would-be swell were at worst no different from the pretensions of "society." In this sense fashion, reflected from the artistes back to the galleries, became more expression than affectation, an expression of sharing, and having to work to share, in the arena of public life.

> The 'Upper Ten' may jeer and say,
>      What 'cads' the 'Arries are,
> But the 'Arries *work* and *pay their way*
>      While doing the La-di-da.[15]

The bowler hat could play its role in this comedy of dress because it was both Sunday and street best *and* fashionable among the steadier middle classes and intelligentsia (Max Beerbohm and his non-cloistered friends). It pointed in both directions at once. Take Tom Foy, "The Yorkshire Lad" (fig. 14), a North Country comedian of the early 1900s. His whole manner expresses that he is only what he is, a country lad in the wrong clothes. His lumpish, checked lounge suit is ill-fitting, the jacket buttoned too high, the pegged trousers an allusion to fashion gone awry. He could be a provincial costermonger in hand-me-downs, ready to doff his

*Fig. 14. Tom Foy, "The Yorkshire Lad" (from Raymond Mander and Joe Mitchenson,* British Music Hall *[London: Gentry Books, 1965])*

bowler and pull his forelock should a real gentleman walk by. His manner is abject, apologetic. Yet his dress is also fashionable, and therefore, as Simmel would have it, both imitative and differentiating.[16] He has saved a few bob and has a getup, and he is ready for something more than might be defined or prescribed by his class.

Indeed, his whole outfit alludes to casual gentry wear, the dress that Oscar Wilde affected in undergraduate days (fig. 15). Tom Foy's ensemble is simply a comic version of Wilde's, and his aspiration to fashion mirrors and parodies Wilde's. The collapse of the gentry image into comedy allows the reality of Foy's working-class identity to be expressed *through* the costume. The audience can sympathize with him, and with his aspiration, while laughing at the ineptitude of his presentation. Class distinctions are at once marked and blurred, and the relatively unvarying bowler can do this better than any other item of fashion. Foy's bowler, while perhaps not as stylishly curled as Wilde's (though flatter brims were more in fashion in Foy's time), is essentially the same hat. Its hard and con-

*Fig. 15. Oscar Wilde as a sophomore at Oxford, 1876 (William Andrews Clark Memorial Library, University of California, Los Angeles)*

sistent shape (*durable* in the root sense) is a constant sign of the mobility between classes, whether working/middle or middle/gentry. Foy's hopeful sportive-
ness is a comment on Wilde's (as both pretentious and exemplary) and on Foy's
origins (as both inappropriate and valued). With such mixed signals, the bowler
becomes a comic chapeau.

## LAUTREC

The bowler was certainly a sender of mixed signals on the head
of the painter Henri de Toulouse-Lautrec Montfa, the nineteenth-century artist
most identified with bowler hats and with the music-hall milieu—specifically,
the dance halls and café-concerts of Paris in the Nineties. Lautrec not only painted men in bowlers in this milieu, we know from photographs that he himself
wore a bowler to his haunts in Montmartre, and in his studio, and on trips and
outings. There he was, a scion of one of the oldest aristocratic families in France,
living in the demimonde of nightclubs and brothels, dressed like a bourgeois!
(See fig. 16.) This qualifies as a social spectacle of a peculiarly modern kind. The
answer to the question, For what part is he dressed? is, by the time of the 1890s,
necessarily complex.

When he was barely twenty years old, Lautrec painted a parody of *Le Bois
Sacré* (*The Sacred Wood*) by Puvis de Chavannes, which just that year (1884) had
been exhibited at the Paris Salon. Puvis's work, commissioned to adorn a museum staircase, was a rendering of classical muses, robed in white, calmly disport-
ing in the woods. In Lautrec's *Parodie du "Bois Sacré" de Puvis de Chavannes*
(completed by students of Fernand Corman; fig. 17), the exhibitors appear as a
crowd lined up to enter the sacred grove and contemplate the muses. They are a
very contemporary crowd, dressed mainly in black, with top hats; they could be
customers at a café-concert. The diminutive Lautrec is among them, bowler-
hatted, his back disrespectfully to the muses.[17]

It is interesting to speculate about Lautrec's motives in regard to this parody.
Clearly the irony cuts two ways, as comic irony always does. Puvis's setting is
made to seem silly and attenuated, its conventionality and gossamer lack of substance exposed by the somber reality of the crowd. At the same time the exhibitors—painted *into* the scene as they are—are made to seem vulgar interlop-
ers, out of place in this antique and traditional site, mere pretenders to the
muses. The painting as a whole is like a comic version of Baudelaire's idea of

*Fig. 16. Henri de Toulouse-Lautrec as a young adult
(Musée Touolouse-Lautrec, Albi)*

*Fig. 17. Henri de Toulouse-Lautrec, detail from* Parodie du "Bois Sacré" de
Puvis de Chavannes, *1884 (reproduced from Gale B. Murray,* Toulouse-Lautrec:
The Formative Years, 1878–1891 *[Oxford: Clarendon Press, 1991])*

"modernity" as "the ephemeral, the fugitive, the contingent, the half of art whose other half is the eternal and immutable."[18] Here the halves clash.

Like all good parody, Lautrec's work is a personal statement about art and technique (he hung it high in his studio in Montmartre). By including himself among the exhibitors, he deflected his motive away from a simple satire of a particular group of artists. Instead, he *posed* the idea of the modern against the academy, as if to imply, What have *we* to do with *these* muses, dressed as we are in the dark fashion of an urban, industrial civilization? At an early age Lautrec saw himself as part of the contemporary Paris scene; Montmartre was to become his sacred grove. His bowler was an accessory to his sense of his modernism.

A biographer describes Lautrec at the Moulin Rouge:

> With his bowler hat either pulled down over his eyes or balanced on the back of his head, Lautrec drew, soaking himself in the noisy, vibrant atmosphere of the dance-hall which was, indeed, more than a dance-hall, a market, a fair of love. The public did not dance. They came to see the quadrille. The over-excited men fell an easy prey to the women seeking "customers." Blue, red, green, white and yellow dresses moved to and fro, mingling with top-hats, felt hats and bowlers.[19]

At the Moulin Rouge he was at once working and out on the town (soaking himself in the atmosphere for both entertainment and art), trying to blend in, one bowler among many bowlers. In this sense it was a disguise for him, a way of not calling attention to himself. He was no longer an aristocrat, slumming among the tradesmen, bohemians and *apaches* (street criminals) of Parisian nightlife. Nor was he any longer a struggling (or, later, successful) artiste. Nor a freak with stunted legs, painfully aware of *not* blending into a crowd. He was precisely what he was not, in reality: a man of the crowd, a middle-class something-or-other, one of the "worthy bourgeoisie" who made up most of the audience.[20] In his typical bowler, impeccable overcoat, waistcoat, checked trousers, eyeglasses and cane, he could stand out respectably from the more decadent and criminal elements and at the same time not seem aristocratically aloof. He could distance himself from both the Chat Noir and the Château Montfa, the home of his ancestors. Like his vivid father, Lautrec loved to dress in costume—as a Japanese, a choirboy, in drag, and so on. At the Moulin Rouge and elsewhere he was acting out his part in a modern social drama. He introduces, for us, the element of costume in the bowler, a sense of theatrical self-consciousness appropriate to the music-hall environment in particular and the spectacle of modern life in general.

Lautrec may also have wished to insist on himself as a serious young man. He was actively ambitious about exhibiting and marketing his work and let his family know of his material success, partly to appease their dismay at his vocation and style of life. He "considered himself to be a working artist, not a dilletante."[21] His dress would certainly have suggested a professional rather than a pretender, one who belonged in the exhibiting crowd in his parody of Puvis. In a photograph of Lautrec among many other students at the studio of Fernand Corman, Lautrec in his bowler and shirtsleeves is the only artist with a hat on: he looks *very* studious. He also wore hats when painting indoors because of the light.[22]

Perhaps, too, there was something neutrally matter-of-fact about the bowler that made Lautrec feel comfortable in his role as spectator of nightlife, an observer who saw and recorded objectively, without flinching and without moral constraints. "He looked on others as implacably as he looked on himself. He neither condemned nor approved . . . he analysed."[23] When he painted himself into the nightclub scenes, he never made himself appear as an artist; he could have been a short and morose *badaud*—a watcher of modern life, which is what he was, one of the first great ones. In *Au bal du Moulin de la Galette* (*In the Moulin de la Galette*, 1899; fig. 18), a painting set in a small dance hall with a folksy atmosphere attended by the petite bourgeoisie, Lautrec painted René Grénier, his friend and an amateur painter, as a stand-in for himself. His alert *watching* of the dancing is the focal point of the painting; his observant attention makes him distinct from the rest. It is as though he were recording this dance, at once apart from and absorbed by it. For Lautrec, just to see what he saw, the gaudy and seamy spectacles of modern leisure, and to paint it objectively, was a modern and bourgeois act. It was to respect the sheer function of things. Henri Perruchot notes that to Lautrec, "every object precisely adapted to its function was . . . a work of art. The logic and efficiency that determined its shape delighted him."[24] Perhaps the very design of the bowler, then, might have pleased him, especially in his role as a keen but neutral observer, a hard worker.

To read Lautrec's bowler in these various ways is not simply to engage in an academic exercise. The point to be made about the dance halls and café-concerts that Lautrec frequented is that the social definitions within them were mixed and blurred: artiste, bohemian, and bourgeois (to isolate only three) were social roles not only to be performed side by side, but often to be performed at once by the same person. Jerrold Seigel says that in Montmartre in the 1890s, there was "a Bohemia for the bourgeoisie, a place where the increasingly organized and regulated life of the modern city could be left behind for an evening by those unable to escape it for longer. Here non-Bohemians might seek release

*Fig. 18. Henri de Toulouse-Lautrec,* Au bal du Moulin de la Galette, *1899 (The Art Institute of Chicago, Mr. and Mrs. Lewis Larned Coburn Memorial Collection, 1933.458; photograph © 1992, The Art Institute of Chicago. All rights reserved.)*

from ordinary social boundaries."[25] This is one aspect of Seigel's thesis that bohemia "was not a realm outside bourgeois life but the expression of a conflict that arose at its very heart,"[26] the conflict between an emphasis on personal liberation and antitraditionalism on the one hand, and the need for stability and respectability on the other. "Bohemia grew up where the borders of bourgeois existence were murky and uncertain."[27] Lautrec, in the café-concerts, could play the bourgeois not being bourgeois (dissolute, released), and the artiste being bourgeois (hardworking, composed). This symbiosis, of course, takes place within the parameters of bourgeois life itself, which was everywhere triumphant. Lautrec's eccentricity was a Brummel-like "manifestation of his desire never to appear astonished,"[28] and his bowler hat enabled him to be at once eccentric and sedate. In this way it had a comic function, and he seems, in his photographs, a comic figure.

The figures that he painted in bowlers were, however, often dissolute, as if

*Fig. 19. Henri de Toulouse-Lautrec,* A La Mie, *1891 (S. A. Denio Collection, and General Income, Museum of Fine Arts, Boston)*

Lautrec wished to pose the hat with which he identified against the life to which he had accustomed himself.[29] In *A La Mie* (*At the Café La Mie*, or *The Last Crumbs*, 1891; fig. 19), he posed a very bleary-looking Maurice Guibert with a model. Guibert, Lautrec's "dark angel,"[30] was a champagne salesman and bon vivant who frequented brothels and was considered a bad influence by Lautrec's family. In the painting his eggplant-colored coat and bowler, and his gaze, are the focal point, in contrast to the several patterns in purples, greens, and oranges (though the woman's white blouse stands out as well, she blends in with the patterns, seems almost decorative). His gaze, directly at us, is ambiguous: drunken, lecherous, amused, cynical, weary, etc. Except for his bowler, he is very unlike the photographs of Lautrec in bars, or Lautrec's appearance in his own paintings (like *Une table au Moulin Rouge*, 1892), in which the painter is respectable and self-possessed. Guibert is like a prophetically fallen Lautrec, utterly absorbed in and encompassed by the milieu in which he keeps his fascination intact, despite his drinking—until, in Lautrec's case, his drinking did him in. In *Monsieur Boileau au café* (*Monsieur Boileau in a Café*, 1893; fig. 20), the bowler-hatted

*Fig. 20. Henri de Toulouse-Lautrec,* Monsieur Boileau au café, *1893
(The Cleveland Museum of Art, Hinman B. Hurlbut Collection, 394.25.)*

Boileau is similarly jaded but much more burgher-like. He seems oversatisfied; perhaps he has eaten too much. Perhaps Lautrec painted his aristocratic father in a top hat in the background, absorbed in a lively conversation that underscores Boileau's isolation and discomfort,[31] in order to contrast the two as a way of distancing himself from the bourgeoisie.

For Lautrec, then, as for Lupin Pooter and Max Beerbohm (though from another social angle), the music-hall/café-concert environment was one in which he could participate in "modernity" through a disguising or blurring of his class. Wearing a bowler, he could at once detach himself from what he observed (for purposes of his respectability and art) and identify himself with it, as a spectacle for his own consumption, or as an arena of fashion. He could watch and be watched—in effect, be part of the subject of his art as well as the artist. That no doubt satisfied his theatrical bent and made his bowler an item of costume as well as dress. It also made his art the most modern in terms of technique *and* subject matter before Picasso, who would, very early in his career, as the new century began, turn to the subjects honored by Lautrec, including Le Moulin de la Galette, and a still life with Cézanne's bowler hat.

# CHAPLIN

In his short but dense essay "At the Music Hall,"[32] Roland Barthes argues that "the music hall is the aesthetic form of work." That is to say, "each number is presented either as the exercise or as the product of labor"—specifically, the labor produced in the industrial cities—and yet is marked by facility, laughter, and grace. In the spectacle of the music hall, continuous time is broken up, disengaged from cause and effect, so that "the crude musculature of an arduous labor" can be expressed in the "visual luxury" of gestures and objects perfected, made "euphoric." Something of this quality, the value of work sublimated as an aesthetic experience, is described by Vladimir Nabokov in his novel *Lolita*, when Humbert Humbert writes, "We all admire the spangled acrobat with classical grace meticulously walking his tight rope in the talcum light; but how much rarer art is there in the sagging rope expert wearing scarecrow clothes and impersonating a grotesque drunk!"[33] The acrobat/clown at once expresses the work involved in maintaining his balance, and makes his art rarer through the sublimation of that exposed work. The comedy is in keeping both grace and effort in play. This is central to the art of Charlie Chaplin.

Chaplin's art was, of course, rooted in the traditions of British music hall, in which he grew up (his father, Charles Chaplin, Sr., was a Champagne Charlie–type performer), and his gradual adjustment of them to the demands of the cinema may well have been made easier by the relation of both forms of entertainment. Films were first run for the public as part of the variety theater of the 1890s. And what is cinematic montage but continuous time broken up and disengaged from cause and effect? Perhaps Chaplin's films could be described as becoming, increasingly as his comic art developed, narratives of work broken up into moments of grace.

The bowler hat, which Chaplin carried from the music hall (and before that, no doubt, from the slums of South London) to world renown—the hat identified with him ever since—was uniquely appropriate as a vestimentary sign of both work and grace. Unlike the top hat, the bowler was heavy with the social history of grubby city streets, the world of costermongers and cabdrivers and newspaper hawkers going about their business under the fine rain of urban grit. At the same time, like the topper, it was an item of fashion, of being at large in a world of Sunday-best politesse and flair. The music-hall comedians could doff a battered bowler with exquisite decorum. This is the double world, both of life and of art, from which Chaplin emerged with such perfect and unconscious timing. In his films—as in most films since, for he helped define the nature of film—a continuous narrative, with its incumbent social context, exists in tension with a series of isolatable moments, with their incumbent iconography. "Stills" are set in motion, and motion-as-duration is interrupted by montage. Cinema, in this way, brought together the arts of the theater and of the spectacle of variety "numbers."

The contradiction between work and grace is expressed in Chaplin's famous costume (see fig. 21). He claimed in his autobiography that he thought up his "Tramp" costume "on the way to the wardrobe" when called upon by Mack Sennett to perform some impromptu comic business on the set of what was surely *Mabel's Strange Predicament* (1914), his second film for Sennett.[34] He recalled,

> I wanted everything a contradiction: the pants baggy, the coat tight, the hat small and the shoes large. . . . I had no idea of the character. But the moment I was dressed, the clothes and the make-up made me feel the person he was. I began to know him, and by the time I walked onto the stage [set] he was fully born.[35]

The nature of this contradiction is clear, both in social and in romantic/existential terms (the latter much preferred by Chaplin when he spoke of his art). From the waist up Charlie (as we shall call the Tramp or the Little Fellow, in order to avoid imprecision about his various roles), with his fastidiously buttoned coat, clean collar and tie, and bowler, was an aspiring member of the *nouvelles couches sociales*. Sobel and Francis, in their study of Chaplin's English origins, describe the Little Fellows as they could be found in turn-of-the-century London,

> behind the counters of corn merchants and grocery shops and dairies. . . . Their fathers might have been comfortably off working men. . . . Their

school fitted them to be clerks and shop assistants. They served the middle class, learned some of their ways, aped their conduct and dwelt in that pale, indeterminate region between the skilled artisan and the prosperous businessman known as the lower middle class.[36]

From the waist down Charlie betrayed his lower origins, so to speak: ugly, baggy pants and bizarrely long shoes. This ensemble, kangarooish in effect, made physically clear the idea of aspiration (from oversized shoes to undersized bowler, the costume pointed upward), while placing limits on it (the bowler as much a hand-me-down as the shoes, and capping Charlie as a "little fellow").

This is how the English tend to read Charlie's costume and manners, probably because they are more familiar with its music-hall origins. For them—if we can assume the remarks of British commentators and critics are representative—Charlie's genteel manners were imitative, and his costume expressed his desire to make his arduous way up the social scale. Sobel and Francis note that Chaplin "was sensitive to the need to keep accurately within class boundaries," pointing to the scene in *Twenty Minutes of Love* (1914) when Charlie "makes a furrow in the crown of his bowler to change it into a Homburg, thereby giving him more status" in the eyes of a girl with whom he is flirting.[37] And David Robinson says that Chaplin's ensemble "indicated brave but ineffectual pretensions to the dignity of the *petit bourgeoisie*,"[38] thereby setting him a bit lower than do Sobel and Francis in this "indeterminate" class.

Chaplin, for his own reasons, did not choose to emphasize the effects of his background, either in the slums of South London or in the music hall, in the impromptu throwing-together of his costume, though surely his experience and training would have played a major role. Stan Laurel (then Stan Jefferson), who was Chaplin's roommate and understudy when the two comics came to America in 1910 in Fred Karno's troupe, recalled that "the bowler hat to me has always seemed to be a part of a comic's make-up for as far back as I can remember. I'm sure that's why Charlie wore one. Most of the comics we saw as boys wore them."[39] Those would have been music-hall comics, of course; Karno's troupe aspired to bring the pleasures of the English music hall to American audiences. The whole costume alluded to music hall, from the shoes like a minor version of Little Tich's to the swell's cane and waistcoat.

In his recounting of the origins of the costume, however, Chaplin stressed the creation of Charlie as a romantic and existential figure, "fully born" at the necessary moment, Chaplin feeling "the person he was" from the clothes and make-up alone. When he told Sennett that the Little Fellow "wears an air of romantic

*Fig. 21. Charlie Chaplin as the Tramp, c. 1915 (author's collection)*

hunger, forever seeking romance, but his feet won't let him,"[40] he described the contradiction, characteristically, in general terms: whereas the "little man," the *petit bourgeois* of the nineteenth century, might have aspired to secure employment and middle-class comfort, the Little Fellow aspires to a more abstract "romance." Winston Churchill remarked astutely in 1935 that "the American scene as a whole has influenced Chaplin—its variety, its color, its animation, its strange and spectacular contrasts," and Chaplin's Tramp is "characteristically American" because he "refuses to acknowledge defeat." Unlike the defeated, spiritless, and homeless English tramps, Charlie has the "indomitable spirit," the "defiance and disdain," of the American hobo, someone who rebels against routine and loves "the changes and chances of the road."[41] If he looks for work, he is content to move on from it. He aspires not so much to a higher class as to a more abstract idea of freedom.

In this more American (or American-inspired) reading of Charlie, he is a figure of declined caste rather than aspiration, a vaguely genteel person fallen on hard times. It is a reading, as it were, from the bowler downward. While it is hard to draw a firm line between English and American perceptions of Charlie, this distinction largely holds true. One American critic points to "the bowler hat with its claim to a lost respectability," and a biographer describes Charlie as a character who has known better days.[42] As Chaplin himself noted, "My character was different and unfamiliar to the American," adding, perhaps with characteristic shyness about his background, "and even unfamiliar to myself."[43] And when the British biographer Roger Manvell refers to Charlie's "overall appearance of disintegrating gentility,"[44] we may assume he means gentility as a form of striving, a faux dignity, rather than as an achieved quality, as Americans might understand it. For Americans, Charlie's decline into vagrancy is the opportunity for him to aspire to something beyond social contingency—one of the regnant American ideals.

In whatever direction we see Charlie crossing the boundary between vagrancy and respectability, the contradictions in his dress and manner are constant. Manvell accurately notes that he "was at once tramp and city man, a hobo and a genteel man of the world"[45]—the first pairing more English, the second more American. The bowler hat, as we have seen, expresses at once gentility and rude practicality, ambition and limitation. Donning his bowler, Charlie could participate appropriately and vigorously in the rough-and-tumble of street life, and also behave with a finicky, if rather rapid, politesse.

He scurries with effort to get into employment queues, but others always cut in front of him at the last moment (*A Dog's Life*, 1918). Perhaps it is his lack of experience but it is also some innate reserve of his, the vestige of some dignity, which makes poignant his frantic attempts to get on in a rough world. If he falls or runs too fast, his hand is always ready to catch his bowler, and if he loses it, he will take great risks to retrieve it, clap it on, and continue. Sometimes, Charlie doffs his bowler to a man before kicking him.

These contradictions were, as we have noted, staples in the music-hall comedians' evocation of lower-middle/working-class life. We can sympathize with as well as patronize this life. Charlie's behavior—especially his manipulation of his bowler and cane—expresses a street gentility, an actual quality and not simply a clash of opposed qualities. His aspiration and his toughness reveal each other, and for both the bowler is the appropriate emblem. Charlie can be fastidious and rowdy, turn and turn about, the bowler suggesting a dandy or a costermonger or both at once, embodied in a figure of "indeterminate" but insistent ambition.

## THE BOYS

The characters that Stan Laurel and Oliver Hardy created in their comic films have ambitions very like Charlie's. They too are trying to get a toehold in the lower middle class, through temporary, unremunerative, and harassed employment, or through suburban rituals like weekend outings (*A Perfect Day*, 1929) and participation in men's clubs (*Sons of the Desert*, 1934). But although their environment is more insistently lower-middle-class than Charlie's, more elaborated as an urban/suburban milieu, the social *gestus* of their costumes and behavior seems even more indeterminate, probably because the social nexus to which they refer had become so familiar, so pervasive, as to seem abstract.

By the time Laurel and Hardy became a bowler-hatted team in 1927, the specific significations of the hat had all but vanished from the world of the silent comic film and from its origins in music hall. Like Chaplin, Laurel was steeped in the traditions of music hall, from which he derived his use of the bowler, among other things.[46] So it was natural for Laurel to wear a bowler (as noted above, he always considered it part of a comic's outfit)—sometimes in imitation of Chaplin—during the years when he struggled as a minor comic film actor between leaving the Karno troupe and teaming with Hardy. "Babe" Hardy, an American whose only training was in film, had been wearing a "derby" since 1914 without being aware he was imitating anyone. Someone once told him that his success could be attributed to his and Laurel's imitating Chaplin's use of the bowler;[47] and while it is true that they make many similar moves, including Stan's doffing and head-scratching, and Ollie's hat-tipping to the ladies (with fussy variations on Chaplin's abrupt and simple tilt), it is also true that by 1927 it was commonplace to see comedians in bowler hats, from Ford Sterling and Fatty Arbuckle to Buster Keaton (on occasion). They were simply a comic accessory of obscure origin.

Leo McCarey, later a famous director of comic films but then a supervisor for the Hal Roach studios, was central in bringing Laurel and Hardy together as a team and in expanding their roles,[48] and it was he who came up with the idea of their wearing bowlers as a trademark.[49] It was somehow important to get this "vestimentary sign" fixed, as it was for Chaplin (and, hats varying, for almost every silent film comic). But what was it a sign of? Barthes (see the Introduction) refers to what Brecht called the social *gestus* of a dramatic work, which in Brecht's terms is the expression through which "the social laws under which . . . [people] are acting spring into sight," a "realm of attitudes adopted by the characters toward one another"[50] that Barthes extends to costume. If we think of Stan and Ollie's bowler hats as not somehow wrong as costume, then we may ask, What do they express and how do they function? Because Laurel and Hardy's roots in music hall are more distant and tenuous, and because their combined English/American origins blur their relation to a particular culture, the answers to these questions are more difficult than they were with Chaplin. The *gestus* is more unconscious, which may be why nobody wants to address these questions with more than a passing comment.

The comments are interestingly vague. Laurel himself is quoted as saying that "stand-up collars were formal and slightly different but never too obviously so. They gave us, together with our derbies, a something we felt these two characters needed—a kind of phony dignity. There's nothing funnier than a guy being dignified *and* dumb."[51] Taking a cue from this, John McCabe in a later book says, "Their bowler hats crowned their essential dignity, and the use and misuse of these hats were the activations of their unceasing battle to maintain that dignity."[52] McCabe makes "essential" what Laurel more accurately called "phony": their strange formality in inappropriate circumstances. "They were gentlemen," says McCabe,[53] but more precisely they—mainly Ollie—*put on* being gentlemen when they felt unsure of themselves and tried to cover for it. We are aware of a formality in them that seems rootless, or something more rooted in their consciousnessses than in their social circumstances. When another critic, referring to their bowlers, says "Both of them *must* be wearing this symbol of class in order to perform even the simplest of actions,"[54] he is pointing to their immature and "fetishistic attachment" to their hats, but is also inadvertently pointing to the vagueness of the bowlers as signs. "Class" presumably indicates behavior detached from specific social conditions, a very American idiom. In any case, Stan and Ollie's dignity, of which their bowlers are the major signs, is unsuitable, dysfunctional, ungrounded—and in contrast to Chaplin's Charlie, who is resourceful and quick-witted, they have nothing more than their dignity going for them.

But although Charlie is more aggressive and crafty and, God knows, more intelligent than Stan and Ollie, the worlds in which they dwell are similar. It is seldom noted how miserable these worlds are: teeming streets, tacky storefronts, employment lines, angry and embittered people, hostile authority figures, dusty roads with muddy and bottomless pools—not to mention "male lechery and drunkenness, female vindictiveness, sexual jealousy, marital discord, infidelity, and violence."[55] These last words describe the environment of the Keystone comedies, which stayed with Chaplin after he left Keystone. It is reproduced in Laurel and Hardy as well, and widened to include the suburban: the tract homes of Culver City in *Big Business* (1929), the duplex in *Sons of the Desert*, and so on. In this world Stan and Ollie were vagrants (especially, and not surprisingly, in the early 1930s), or deliverymen, or housepainters, or such. They have no skills, only the kind of anxiety and bewilderment that comes from not having any, and knowing it, and knowing that skills, however rudimentary, are expected of them. This lack and this anxiety extend to their domestic arrangements; they often have wives, but can't begin to understand or interact with them naturally or usefully, except as children.

The unrelenting childlikeness of "the Boys" (as they are sometimes called in their sound films and have been called ever since) is of course their most remarkable and remarked-upon characteristic. Hardy described the Boys as "nice, very nice people. They never get anywhere because they are both so very dumb but they don't *know* that they're dumb,"[56] a version of what Laurel has already been quoted as saying about their being "dignified *and* dumb." They're dignified because they don't know they're dumb, because they're dressed like adults but don't know how to be adults, and their incompetency (especially at anything requiring organizational or mechanical ability) is ingratiatingly laughable because it is so childlike. They're dumb in the way kids are dumb. They seemingly have no past experience, no sense of how things are done; they mean no harm to anyone yet take an unconscious delight in disorder—that is, the considerable, even surreal, disorder they cause is what they are most comfortable with, even as it frustrates them (or, to be more precise, as it frustrates Ollie). They get assigned chores and have no work habits. They invent Rube Goldbergian ways of climbing onto a second-story balcony (*Way Out West*, 1936). Almost everyone scares them; Stan's famous whimper is only the more direct expression of Ollie's tie-twiddling. In the person of Stan—the more overtly childlike of the two (he wore a flat-brimmed Irish children's bowler[57]), and the funnier—the infantilism extends to language: his garbled attempts to convey information or to put things verbally in perspective. As one critic puts it, Stan "has no rehearsal capacity, and cannot properly store his own speech."[58] In sum, they are overgrown boys trying to make their way in a hostile adult world with its own and (to them) indecipherable codes and demands. They have only their indefatigable innocence and persistence, and the politeness of scared or lost kids

On one level, then, their bowlers have a "light" function: as the practical hats of men of affairs, they stand in contrast to the Boys' stupidity, and as relatively formal headgear, they stand in contrast to their chaos-making, sitting firmly in place even when Ollie falls headfirst down a manhole or emerges from under water. But on another level, their bowlers are signs of what the modern world has become for the middle class who created it. The social *gestus* of the Laurel and Hardy films—their interactive behavior in a modern milieu, their hats as they help define this behavior—expresses a darker and more all-absorbing environment than the one into and out of which Chaplin's Little Fellow tramped: an environment that reduces people to the helplessness of children. Laurel and Hardy's popularity reached its peak in the Depression years, when so many had no grasp of the external and impersonal forces that were making them miserable. On the one hand the Boys' bowlers signified their practical aspiration to a middle-class world of available work and a certain amount of class flexibility: if you can look the part, you can get the job, and if you can do the job, you might wind up secure. On the other hand, their bowlers are signs of a déclassé comedy, of aspirations necessarily frustrated, not, for example, because of the innate individuality and independence of the Little Fellow, but because the mechanisms of modern life are themselves beyond the capacities of the class that invented and developed them. Modern life is seen by those most caught up in it as the adult world is seen by lost children. Any machine baffles Stan and Ollie; they cannot master it, as Keaton did, or turn it into play, as Chaplin did. Because bowler hats have been identified with so many of the mechanisms (trains, bicycles, autos, factories) and processes (business, e.g.) of modern life, it is not surprising that if these mechanisms, as they clash with the human, are viewed comically, the bowler would become, as it had with the later Chaplin, the comic hat of modernity.

So pervasive had the middle classes become—especially after the Great War rang the death knell over so many of the *anciens régimes*, and especially in the United States—that their triumphs and travails represent "humanity," certainly the humanity of the film audiences. Modern middle-class man became, in the words of Walter Gropius, founder of the Bauhaus, "modern man, who wears modern not historical dress."[59] This is the iconographic route that Magritte and Beckett, among others, were to take. It is probably one reason why Toulouse-Lautrec, who was so engaged in the technology of printmaking and lithographic reproduction, wore a bowler hat; why Cézanne painted a self-portrait (1883–87) in a bowler hat; why Picasso painted *Still Life with [Cézanne's] Hat* (1909), an homage to Cézanne's modernism; why the modernist composer Erik Satie and the Dadaist painter Francis Picabia wore bowlers; and why there was an explosion of bowler-hatted men in Weimar art (see Chapter 4). It is why Leopold Bloom, a middle-class Jew, is given a bowler hat in Joseph Strick's film version of *Ulysses* (1968), though James Joyce never gave him one: this hapless and encyclopedic comic hero had become modern man. So would Charlie and Stan and Ollie, each icon responding to a different, and abstracted, aspect of modern life.

In this, Laurel and Hardy look forward to Samuel Beckett (as we shall see) and backward to, for example, Harry Tate's comic sketches of modern life. Tate, who made his debut on the English music-hall stage in 1895, had become by the Twenties very well known for his sporting sketches, which included "Golfing," "Selling a Car" and "Motoring." He played a "would-be gentleman"[60] and "self-important sportsman in a world drifting away from sense and logic, cause and effect."[61] He often performed these sketches in cross-talk with his "son" (at first played by an actor, then by his real son Ronald).[62] In a publicity still from "Motoring" (fig. 22), we can see Ronnie Tate as the bowler-hatted modern man, who cannot control the machine which he is dressed to drive, who is overwhelmed by and entangled in its misplaced and misused parts. This recalls the Boys' frustrations with automobiles, notably in *Two Tars* (1928) and *A Perfect Day*. Modern man, often posing bowler-hatted and serene in his automobile in photographs and advertisements, the figure of the mobile and industrial age, his car a little factory engineered for his freedom, had become, in the history of comedy from music hall to film, a man ridden *by* the modern world, rendered childlike before its products: a befuddled Ronnie Tate looking up to his pompous, faux-gentry father, who also hasn't got a clue. He is a middle-class man at once set practically to perform his technological tasks and frustrated by them, his bowler the sign of both aspects. Just so, the Boys' "derbies" signify their aspiration to a world they cannot understand and in which they certainly cannot compete.

*Fig. 22. Harry and Ronnie Tate in the sketch "Motoring," early 1900s
(from Raymond Mander and Joe Mitchenson,* British Music Hall
*[London: Gentry Books, 1965])*

In their comic business with their bowlers, which much exceeds Chaplin's, Laurel and Hardy express, simultaneously, their intense engagement with and addled detachment from their environments. The bowlers either stick to them like glue, no matter how often they fall down or what they fall through, or are blown off their heads easily. That is, they either adhere to them like appendages or are swept away as minor accessories. Insofar as the bowlers signify their sense of themselves, their stored-up consciousness (we will discuss the psychology of hats in Chapter 5), Stan and Ollie are both comically individual, at odds with whatever and whomever they come up against, perennial dudes in the Way Out West of the world—and typical, to the extent that they are going through what others (in the film, in the audience) are going through. After all, the hat mix-ups and exchanges can occur because the bowlers are stereotypical, generic hats that a good many others in their films wear. And yet they don't fit any more than the Boys do. The Boys remain sweetly and ludicrously individual even as they partake in social and communal rituals: trying to better themselves, starting a new job, taking an outing, being stuck in a traffic jam, escaping their vexed and shrewd wives. The very middle-class world that offers them the opportunities to join in, work and play, takes away those opportunities easily, keeping them constantly and childishly trying to make sense out of what doesn't yield itself to the operations of sense.[63]

In the first film in which Laurel and Hardy appear together with their bowlers, *Hats Off* (1927)—a film of which no known print exists—their vagrant hats touch off a hat frenzy. They recover the wrong hats when theirs fall off, initiating the first of their trademark never-ending hat routines, which will surface, as we shall see, in *Waiting for Godot*. At the end they kick each other's bowlers into the street, and there ensues a finale in which they and a crowd of other men knock off each other's hats. When the police arrive to drive everyone else away, the Boys remain sitting in the street surrounded by a variety of forlorn hats, many of them crushed (fig. 23). They conclude by putting on the wrong hats "for the umpteenth time."[64]

Clearly, in their world everyone needs his own hat; others' hats don't fit. Stan's and Ollie's bowlers, like Charlie's, are so identified with them, so often in place in the most outlandish circumstances, that losing them requires their immediate recovery at whatever cost. Without their hats they are lost; whatever formality the bowlers lend them gives way to the very chaos their behavior is creating. With their hats on, they can maintain their dignity *while* being dumb, they (and others) can maintain a stately decorum during their famous exchanges of violence, their

*Fig. 23. Laurel and Hardy in* Hats Off, *1927*
*(© Richard Feiner and Company, Inc.)*

tit-for-tat routines, notably in *Two Tars* and *Big Business*. They need to seem to
be in control. The fact that the other characters in their films, especially in the
two-reelers, can get caught up in their mayhem (everyone losing his hat or his
pants, or getting a pie in the face) and participate in their tit-for-tat aggression,
suggests that Stan's and Ollie's anxieties and problems are shared, and that the
forms of order and authority with which the world browbeats the Boys are easily
penetrated facades covering violence and anarchy. These are Depression films.

In *Habeas Corpus* (1928), the Boys, again eager for employment, are hired by
a mad scientist to bring back from a graveyard a body for experimentation. A de-
tective follows them and crawls into a sheet in an open grave to entrap them. The
Boys haul him away in a sack (fig. 24); he winds up taking Ollie's hat, and so on.
Despite the "ceremonious pacing"[65] that enabled Laurel and Hardy to include
their gags in a more realistic narrative and so manage easily the transition to
sound films, there is no disguising the dark wonderland of sudden changes and
hidden plots that constitutes their world, against which the Boys' bowlers are like
icons of futile thought, seemingly stable when all else is collapsing, then sud-

*Figs. 24 and 25. Laurel and Hardy in* Habeas Corpus, *1928*
*(The Museum of Modern Art, Film Stills Archive, New York)*

denly detached by circumstances, proven wrong again. This is very like the nowhere landscape of *Waiting for Godot*, in which two bowler-hatted men try to maintain a frail hold while mysterious plans and physical embarrassments operate outside their control. No wonder Laurel and Hardy influenced Beckett and were probably the models for Didi and Gogo (see fig. 25).[66] Their mise-en-scène may be much more specific than Beckett's, but the germ of abstraction is there—and it is there because the middle class has claimed the modern world as its own and has to suffer the consequences.

# THE WEIMAR BOWLER

## THE BOWLER AS ICON

By the time of Germany's Weimar Republic (1919–33) the bowler hat had accumulated such a complex semantics of the middle class that its various significations could be made unconsciously, or taken for granted. The bowler was on its way to being used more in the arts than in life, to becoming more icon than object, more an item of costume or design than of everyday dress. By the Twenties it was not as ubiquitous as it was at the turn of the century. A perusal of *The Gentleman's Tailor* between 1907 and 1920 reveals a trend in men's apparel toward the formal. More and more the bowler was worn with lounge suits and chesterfields and was referred to as the "next most dressy style of hat"[1] to the topper. A flatter, less curled brim became popular, as did shades of brown and gray. Hats in general were becoming dressier; for example, soft hats, like fedoras, were replacing cloth caps. Businessmen's dress was becoming more elaborated, and the bowler more strictly identified with it. The stereotype of the Man in the Bowler Hat was well in place in fashion magazines (see fig. 26) by the time Magritte, in Belgium, began to depict it in 1926. It is remarkable that the bowler survived as it did, given that the middle class, as it settled into its ascendancy, would eventually adopt and invent more various styles of dress—more kinds of hats, for example. Its survival was partly, or even largely, due to its becoming more iconic than practical, a more potent and impersonal sign—like the middle class it signified.

In D. H. Lawrence's *Women in Love* (1920), the bowler hat represents a country and a way of life. Toward the end of the book, Gudrun Brangwen, considering her future with Gerald Crich, who she knows "could reorganise the industrial system,"[2] is seized with a corrosive irony:

> What did she care, that Gerald had created a richly-paying industry out of an old worn-out concern? What did she care? The worn-out concern and the rapid, splendidly organised industry, they were bad money. . . . And who can take political England seriously? Who can? Who can care a straw, really, how the old patched-up Constitution is tinkered at any more? Who cares a button for our national ideas, any more than for our national bowler hat? Aha, it is all old hat, it is all old bowler hat! (409)

Here the bowler hat, in representing England, or England's "ideas," seems to stand at once for the old and the new, for worn-out and for modern things. For Gudrun, the latter only grows out of the former, through organizing and tinkering; the ideas remain the same, and these ideas, as the novel makes clear, are middle-class, commercial, industrial, mechanistic, materialistic. Earlier, when the difference between Gerald and his industrialist father is discussed, the father's "Christian attitude of love and self-sacrifice" is regarded by Gerald as "old hat" —what mattered now were "position and authority" (219). Both of them wish to promote industry—that energy is sustained—but Gerald, being more modern, is also more impersonal and mechanistic. So the bowler signifies the bourgeois, mercantile spirit as a whole, corrupted by materialism at its heart. Gerald has abandoned "the whole democratic-equality problem," as well as the Christian ethic, in favor of "the great social productive machine" (219), yet even democracy and equality were mechanistic ideals, weapons of "chaos" and "disruption" (218–19).

Although Gudrun's thinking is qualified by her mood ("everything turned to irony with her"), her thoughts, though exclamatory, are confirmed elsewhere with the authority of Lawrence's third person—as in the passages, already quoted, on Gerald and his father. For Lawrence, the bowler hat had become an icon of everything wrong with England: a middle-class, commercial materialism ("the substitution of the mechanical principle for the organic" [223]) that already had the alarming depth of its own history. It is, for him, a weighty sign, and a rather simple and declarative one, having behind it the dull edge of denigrating the modern that would become a costly pastime in Weimar Germany.

*Fig. 26.*
*Model from*
Grafton Fashions
for Gentlemen,
1924–25
*(The Fashion*
*Research Centre,*
*Bath)*

Nowhere in the world, in the Twenties, was the middle class more in crisis than in Germany, and nowhere did the bowler hat have such importance as an icon. The German burghers during the Weimar years were suddenly and at once at the center of things, intensely vulnerable, and under grave and finally catastrophic attack. Modern industrial life came to Germany very quickly and was never assimilated. Weimar Germany was born, and died, in trauma. The bowler, identified with England and with American film, was not indigenous, and its fit, like the fit of everything else in Germany, was not comfortable. It became filled with various and transferable anxieties: about industrial, functional, urban life; about rootless entertainment; about machines; about finance; about Jews; and about a lower middle class that, if it was new to England and France in the latter half of the nineteenth century, was almost alien to a Germany en route from an atavistic and antimodern monarchy to an atavistic and antimodern dictatorship.

## PINNEBERG AND BIBERKOPF

One of the most popular novels in Germany during the years of the Weimar Republic was Hans Fallada's *Little Man, What Now?* (*Kleiner Mann, was nun?* [1933]). Perhaps it was popular because it focused on the lives of the lower middle class with sympathy rather than with hostility and contempt. The contemporary Germany that Fallada describes is, of course, a nation of inflation and money depreciation, in which "millions" of the class of clerks and cashiers are threatened with unemployment at any time, without having any working-class trade unions for support and solidarity. "Clerk, eh?" says a working-class woman to her prospective son-in-law, "I'd sooner you were a working man."[3] Her husband agrees: "I'd rather have a working man for my daughter. When my boy works overtime he gets paid for it" (17). In Weimar Germany, as Fallada sees it, the "little" people are the lower middle class of respectable and impecunious clerks who work hard, live carefully, maintain their self-respect (the only "luxury" they have [376]), and imagine themselves superior to the laborers, whose lives are cruder but more secure.

The clerk in question is the novel's protagonist, Hans Pinneberg, the "little man" of the title. He is one of the watchers of modern life, one of those who do not wish to be followed home. All through the novel, which is set in 1931, he struggles, with his wife Bunny and, eventually, their infant son, to contrive a life of minimal security and respectability, but at the end he is less well off than he was at the beginning. We are given to understand that Pinnebergs are legion, and Fallada asks—in his affectingly simple and straightforward way—what will happen to these people, "insignificant little being[s], crying and struggling and elbowing to keep [their] place in life" (215), buying cheap Sunday excursion tickets, wearing collars when the rest of their clothes are shabby, raising nuclear families in impersonal cities, pitted against each other in workplaces where bosses say "give me your sales-book . . . and I will tell you what sort of man you are" (201), and unable to achieve any clear social or political identity?

In the countryside, "those that stayed, the poorest, the most enduring and courageous, felt somehow that they ought to hang together, but unluckily they did not hang together at all. They were either Communists or Nazis, and thus involved in constant quarrels and conflicts" (347). Pinneberg does not join either party. Bunny, like her working-class parents, plans to vote Communist. She tells her husband, "The way they've treated the workers for a long while, and us too, will turn them all into wild beasts, as they'll find out one of these days," and Pinneberg replies, "They certainly will. . . . Most of us are already Nazis" (194). Fallada is alert to this delicate and very dangerous sociopolitical situation. The working class and the lower middle class are treated equally poorly, the former becoming Communists, the latter Nazis, and both fighting each other even though both are roughly in the same inflated raft. Pinneberg says, "I only wish we were working people. They call each other 'comrade,' and they really are comrades" (309), yet he is too respectable for Communism, and his wife reminds him that he's sentimentalizing working-class solidarity.

This provides us with some Weimar background, to which we will return. But for now, an important sequence of incidents in the novel brings Pinneberg to our special attention. Hans and Bunny go to see a Chaplinesque film featuring a "little man" in a bowler hat "making his way through the great city" (294). He is a "bank-cashier" with no money and a small family. He borrows money from a friend who eventually steals his wife. This latter development is probably behind Pinneberg's failure to see the character as his clear alter ego; he tells a friend, "Of course we know it isn't all of it true to life. . . . There's no one like the little cashier with the bowler hat" (299). (Hans wears a "hard black hat" as part of his respectable "outer husk" [136], but we can't be sure it's a bowler.)

The actor who plays the cashier, Franz Schluter, is clearly a Chaplin figure. He has an expressive face that can transform itself from careworn to happy. His acting helps point the reader to the Chaplinesque qualities of the little man Pinneberg himself, with his "outsider" status in regard to authorities (bosses, policemen) and workers alike, his marginal existence on the borders of class, his obsequious politeness and anxious respectability. Later in the novel Schluter himself turns up at the department store where Pinneberg works. Desperate to meet a quota and keep his job, Hans tries to sell him clothes that he seems interested in and in the process strikes up a conversation about the film and Schluter's acting. Pinneberg says that he liked it best when the actor "became quite small and shrunken, it was dreadful. . . . I felt it was so like us" (331–32). Pinneberg, almost unhinged with anxiety about his job, can now acknowledge his relation to the little man on the screen. This intimacy is too much for Schluter, who replies, "The voice of the people . . . Right, my friend, and now we must return to the serious affairs of life and find that suit" (332). It turns out the actor has no intention of buying, coldly rejects Pinneberg's pleas, and winds up getting him fired.

There are, then, paired confrontations between the bowler-hatted silent film comedian and his city-life counterpart. Pinneberg sees his life reflected on film, and Schluter sees his film persona reflected in real life. Neither one can identify with the other's realm, except for Pinneberg in the store when, feeling small and frail himself, he can appreciate his depiction on the screen, only to be given a rude reminder of the difference between art and life. There *is* no "voice" for these people. "The people" is an abstraction for the masses, those whose organized solidarity has made their numbers expressive. But the "little" people, despite their numbers, have no expression, and no power. For one thing, they are too identified with—and identify themselves with—"a world of respectable and blundering captains of industry" (319). "People like you, so I've heard," his prospective father-in-law tells Pinneberg, "think you're a cut above us working men."

> "No."
>
> "Yes. And why? Because you're paid by the month instead of the work. Because you work overtime without pay. Because you don't mind being paid under scale. Because you never go out on strike. Because you're always scabs."
>
> "It's not just a matter of money," said Pinneberg. "We think differently from most working men, our needs are different." (18)

The needs of the lower middle class are not different, but their thinking is, and therein lies their plight. Later, Pinneberg realizes that "we're people who don't count. We're quite alone," and echoes his father-in-law: "We think ourselves a cut above the workers" (309). One of Fallada's points is that not counting is a matter of not being included in "the people." In the end Hans has been cast out from "respectable people, people who earned money" (364), and stands alone, except for his family.

Though it does not conclude sentimentally, or even positively, *Little Man, What Now?* has been called a sentimental novel. This may have as much to do with its popularity as anything else, but it may also have to do with Fallada's affection for Hans and Bunny. They are never heroic—indeed, their lack of heroism is one of the novel's concerns—but they are, like Chaplin, engaging and touching in their small and fragile aspirations. They are also, like Chaplin, crucially and ultimately alone, having neither solidarity nor solidity.

The same is true of Franz Biberkopf, the protagonist of Alfred Döblin's *Berlin Alexanderplatz* (1929), widely regarded as the greatest novel to come out of the Weimar years and as one of the great modernist novels. Franz, an uncouth ex-con who returns to his Berlin neighborhood, "has sworn to all the world and to himself to remain respectable. And as long as he had money, he remained respectable."[4] Like *Little Man, What Now?*, this novel is about how impossible it is to *be* respectable when inflation is so bad that lower-middle-class people have become thieves (196). Franz is much cruder and much less sweet-natured than Hans Pinneberg, and the world he faces is much harsher, but he is just as dim about how the Weimar society in which he finds himself works against him. Both little men are brought to slow realizations of conditions which trap them because of their very ambition, as Franz puts it, to "stay respectable and keep to yourself! That's my idea" (73).

Franz characteristically wears a bowler hat (42, 75). After selling anti-Semitic, pro-Nordic newspapers (he is "not made" for but can't get away from politics [367, 375]), he becomes a fence and a pimp, though he "looks like a well-fed, good-natured saloon-keeper, or butcher, with creases in his trousers, gloves and a derby hat," and "enjoys the respect of passers-by and the anger of proletarians" (346). The boundaries between the middle and the criminal classes are blurred. Indeed, Franz's very desire to be a bourgeois ("I'm a self-provider, I am!" [373]) involves him in the underworld, where his uncommitted and apolitical nature proves useful. The evil Reinhold, who murders Franz's girlfriend, wears a derby as well (523), as though he were a dark alter ego (Franz was in jail for causing the death of a girlfriend). When, near the end of the novel, Franz walks through the city, five sparrows who are "five slain evil-doers," fly over him, crying out that he is a criminal, not a gentleman, that he's "aping the honest man." They want to "let something drop on his hat" (539), which of course represents his respectability. The solid sobriety of the bowler only lasts as long as Franz's oath to remain respectable—that is, as long as his money doesn't run out.

Without it, the self-help autonomy that Franz cherishes dissolves, and his bowler becomes, for the fantasy sparrows, an item of costume, covering over criminality. And Franzes, like Pinnebergs, are legion; Döblin, who intrudes on his narrative as a storyteller, says he is "following the traces of my little man in Berlin" (257), "an ordinary man only in the sense that we can clearly understand him and say: step by step, we might have gone the same way" (292). Franz goes insane with rage and suffering and, returning from a mental hospital, is offered a job as "assistant door-man in a medium-sized factory" (632), ready to be conscripted if war comes along. For, as Döblin prophesies, Weimar will go the same way as Franz Biberkopf, "tramp[ing] to war with iron tread" (634). And Weimar, too, as we shall see, wore a bowler hat.

## CHAPLINESQUE

There are several reasons why the bowler was prominent in Weimar art and Weimar culture. In the first place, Chaplin had an enormous influence. Chaplin and the Russian director Sergei Eisenstein were the dominant figures in film,[5] especially in 1926 when both *The Gold Rush* and *Battleship Potemkin* appeared. Stills from *The Gold Rush* were published in a Berlin art journal, *Das Kunstblatt*, that same year, and the playwright Bertolt Brecht went to see the film because theater people he knew who saw it felt the drama would never match it.[6] Well before *Modern Times* (1936), Chaplin was a topic among the German intelligentsia of the Left.[7] Indeed, in 1929, the polemical weekly *AIZ* (*Arbeiter-Illustrierte Zeitung* [*Workers' Illustrated Newspaper*]), founded by the revolutionary socialist organizer Willi Muenzenberg, featured a cover showing "three people pulling in the same direction": Chaplin, dressed up as Charlie, flanked by the Communist journalist Egon Kisch and the American socialist novelist Upton Sinclair (fig. 27). This direction seemed to be toward an egalitarian society in which the machinery of bourgeois civilization would be dismantled and the little man would come into his own; the aesthetician Elie Faure described Chaplin as "obstetrician to a new world."[8]

Recognizing or imagining a socialist agenda in Chaplin's work probably had as much to do with his public statements as with the world expressed in his films. In the early Twenties, Chaplin, beginning to conceive of himself as a man of ideas, spoke neutrally or warmly of his interest in Bolshevism, Trotsky, and Lenin, and of his friendship with the American leftist Max Eastman. Chaplin re-

*Fig. 27. Charlie Chaplin, with Upton Sinclair (left) and Egon Kisch (right), on the cover of* AIZ, *1929 (from John Willett,* The Weimar Years: A Culture Cut Short *[New York: Abbeville Press, 1984])*

vealed a social consciousness about unemployment, the poor, the outcast. Much of this was expressed in *My Trip Abroad* (1922), an account of his one-month trip to Europe in 1921,[9] including only three days in a "depressing" Berlin, in which his films had not yet been shown.[10] Chaplin's sociopolitical ideas were always more personal, emotional, and occasional than intellectual and programmatic; he described himself best in his autobiography as "intellectually a fellow traveler" with those he met in Greenwich Village.[11] He did include in his autobiography a photograph of himself and his "mentors" Upton Sinclair and Rob Wagner, a friend, and declared that Sinclair had provoked his interest in socialism.[12] These friendships, and remarks, in turn made people see more social and political content in his films. In this way Chaplin the little man of the lower-middle class came to represent "the people," a development that Fallada later reflected on rather shrewdly.

The artist Fernand Léger, who painted mechanistic Utopias in which people are interconnected through their machine parts, drew Cubist Chaplins for the writer Ivan Goll's *Die Chaplinade* (1923; see fig. 28) and for his and Dudley Murphy's film, *Ballet mécanique* (1923–24).[13] For the latter, Léger's Chaplin is constructed of mechanical pieces that can fly apart, including his severely drawn bowler, a perfect half-circle on a straight line. His Charlot is a marionette who introduces and concludes a film that celebrates a discontinuous, fragmented, modern urban life. Observing two men carrying huge golden letters in a wheelbarrow, Léger remarked, *"There is the origin of the modern performance. . . . The street thought of as one of the fine arts?"*[14] Later, in an essay titled "A New Realism—the Object" (1926), Léger, discussing the need for a new and nonromantic, nonliterary cinema, wrote "that in the new realism the human being, the personality, is very interesting only in these fragments ["parts of the human body"], and that these fragments should not be considered of any more importance than any of the other objects."[15] With this motive objects could be discovered as having "a new lyric and plastic power" as part of a modern and geometric age.[16] Film can enlarge and isolate objects; indeed, "before the invention of the moving picture no one knew the possibilities latent in a foot—a hand—a hat." Chaplin, the creation of a sped-up and fragmenting medium, is imagined by Léger as an assemblage of geometric parts. Léger may well have had Chaplin in mind when he selected a hat as a representative object in the passage above: the geometric bowler was a perfect design object for the "new realism" of German art, of which Léger's essay is a document.

It was not only Chaplin whom Léger thought of as bringing style and humor to the troublesome discontinuities of modern life. Léger used the bowler hat itself

*Fig. 28. Fernand Léger, drawing of Charlie Chaplin
for Ivan Goll's* Die Chaplinade, *1923 (from John
Willett,* Art and Politics in the Weimar Period:
The New Sobriety, 1917–1933 *[New York:
Pantheon Books, 1978])*

for roughly the same purposes in his *Umbrella and Bowler* (*Parapluie et melon*, 1926). The painting is composed of blocks of geometric objects, including the two businessman's appurtenances. The arrangement seems staid and male except for the bowler, a high-crowned one with a satin band that is softer looking and more curved than the other forms. If Léger is imagining a cold, rigid world, the bowler makes it a stylish one. Léger's bowler is a Cubist object with flair; it both fits and lightens the modern world.

The bearable lightness of the bowler—its connections with style and gaiety and change—is carried further by Hans Richter in his experimental film, *Ghosts before Breakfast* (*Vormittagspuk*, 1928). Richter, a leftist painter who turned to film, showed bowlers flying through the air, free of their wearers, like a flock of low-flying birds (fig. 29). Siegfried Kracauer describes these as "inanimate objects in full revolt against the conventional use we make of them,"[17] mocking their possessors, and indeed, bowlers under their own power, free of their staid environment, have a peculiar rebellious power, a power Magritte would make signal use of. Always within the bowler's sober shape and heavy, respectable contexts has lurked a sporty design object, a piece of sleek costumery, that wants to fly free of its contexts.

*Fig. 29. Stills from Hans
Richter's film* Ghosts before
Breakfast, *1923 (from John
Willett,* Art and Politics in
the Weimar Period: The New
Sobriety, 1917–1933 *[New York:
Pantheon Books, 1978])*

# MATTERS OF FACT

The spirit of sober realism that would permeate everything in Weimar culture from graphics to music to architecture is another reason for the importance of the bowler hat in Germany. The bowler became a common object of what was termed, in painting, *Neue Sachlichkeit*, the "new matter-of-factness," a hard-edged and functional style (*Sachlichkeit* signifies "a mixture of utility, sobriety, practicality and objectivity."[18]) This was the art of a less lyrical and more urban modernity, "inspired partly by the new technology, partly by the tasks being set them by a self-renewing society which treated design as an aspect of social engineering and economic advance."[19] From its utilitarian use for William Coke's gamekeepers, the bowler was both functionally and stylishly designed, and this combination of contemporaneity and everyday usefulness made it a hat "for the times," as they said at the time.

Eberhard Kolb calls the mood of *Neue Sachlichkeit* "republic-oriented,"[20] and indeed it coincided with the relative stabilization of the Weimar government in the mid-Twenties. The aesthetic and political passions of Expressionism, which marked the second decade of the century in Germany—passions of outcry, revolt and Utopian dreaming—had expended themselves by about 1923, and the artistic focus shifted to the qualities we have come to identify with the Man in the Bowler Hat: sobriety, functionalism, impassivity, neutrality, a concern with the business of everyday life: "People were disillusioned, mistrustful of emotion, and determined to survive the economic crisis."[21] The Expressionist playwright Paul Kornfeld had a character of his cry out for another attitude toward life: "Let us hear no more of war and revolution and the salvation of the world! Let us be modest and turn to other, smaller things."[22] The Weimar republicans, eager to put the Great War and the Bolshevik Revolution of 1919 behind them and to try to meet reparation payments, could not have agreed more.

Men in Bowler Hats were precisely the subjects that many *Neue Sachlichkeit* artists painted. The name itself was conferred by a journalist describing the work of a group of painters who staged a collective exhibition at the Mannheim Kunsthalle in 1925. Their "matter-of-factness" was "new" because *Sachlichkeit* had been one of the aims of the German Werkbund, a group of artists and industrialists organized in 1907 to improve the quality of German manufactured goods by reconciling industry with arts and crafts.[23] Walter Gropius joined the Werkbund in 1912, and through him and others the Bauhaus, which Gropius founded in Weimar in 1919, was influenced by the aesthetic of *Sachlichkeit*. By 1922 the

Bauhaus—arguably the most important modernist school of art and design in the twentieth century—had shifted toward the functional and practical, a shift that occurred in all the arts.[24]

By the time the Bauhaus was moved to Dessau in 1925, the style by which it became known had evolved: geometric, functional, boldly primary in color, and of modern materials.[25] All of this is by way of pointing out that the bowler hat figured so strongly in Weimar art and life partly because it fulfilled the aesthetic interests of the time. The style of *Neue Sachlichkeit* "expressed the hope that thinking men, through self-control, scepticism and discipline, could still master both mechanization and the darker side of human nature."[26] The bowler could have been a Bauhaus design; it had never ceased being "modern." And, despite the Bauhaus's later leaning to the Left, to be modern was to be middle-class.

Bowlers were, of course, identified with city life, and a comparison between an Expressionist and a *Neue Sachlichkeit* rendering of bowlers and cities is instructive. In Ernst Ludwig Kirchner's *Street, Berlin* (*Die Strasse*, 1913; fig. 30) we have the tilting planes, the jagged lines and angular distortions, the toxic colors, and the aura of anxiety that marked so much of Expressionist art. Kirchner's bowlers, in this and in other paintings like *The Red Cocotte* (1914–15), are elongated, as though trying to be top hats. Such bowlers did exist—they can be seen in photographs of English street scenes and in Picasso's *Still Life with Hat*—but I have never seen one advertised or remarked in fashion books, and certainly the elegant figures in *Street, Berlin* didn't wear them. No, they are as distorted as the women's hands. As was common in Expressionist art, all figuration is affected and shaped/misshaped by the emotion(s) to be expressed, and in this painting contempt for the fashionable is strong. Kirchner's creatures of the boulevard bear the dehumanizing marks of the modern life that has produced them. They are as thin and hard and featureless (except for the women, who simper) as mannequins. They crowd together, parade for each other, look in store windows. In the upper left background, they seem a line of faceless ghouls. The light is candescent and harsh, the light of unhealthy night streets. Kirchner's vision is of a machine age having finally produced its bourgeois progeny, defined only by their clothes. Fashion and modernity are conflated as subjects of anxiety.

There is anxiety in *Neue Sachlichkeit* painting, but it is much more coolly conceived. In Anton Räderscheidt's *Portrait of the Davringhausen Painters* (*Bildnis des Malers Davringhausen*, 1925; fig. 31), the more naturally drawn bowlers are part of the businesslike objectivity of the scene. The painting seems realized by a man in a bowler hat, and indeed these pre-Magritte figures are painters. Like Kirchner's figures they are smartly dressed and crowded in the picture frame, but

*Fig. 30. Ernst Ludwig Kirchner,* Street, Berlin, *1913 (Collection, The Museum of Modern Art, New York. Purchase.)*

there the resemblance ends. These men are allowed to be self-possessed; if their expressions are hard, impassive, as businesslike as their clothes, they are comfortable in their angular milieu. Kirchner's dynamism results from a clash between the superficial and featureless subjects and the emotional distortions of the composition; outer and inner are in violent conflict. Räderscheidt expresses

*Fig. 31. Anton Räderscheidt,* Portrait of the Davringhausen Painters, *1925
(© 1992, ARS, New York / Bild-Kunst, Bonn; Fackelträger-Verlag)*

*Fig. 32. Georg Scholz,* Self-Portrait, *1926 (Staatliche Kunsthalle, Karlsruhe)*

no conflict with his subjects; indeed, what anxiety the painting conveys comes from this seamless objectivity. The bowlers seem natural extensions of the subjects' heads, snug and appropriate. In Georg Scholz's *Self-Portrait* (1926; fig. 32), the bowler-hatted man, individually realized, is seen in a city street that is clearly and comfortably his home. The automobile, nosing out like the one in *Street, Berlin*, parked in a much calmer, more staid composition, is merely on display. The machine, like the streets, is accepted. The painter seems energized, made alert, by the environment. Even his bowler has a dynamic brim. Max Beckmann and Ernst Fritsch also painted self-portraits in bowler hats, as had Cézanne before them.

These are the facts of life, say these Weimar painters, with their own somber brand of modernity. There is no reason to take any special attitude toward these facts, whether of outrage or satire or celebration. The many bowler-hatted men featured in Räderscheidt's paintings are like frozen Chaplins, haunted but affectless men in black suits and black ties who are almost scarily sober. One, *badaud*-like with large eyes and his hands joined behind his back, looks straight out at us, although a naked woman splayed on parallel bars is almost in front of him (*Act on the Bars* [*Akt am Barren*], 1925); her nakedness makes us aware, not only of his lack of attention to her, but of his formal dress as well. As in Magritte's paintings, the woman seems to express something—expose herself—that the man is keeping under wraps.

Perhaps Räderscheidt's most representative use of the bowler hat is in his almost generically named *Man with a Stiff Hat* (*Mann mit steifem Hut*, 1922; fig. 33), in which a formally dressed bowler-hatted man, through a foreshortening of perspective and an almost mathematical relation of lines and volumes, seems to become one with an urban building that looks like a cell door in a jail. He is a severe, formal figure in a world of severe forms, the ultimate model of urban life. He stares straight ahead at nothing, impassive, a hard shell having formed around his inner life in response to the city.

The bowler hat was so much a property of *Sachlichkeit* that in Albert Henrich's *Still-Life with Collar and Hat* (1925) a handsome bowler takes its place on the traditional table of goods, as common and as pleasing as fruit or flowers. Postwar Germany clearly needed a formality, some sense of composedness—which it could only hope to feel briefly in the mid-Twenties. Weimar life was almost never still.

## THE REPUBLIC OF THE BURGHERS

The third and most important meaning that the bowler had for Germany in the Twenties was as a sign of Weimar itself, the "republic of the burghers."[27] Republican democracy came to Germany later, of course, than to England and France, and came in an atmosphere of postwar trauma and humiliation. Modern life, which always developed under the aegis of democracy in one form or another, arrived in Germany in the Twenties precipitously, and in an atmosphere at once liberating and foreboding, that would heighten all its qualities, as well as the reactions against those qualities. The story of Weimar's volatile mixture of avant-gardism and fascism, experimentation and reaction, is a fairly familiar one and requires no elaboration here. Suffice it to say that the various republicans who ruled Germany until Hitler came to power in 1933 effected a kind of political and cultural revolution without having any fervor, program, agenda, or identity to speak of, and only intermittent energy. The change of government from monarchial and imperial to parliamentarian "would be inspired by that middle-class Kultur, the property of the ten per cent who had gone to a gymnasium,"[28] but it was unable to inspire anyone else. A large number of its supporters

*Fig. 33. Anton Räderscheidt,* Man with a Stiff Hat, *1922 (© 1992, ARS, New York /
Bild-Kunst, Bonn; Das Rheinische Bildarchiv)*

were called *vernunftsrepublikanisch*, that is, prorepublican by virtue of reason
(expedience) rather than conviction. And there was about the government the behavior and atmosphere of *Sachlichkeit*,[29] a tepid and businesslike sobriety, a pas-
sionlessness that struck many as expressing a petty bourgeois mentality. One
journal editor wrote that he could not live in a "republic of hairdressers, postal
clerks, and salesmen."[30] And yet the Weimar Republic established a parliamen-
tary democracy; nurtured a social, political, and regional pluralism; "rational-

ized" production methods; and, of course, shifted power from the military and aristocracy to the middle class. And, in effect, it allowed (if it could not inspire) a "Weimar culture" of the arts, second to none in the Twenties, that would displace in most people's minds any culture to which the Republic itself would have wanted to attach its name.

It is certainly not surprising that a government thought of as lower-middle-class (that is, unsolidly bourgeois), commercial-minded and politically "modern" (in the sense of untraditional) would be identified with a bowler hat. The *Neue Sachlichkeit* figures have the passionless insubstantiality of burghers connected to a geometry of city surfaces rather than to any community or even a space of any perspectival depth. But these paintings are, as their collective name suggests, objective—the work of artists, like Magritte, who saw each other, and themselves, as middle-class. These painters were relatively apolitical—that is, their politics was largely unprogrammatic and unconscious.

The same cannot be said of Georg Grosz. In his *Republican Automatons* (*Republikanische Automaten*, 1920; fig. 34), the dispassionate style of *Neue Sachlichkeit* and Léger's modernism becomes politically satiric. "Objectivity" becomes in Grosz's hands a weapon with which to expose the Republic's lack of a German heart. Two robot figures are posed in the cool, angular urban milieu favored later on by the *Neue Sachlichkeit* painters (with whom Grosz was lumped) and inspired by de Chirico. These figures strongly resemble Léger's automatons, people constructed of tubes and balls and linkages, except that they lack a harmonious relation to the overall composition that makes Léger's figures seem part of a mechanical Utopia. (If these Utopias seem cold Dystopias, that is only true of Utopias in general; Grosz never depicted ideals of any kind.) Grosz's figures of urban modernity share with the beige and cream-colored cityscape a sharp functionalism (they are, after all, functionaries), but they are awkwardly placed and isolated, even from each other.

*Republican Automatons* is Grosz's imagination of the Weimar Republic. It is a government of patriotic robot bourgeois, whose loyalty—expressed by the cheer of advertisement typeface coming out of (entering?) one's empty head and the waving of the Republic's black-red-gold tricolor by the other—is strictly mechanical and mindless. And these figures don't even seem to function clearly. The gestures of the one on the right, with his veteran's Iron Cross, are made obscure by what seem to be missing arm parts. Their left arms end in useless surfaces, their right arms in tiny and incomplete-seeming fittings; the flag rests unsteadily in one of these. And one has a peg leg, probably because he's a war veteran, like the other. These are not machines designed to accomplish any task

*Fig. 34. Georg Grosz,* Republican Automatons, *1920 (© 1992, ARS,
New York / Bild-Kunst, Bonn; The Museum of Modern Art, New York.
Advisory Committee Fund)*

but to embody and represent their government. Since the Weimar Republic was
fundamentally middle-class, at the center of Grosz's composition is the featureless disk face, mounted by a bowler hat, of one of the automatons. The bowler
goes with his business suit. We may imagine his head as incomplete and empty
as his tuxedoed companion's; the first two letters of the companion's cheer are

stamped on his face, the number 12 replacing his features (and perhaps signifying him as a chauvinist apostle of the Republic).

Here we have the satiric expression of the qualities of the Man in the Bowler Hat. Sedateness, impassivity, stiffness of bearing—all are realized now in pure mechanism. Stereotyped or hidden facial features have been expunged. The anonymous commercial man is a robot, having truly lost the humanity people suspected him of lacking. And these being the early and most difficult years of the Republic (c. 1920), when the economy was collapsing, he cannot even function except as a well-dressed cheerleader; he is not even commercially viable. Walter Lacqueur wrote that "Wilhelmian Germany had been governed more or less automatically by a clearly defined elite; it was far more difficult to define with any degree of accuracy the identity of the new republican establishment."[31] Grosz wasted no time in depicting its anti-identity as feeble, crippled, soulless automatons, the product of a commercial machine age, the futurist dream as a banal nightmare.

The bowler hat here not only caps a soulless commercialism, it is a sign of mercantile Britain, one of Germany's conquerors. Grosz wants to reveal the ascendant middle-class modern world for what it is. But what does Grosz reveal of himself? In 1920, the year of *Republican Automatons*, he began a series of "objective" mechanical works. A year later he wrote: "People are no longer individual, they are collective, almost mechanical concepts. Individual fates no longer matter. . . . The straightforwardness and clarity of engineering drawings are a better guide than uncontrollable gush about the cabbals and metaphysics and saintly ecstasies."[32] Three years after joining the Communist Party and becoming a well-known satirist of what was philistine, brutal, and militaristic in the German character, Grosz was calling "mechanical" ideas about the "People" and the "collective." Indeed, after his first trip to the Soviet Union in 1918, he wrote of the Party functionaries that "many of them seemed like animated, red-covered pamphlets, and they were even proud of the fact. And naturally, since this was supposed to be the mass era, they tried to suppress what little individuality they had, and would actually have been glad to have grey cardboard discs for faces with red numbers on them instead of names."[33] So Bolsheviks and republicans alike are part of the anonymous, numbered herd. This would seem to leave Grosz in the dwindling camp of the individualists, but the style of *Republican Automatons* belies that: it is just as heartless and categorical as its subjects. Matthias Eberle is right when he criticizes Grosz for mechanizing "social phenomena" with a politics to which even he couldn't be faithful.[34]

With this reading in mind, we can understand *Republican Automatons* as about the unintended conflation of a mechanical politics and a mechanical culture: the bowler hat points with disgust to the Social Democratic burghers running the country, and at the same time points with self-loathing to the matter-of-fact style of a culture identified with the Republic. Grosz turns the fashion, if you will, of this culture against itself, thereby inscribing himself within it, as surely as he wanted to circumscribe it, himself outside, drawing the lucid and telling lines.

But this is not merely to expose the aesthetic and political limitations of an artist. The point to be made is that the sentiments held by Grosz were legion. Contempt for the middle class by people (intelligentsia included) who were middle-class, and whose claim to be outside its influence was staked only by the expression of this contempt, was a hallmark of Weimar life, and of what has come to be known as "Weimar culture."

One of the major reasons for the eventual and devastating collapse of the Republic was that this attitude was shared by both the Right and the Left, by Bolshevik and imperialist intellectuals. Both hated the *embourgeoisement* of Germany. (Indeed, in 1928, according to Henry Pachter, the Communists declared the Social Democrats to be the "main enemy" and began to campaign with the Nazis to overthrow the Republic.[35]) Both ends of the political spectrum offered a *Gemeinschaft* of community (whether German or Communist) against the *Gesellschaft* of modern business society,[36] the society of the Man in the Bowler Hat. The sad fact is that *Republican Automatons* could have been painted by a Nazi artist. As Pachter notes, the proto-Nazi, right-wing movements had in common

> a fanatical hatred of rationality and of the bourgeois system of values, life styles, and mental attitude. . . . They tried to escape from the mediocrity of the "nouveau-riche" empire and of business materialism into the fantasies of a nobler existence of Wagnerian knights, noble Conquerors . . . a social order instead of wild competition, artistic values instead of mercantile hypocrisy and venality, respect for the great individual instead of democracy.[37]

What fantasies of order Grosz meant to imply are not clear; for him, as for the leftist intellectual Kurt Tucholsky, disgust was often enough. In an alarming volume of essays, poems, and captions (to John Heartfield's photographs of German life in the Twenties) titled *Deutschland, Deutschland über Alles* (1931), Tucholsky decried a state "that has been drowned in faceless anonymity"—a bureaucratic, cowardly, class-ridden, conservative and, above all, middle-class republic.[38] What marks the republicans are their cold, petty mercantile attitudes; they are underlings reveling in being on top for a change.[39] Tucholsky, himself a Jew, had no trouble extending his satire to middle-class Jews. In a poem entitled "Small Official Journey," he wrote,

> It's family, it's pound-cake, the good old German pattern—
> you can hunt out democrats with your *Reichswehr* lantern;
> the notables, at evening, sit solidly spread,
> calling down damnation on the Jew Republic's head.[40]

The good old Germans are the targets here, but Tucholsky has been damning the Republic all along. Having satirized "the educated, north-German middle-class ideal" as being, in reality, "rigid, abrupt and cold officials or merchants,"[41] he is brought face to face with the German right-wing stereotype of Jews, who "incarnated all the evils of capitalism, above all its impersonal anonymity and its cold rationality."[42] So the democratic Republic and the Jews were brought together in a demonology of the middle class shared by the Right and the Left. Pachter claims that "Romanticists, nihilists and reactionaries found the Republic odious not because it was Jewish but because they realized that the Jews identified with it,"[43] but in general it is difficult to know whether anti-Semitism, especially in its modern forms, is a cover for hatred of the middle class, or the reverse: that attacking the commercial anonymity of the bourgeois is safer than attacking rootless moneylenders. We may leave Tucholsky with his intellectual's *Hassliebe* (hate-love) for his own kind, and Grosz, too, with his cartoon German characters expressing his own cartoon politics. Both of them, and many others, mirrored their sworn enemies on the Right in hating the same targets, and therein lies much of the fate of Weimar Germany.

## THE JEWS' STEEL HELMET

Given this background, it is not surprising to note that Jews not only commonly wore bowler hats in Germany, they were actually identified with them in the Thirties. Of course the bowler was the "hat of the decade" in the Twenties.[44] It was sported by everyone from Franz Kafka and his father Hermann, middle-class Jews involved in business, to T. S. Eliot, natty in his banker's clothes and eager to identify with the British, to George Gershwin and Jack Dempsey. It was Mussolini's favorite hat. In the 1924 and 1928 American elections, Al Smith made the brown derby famous as his trademark. The derby gave him, as it gave Mussolini and Dempsey, at once a formal dignity and a street-wise solidity. With this kind of popularity, the bowler's referents are in danger of becoming too diffuse to be resonant. Yet its connection with the business world remains unmistakable, even when it is worn by silent film comedians, who are, after all, often pounding the streets looking for employment. The bowler, as we have seen, can be a sign of middle-class commercialism on the heads of everyone from aspiring cashiers to wealthy industrialists. Within this spectrum were many Jews.

Since the vast majority of German Jews were engaged in bourgeois occupations—over 61 percent in trade or commerce, especially retailing[45]—it is not surprising that the bowler hat was common headgear among them, especially since many were interested in assimilating into German middle-class culture. Hatred of capitalism and the Republic from the Right and Left was easily conflated with hatred of the Jews. As W. E. Mosse notes in his study of Jews and the German economy, "General anticapitalism could all too easily be directed into anti-Jewish channels, given the prominence of Jews in capitalist development."[46] Jews were politically moderate and held high positions in the Social Democratic Party, the bulwark of the Republic. Jews were enormously important to the cultural and intellectual life of Weimar. So the Right (monarchists, industrialists, proto-Nazis, et al.) sneered at Weimar as a *Judenrepublik*.[47] And by the Thirties, the bowler hat became so identified with Jews that it was called by the Nazis a *Judenstahlhelm*, or "steel helmet of the Jews," a term of contempt by which the Nazis expressed their view that the Jews profited from the war although they did not fight it ("Stahlhelm" being the name of a paramilitary veterans' league in the Twenties, derived from the descriptive name of the headgear that had been worn by soldiers on the frontlines). After the Nazis seized power in 1933 and Jews were everywhere threatened, the bowler hat went out of fashion in Germany and was worn only by the rare few who wished to advertise their political sympathy with Jews.[48]

An anti-Semitic poster by O. Caniche designed for the Vichy government of France in 1943 (fig. 35) depicts an ugly, villainous Jew in a bowler hat. The caption reads, "Behind powerful enemies: the Jew." Those enemies are Great Britain, the Soviet Union, and the United States, identified by their flags. The Jew is almost wrapped in the American flag; "Americanism" signified, for the philosopher Heidegger on the Right,[49] as well as for Tucholsky on the Left, all the manifestations of modern capitalism: technology, faith in science, consumer culture, unabashed commercialism (abashed commercialism is as old as any

*Fig. 35. O. Caniche, poster for the Vichy government, 1943
(Musée d'histoire contemporaine–BDIC)*

aristocracy), and "inauthentic" egalitarianism. The conjunction of the bowler hat with the American, British, and Soviet flags signifies a practical, hard-headed commercialism with treasonous, revolutionary aims. After all, Jews had played a leading role in integrating the German economy into an international trading system, for which cosmopolitan and "un-national" endeavors they were attacked by the protectionist right wing.[50] This is not to mention the left-leaning Jewish intellectuals. So here, in Caniche's poster, we have the modern middle-class cosmopolitan Bolshevik Jew as ugly thug.

Yet there is a relation between his hook-nosed, thick-lipped physiognomy (the Jew as the villain of melodrama, the heartless landlord) and Grosz's featureless and numbered automatons. The key is a shared soullessness. The "faceless anonymity" that Tucholsky felt was drowning the state[51] has given way to the evil energies of internationalist treason, but both represented a *geistlosen Staat*, the "spiritless state" of Weimar.[52] The crosses that dangle from the breast of one of Grosz's robots and hang like a timepiece (time is money) from the fob of Caniche's Jew—the former signifying an archaic and atavistic nationalism, the other signifying a religious and conspiratorial internationalism—are both emblems of the modern burgher. We can see this also in photomontages of bowler-hatted fools by the Dadaist John Heartfield (a.k.a. Helmut Herzfelde). In one of them, *The Reichsbishop drills Christendom* (*Der Reichsbischof richtet das Christentum aus*, 1934), the new Nazi bishop of the Reich church, appointed by Hitler, struts in inspection before a rank of ecclesiasts holding Nazi rather than Christian crosses. He is bemedalled and bowler-hatted, crisp, officious and impersonal.[53] The bowler could float from Right to Left because its identification with nineteenth-century respectability made it a conservative sign, and its identification with the modern made it a sign of threatening change. The Nazi-as-burgher, as imagined by the Left, brought these signs together. Nazi, Republican, Jew—whoever felt that *Geist* was missing from their antagonists imagined those antagonists in bowler hats, respectably selling off Germany. Nothing could be more tellingly typical of Weimar politics—and, I would argue, of twentieth-century politics in general—than this unconscious collusion of Right and Left in execrating the commercial and progressive middle class.

In his anti-Semitic study *The Jews and Modern Capitalism*, Werner Sombart remarks the similarity between capitalism and the Jewish character. Both, he says, are marked by "extreme intellectuality":

> The quality of abstraction in capitalism manifests itself in the substitution of all qualitative differences by merely quantitative ones (value in ex-

change). Before capitalism came, exchange was a many-sided, multi-coloured and technical process; now it is just one specialized act—that of the dealer: before there were many relationships between buyer and seller; there is only one now—the commercial. The tendency of capitalism has been to do away with different manners, customs, pretty local and national contrasts, and to set up in their stead the dead level of the cosmopolitan town.[54]

The result is a "drab uniformity" in which "money is the common denominator." Who could tell from this passage alone whether Sombart was a Nazi or a Marxist?

Henry Pachter reflects eloquently on this attitude as being expressed in a language (for example, of the German youth movement) on which the Nazis would build their myths:

[Walter Rathenau] quoted the sociologists who had denounced the trend toward the "termite state," the total rationality, the seamless community of production and business, the rule by purpose-oriented organization men. Like Marx he saw these developments as necessary consequences of capitalistic rationality: the abstract, calculable, infinitely divisible and flexible, exchangeable and functional character of the division of labor. The organization of mass production had rationalized man's relationship with his environment, taken the soul out of production, destroyed free creativity, and substituted for it specialization and mass culture.[55]

Most of this rhetoric could serve as a long caption to Grosz's *Republican Automatons*. And to the figure of the Man in the Bowler Hat. Rathenau, an assimilated Jew and successful industrialist, who warned against soulless commercialism, was the liberal foreign minister of the Republic until 1922, when he was assassinated by right-wing terrorists who no doubt thought in the same terms in their hatred of the Republic with which Rathenau was identified.

Using Jeffrey Herf's list of "conceptual opposites" that made up the "cultural system" of Germany, we can imagine that the Man in the Bowler Hat—whether burgher, robot, or Jew—represented civilization (*Zivilisation*) against culture (*Kultur*), mind over soul, society over community, passivity over will, quantity over quality, etc.[56] The aspiring lower middle class, the termites of the "termite state," had passively taken over Germany's vital soul. In the cultural imagination of both the Right and Left, Chaplin had become a republican Jew, hardening from tramp to cosmopolite, his spirit of practical enterprise become a cold and settled rationalism. The little man—he who, as we learned from Fallada's novel, suffered as much if not more than other Germans from reparations, inflation, and finally the Depression—became vilified for precisely those qualities that motored his aspiration.

Another, more pointedly tragic version of the transference of qualities comes from a 1955 comic strip by William M. Gaines, an American.[57] It is called "Master Race" and it concerns a refugee from World War II Germany named Carl Reissman, who is haunted, as he rides an American subway, by a figure from his past. The narrative leads you to think that Reissman is a Jew, "escaped from Belsen concentration camp," confronted by a Nazi who has vowed to get him. But at the end we realize that Reissman is an escaped Nazi, the former commandant of Belsen, and that the man who recognizes and then pursues him (to his accidental death on the subway tracks) is a Jewish survivor of the camp. This figure is represented as a cadaverous man in a bowler hat and black overcoat. So clad, he can effectively sustain the irony of the story: he could be a Nazi, he could be a Jew. Historically, as we have learned, he would be a Jew rather than a Nazi, since the Nazis never identified themselves with bowler hats (when Chaplin played the dual role of Jewish barber and Hitler in *The Great Dictator* [1940], he never wore his bowler in playing the latter); indeed, they identified Jews with bowlers. But the reason Gaines can fool us is that this unnamed man, because of his bowler hat, could represent some official, respectable, and dangerous world (as did Mussolini with his bowler on, and do the assassins in Magritte's *The Menaced Assassin*).

In a long frame of this not-so-comic strip which depicts Reissman's memory of the concentration camp, there is a line of heads of cadaverous men in bowler hats, pictorially unrelated to the guards beating Jews in the background so that we can identify the heads with either side (fig. 36). They seem to be the grim visages of the sadistic master race—but as we learn, they are the skeletal faces of Holocaust victims. The point to be made is that they are in a row, as Magritte's bowler-hatted men sometimes are. They are replicatable, men of the crowd. As such they seem menacing to us: eyeless, soulless, unfeeling. Yet this very image, when "read" again after we realize the man in the subway whom they resemble is a Jew, is one of ghostly victimization: so many of them, alike in having been reduced to walking corpses.

Probably unintentionally, Gaines has touched on the terrible sadness of Germany between the wars, and of German modernity. The ascendant middle class became such a lightning rod for everybody's flashes of anger and discontent and humiliation, including its own, that it was finally burnt up. The Weimar govern-

LOOK, CARL! LOOK AT THE FACE OF THIS MAN SITTING ACROSS FROM YOU IN THIS NOW DESERTED SUBWAY CAR! LOOK... AND REMEMBER! REMEMBER THE GUARDS THAT GLEEFULLY CARRIED OUT THE SADISTIC ORDERS OF THE MASTER RACE... WHIPPING... KICKING... BEATING!... THE GUARDS THAT EAGERLY DRAGGED THE WOMEN AND CHILDREN TO THE WAITING, SMOKING OVENS!...

*Fig. 36. William M. Gaines, frame from comic strip "Master Race," 1955 (© 1954 by I. C. Publishing Co., re© 1982 by William M. Gaines; used with permission from William M. Gaines, Agent, Inc.)*

ment was not only assailed as a "republic of the burghers" but as the "republic of the Jews." Hitler held Jews "responsible for . . . [a] cultural modernism"[58] that had been bred in a middle-class, urban milieu. The Man in the Bowler Hat became the Jew of the Holocaust. Everything modern in both—the sober, the reasonable, the commercial, the middle-of-the-road—became demonized and despised.

# MACHEATH

A final version of this bowler-hatted man, and a subtly demonized one, is the London gangster Macheath in Bertolt Brecht and Kurt Weill's *Threepenny Opera* (*Die Dreigroschenoper*, 1928). Brecht's point in having this criminal wear a bowler (see fig. 37) is not that Macheath is a low-life who aspires to the middle class, or that he is a bourgeois reduced to crime, but that bourgeois and gangster are one and the same, part of "a bourgeois phenomenon," "a bourgeois structure of the world" with "a specific view of the world."[59] Or as Brecht put it more bluntly in a later essay, "The play showed the close relationship between the emotional life of the bourgeois and that of the criminal world."[60] The middle-class audience that Brecht expected for his play would be entertained by the comic spectacle of gangsters behaving like the middle class, and drawn to the play because of that, but then would have to confront the idea of the middle class

*Fig. 37. Macheath and Polly Peachum in the original production of Bertolt Brecht's* Threepenny Opera, *1928 (from Werner Hecht,* Brechts Dreigroschenoper *[Frankfurt: Suhrkamp, 1985]*

as gangsters. In Brecht's terms, the bourgeois spectator "sees his wishes not merely fulfilled but also criticised (sees himself not as the subject but as the object)."[61]

Macheath's underworld gang fuss over the quality of the goods they have stolen (when the chief of police reads the store name from the label of a stolen oriental rug, Macheath replies, like a suburban housewife, "Yes, we never go anywhere else" [25]), worry about what "polite society" says (17) and what makes a gentleman (18), and figure they "will never rise in the world" if they cannot get credit for setting fire to the children's hospital (38). The beggars speak of their investments, and the whores, off-duty, iron and play cards and wash themselves in "a bourgeois idyll" (41), as Brecht puts it in his stage directions. But more pointedly, everything—from marriage to betrayal—is conducted, as Polly Peachum says (echoing her father), "on a strict business footing" (67). Or, as Macheath sings,

> What keeps mankind alive? The fact that millions
> Are daily tortured, stifled, punished, silenced, oppressed.
> Mankind can keep alive thanks to its brilliance
> In keeping its humanity repressed. (55)

Or, as Mrs. Peachum puts it, "money rules the world" (31). This is a world where all people unsentimentally keep accounts, in hopes of advancing themselves. As Polly raptly says to her father concerning Macheath's activities as a "first-class burglar," "A few successful ventures and we shall be able to retire to a little house in the country" (30). In such a world, with such an ideology, distinctions among the middle classes are beside the point.

It is true that Macheath, the arch-gangster, thinks of himself as lower-middle-class. Let out of jail to be hanged, he announces,

> Ladies and gentlemen. You see before you a declining representative of a declining class. We lower middle-class artisans who toil with our humble jemmies on small shopkeepers' cash registers are being swallowed up by big corporations backed by the banks. What's a jemmy compared with a share certificate? What's breaking into a bank compared with founding a bank? (76)

But Brecht is not intent on any sentimentalizing of the upper middle swallowing up the lower middle class. The more successful of the latter simply want to become the former, and Macheath is a first-rate gangster. To Polly he says, "It's only a matter of weeks before I go over to banking altogether. It's safer and it's more profitable," and then he tells her to turn the names of his fellow gangsters in to the police once the financial switch is made (37). Business is business, after all, and the weltanschauung of the middle class extends in every direction in "a picture of bourgeois society." At the end, in a parody of what the middle-class audience expects in representations of its world,[62] a royal mounted messenger appears and announces that the queen has pardoned Macheath, and that he is to be "raised to the hereditary peerage" (78). In this way, the ultimate aspirations of the middle class are realized, at the same time that the aristocracy and monarchy are revealed as part of the same social system and worldview.

All this bourgeois ideology is expressed in Macheath's bowler hat. In the song in which Polly informs her parents of her recent marriage to Macheath, she mentions his hat as one of the sartorial and behavioral traits that marked him as different from her other, richer suitors. Unlike those suitors, whom she had refused, he hung his hat on a nail and got right down to business, as she recalled,

> And as he'd got no money
> And was not a nice chap
> And his Sunday shirts, even, were not like snow
> And as he'd no idea of treating a girl with due respect
> I could not tell him: No. (28)

In some translations and in most productions of *The Threepenny Opera* his hat is a bowler, and is matched by "fashionable evening dress" (15) and well-shined shoes. In his notes for the play, Brecht speaks of him as "emphatically staid" (while the other bandits are but "naturally" so), a description of men in bowler hats echoed in Brecht's remark that Macheath strikes women as "well situated."[63] Indeed, Macheath is captured by the police the first time because he refuses to disturb his habits and visits his whores, hanging his hat on a nail and demanding coffee (41)! The bowler is an item in his homely bourgeois rituals, all of which signify his aspirations. For as the passage above points out, Macheath is neither rich nor nice nor gracious, and it is his sheer physical forcefulness, the element of danger in him, that appeals to Polly in her rebellion against her parents. Macheath reveals to us the ugliness, violence, and cynicism beneath the facade of respectability with which the middle class dresses itself. As the "Ballad of Mac the Knife" tells us as the play begins, though crimes are committed, "Mac the Knife wears white kid gloves which / Give the minimum away" (3). In this way, the bowler signifies Macheath's "street" status, his criminal "Soho" milieu. It is not simply that the bowler be removed and hung on a nail so that Macheath can apply himself to Polly without niceties; the bowler is also the sign of his amoral practicality, the matter-of-factness of his seduction, the street-smarts of his aspiration.

Brecht regarded the *Neue Sachlichkeit* movement, which was strong during the formative years of his "epic" theater, as "reactionary" in the sense that matter-of-factness intervened in the "flabby" emotionalism of the bourgeois theater, and so was welcome.[64] The objective, the analytical, the sober and dry—these were qualities Brecht associated with what was necessary in the theater to counteract the realism and illusionism of bourgeois drama, which according to him absorbed but did not enlighten its audience. Brecht identified the "epic" with "clear description and reporting" and "documentary projections."[65]

What complicates the middle-class-as-gangsters theme of *The Threepenny Opera* is Brecht's appreciation of the lack of sentimentality among the thieves and whores, their matter-of-fact awareness of the nature of their conditions—a quality mirrored in the dialogue and dramaturgy of the play itself, which is meant to be bourgeois in form as well as in subject matter.[66] The hard-headed (hard-*hatted*) practicality of the middle class appealed to Brecht as "modern." His early plays, like the *Neue Sachlichkeit* paintings—and to some extent the Bauhaus designs—were meant to *be* modern while commenting *on* the modern, to be at once analytical and symptomatic. Brecht described the "A-effect (alienation effect)" of his epic theater, which prevented the merging of subject and dramatic demonstration, the appeal to empathy, and therefore allowed "the spectator to criticize constructively from a social point of view,"[67] in ways that also described *Neue Sachlichkeit* art, an art that at once depicted and participated in an objectified reality.

So Macheath's bowler hat is a sign of the bourgeois qualities that could be effectively used to expose the bourgeoisie. The road that "leads over capitalism's dead body," said Brecht, "is a good one,"[68] and is decisively capitalistic: practical, objectifying, down-to-earth. *The Threepenny Opera*, as a version of Brecht's epic theater, is designed to sway a modern audience in such a way as to make it understand critically its own modernism. Macheath is both a cynical, ambitious hero/gangster whom a modern audience can identify with against a system that would persecute his criminal energy, and the exemplum of that very system and its murderous hypocrisy. He's an American-style gangster in a London underworld: the New Industrial Age personified in all its cold, heartless style.

One aspect of this style—and an aspect of *The Threepenny Opera* as a whole—is its fun. Fun (*Spass*) is what Brecht felt the theater was lacking, and what he needed in his plays. When asked for whom he wrote, he replied, "For the sort of people who just come for fun and don't hesitate to keep their hats on in the theatre,"[69] and he didn't separate fun from reason and analysis. Indeed, he thought that "we had to make something straightforward and instructive of our fun," and "to develop the means of pleasure into an object of instruction."[70] The complication of Brecht's social instruction about bourgeois habits and ideology with his attraction to and employment of popular means of entertainment (gangsters, songs, spectacle, title-boards, the self-conscious and detached theatricality he called the epic style) had to do with his avoidance of the didactic and with his sense of fun—at least in his early theater, before his "teaching plays." He was able to make use of comic and cabaret/music-hall business that would draw a modern audience.

One source of this was silent film comedy. Brecht was particularly interested in Chaplin, regarding him as one of the masters of "the epic, story-telling" form of acting. In an interview in exile in 1934, he said this kind of acting was used in *The Threepenny Opera*:

> The actor [of the epic, story-telling kind] doesn't have to be the man he portrays. He has to describe his character just as it would be described in a book. If Chaplin were to play Napoleon he wouldn't even look like him; he would show objectively and critically how Napoleon would behave in the various situations the author might put him in.[71]

Here he connects comedy and objectivity, stressing Chaplin's detachment rather than his empathy. Earlier, in 1930, in reference to having seen *The Gold Rush*, Brecht called Chaplin a "document," and in a fragment on big-city theater he wrote, "The only kind of art produced by these cities so far has been *fun*: Charlie Chaplin's films and jazz."[72] So fun, matter-of-factness, and linear storytelling are related for Brecht. For these reasons Macheath's bowler carries the lightness of its comic history, a lightness which can bear a social weight. Macheath is a character who can fuss over being respectable, plan his business, lie and betray his friends, and then step forward to sing "The Ballad of Immoral Earnings" with a whore who will betray him. In all these roles, the bowler is his appropriate hat, the only hat that *could* be appropriate to them all.

The bowler expresses Brecht's ambivalent attitude toward modernity. The people he said he wrote for, who came to the theater to keep their hats on and have fun, were essentially a music-hall audience. But this audience would necessarily be middle-class, and would need instruction about itself. If, in the process of offering fun, the production set the audience's "reason to work," brought out "the material incidents in a perfectly sober and matter-of-fact way,"[73] then the middle class could come to understand itself through the very processes that it honored.

The epic theater, like the middle class, was to be "eminently practical"[74] without moralizing and enjoyable without being frivolous. Brecht said *The Threepenny Opera* "has a double nature. Instruction and entertainment conflict openly."[75] Macheath's bowler, like Chaplin's (as Brecht conceived Chaplin) is a sign of both reasonableness and fun, of the modernity of the bourgeoisie, and no matter how critically Brecht regarded this class, he recognized it as the center of "reality's headlong development,"[76] with which the theater had to keep pace. Brecht's sense of the theater, as many have noted, was greater than his politics, and so he was able to fill Macheath's bowler with as wide a range of reference as it would get in Weimar Germany. By conflating the weight of the bowler's history with the lightness of its style, he was able to help do for his opera, and for the theater, what Weimar was not able to do for itself. He was able to accept modernity.

# MAGRITTE'S MANNEQUINS

## DREAM ADVERTISEMENTS

The first thing to be said about René Magritte's bowler-hatted men is that they are figures of fashion. Magritte painted these figures at least twenty-five times, four between 1926 and 1929, twenty-one between 1948 and 1966.[1] As early as 1922 he was drawing advertisements for fashion houses,[2] and from 1924 to 1927 he did publicity work for Norine, a Brussels couture house.[3] Like Magritte's men, male figures in fashion advertisements of that time were often posed stiffly in their dress suits and hats, arms at their sides, facing away from us as well as toward us, or in profile, in order fully to display the clothes. They have been called mannequins,[4] and so they are, with their bland, almost featureless faces and their seemingly interchangeable and detachable parts. They are *hommes-objets*,[5] *hommes types*,[6] painted, like all of Magritte's generic objects, with the "glossy definition"[7] of magazine ads.

Pere Gimferrer, one of the few critics to discuss Magritte's background in publicity, calls his paintings "authentic 'dream advertisements.'"[8] His point is that Magritte's "meticulously realistic technique" in the service of making illogical and magical associations, is analogous to the technique he used for "advertising campaigns." Something very clearly delineated, familiar, and easy to absorb is presented in such a way as to stimulate associational rather than logical or causal thinking.[9] Magritte places his bowler-hatted men, as banal as his other generic objects—his pipes and rocks and eggs and balusters—in lawless and oneiric environments, obviously for purposes of contrast. The mysterious and the everyday interact. Interesting advertisements, the kind that would attract artists like Lautrec and Magritte, make their products (or events) seem glamorous. And indeed, Magritte's paintings, or objects lifted from them, are often used in other people's advertisements, or for the covers of books and the illustration of texts. With their objective clarity they engage us immediately, and then provoke or subvert that very engagement. But why? Surely Magritte is not selling anything, surely not the mannequins' hats and suits. We could carry Gimferrer's idea of "dream advertisements" further and say that Magritte's paintings advertise mysterious and unnamable products, or are posters for unnamed and unnamable events—which are ways of saying that they wish to impart "mystery" (one of Magritte's favorite words) to the everyday. The paintings of bowler-hatted men announce something contemporary, modish, *in fashion*, very much of the world, not in order to sell it but to reveal something concealed in it.

The bowler-hatted men are *badauds*; they only stand and gaze—but at what? Many critics are tempted to say: at a mannequin universe, a world just as standardized and impersonal as they. These critics reduce the bowler-hatted men to figures of satire or social criticism: soulless, anonymous, twentieth-century figures, cookie-cutter people, men of the crowd. This last phrase, from Edgar Allan Poe, is used by one art critic to evoke the history of the lower middle class:

> In "The Man of the Crowd" Poe created figures belonging to "the tribe of clerks," who are forerunners of the nineteenth- and twentieth-century bourgeois, with his ready-made clothes and bowler hat, as depicted by Magritte: the strikingly unstrikingly figure temporarily singled out from the crowd without which he is inconceivable.[10]

We are by now familiar with this point of view: the clerks buy their clothes off the rack, and by doing so, become as standardized as their apparel. Their identity is in their numbers. Commenting on Magritte's *The Man in the Bowler Hat* (*L'homme au chapeau melon*, 1964), this same critic goes further:

> The identity of this nineteenth- or twentieth-century body, dressed by the masses (from the clothing stores), with a human being, the human being, has been lost. It is no longer a joke. Will he be resurrected? Magritte painted a representation of the void: the penetrating power of *The Man in the Bowler Hat* lies in this void, this emptiness.[11]

We will pass over the implication that *the* human being has his clothes tailor made; at least this critic points to clothing stores as the proper site of origin for this figure. But the error is to simplify—and, so simplifying, to elevate oneself above the "masses," which can more easily be condescended to, even vilified, as inhuman because they are middle- rather than working-class. The error is to place these figures back into contexts from which Magritte has slyly removed them. The key is to recognize that the social history they bear is one element in an interplay with their unconventional environments.

In a 1940 lecture-cum-autobiographical essay, "Lifeline" ("La ligne de vie"), Magritte made an illuminating remark on the nature of his art:

> I made paintings where the objects were represented with the appearance they have in reality, in a style sufficiently objective so that the subversive effect, which they would reveal themselves capable of evoking through certain powers, might exist again in the real world from which these objects have been borrowed—by a perfectly natural exchange.[12]

The bowler-hatted men are just such objects, borrowed from a fashion and business world with which we are familiar, and returned to that world bearing secret powers. They are charged with a mentality that we imagine fills the conventional shape of their bowlers.

Take the generically titled *The Man in the Bowler Hat* (fig. 38). Our critic claims that "we know exactly what sort of face is hidden behind the pigeon."[13] Then why conceal it? And why conceal it with a pigeon (or, more suggestively, a dove)? Magritte creates his context through his associations, and they are no easier to interpret than dreams—at the same time that, like dreams, they compel us to interpret them. A staid figure stands before us, as definitive in design as the bowler he wears. His plain beige tie is almost too drab. It is true that we can see enough of his face to surmise that he has the generic, expressionless visage of Magritte's other bowler-hatted men. But in effect the dove-in-flight becomes his face at the same time that it contrasts—in its grace, in its flight—with his frozen figure. The bird reminds us of what the man is *not*, and yet, in front of his face (is it frozen there forever? that is, is it *his*?) it becomes part of his expressive life, as distinct from his inexpressive style. Bernard Noel nicely says that in Magritte "the mental object is enlightened, so to speak, by a questioning that nothing can exhaust—no answer . . . just the pulsation of an inexhaustible interrogation."[14] The pulse is set vibrating through contradiction: in this case, between the (spiritual) grace of the bird in flight and the stolidity of the fixed figure whose face it (momentarily?) obscures. In the "exchange" between these two, the bird expresses him as much as it conceals him. Indeed, he is more expressive because he is concealed.

Georg Simmel speaks of the "reserve" of those who follow fashion; since fashion treats individuals alike, one's nature is not affected by it.[15] That is, the fashionable person can maintain a reserve (keeping something of his self for the future) behind a facade of contemporaneity. By dressing his bowler-hatted men in a uniform style, Magritte gives himself the same freedom the man has: to express himself freely in contradiction—a use of the bowler hat that makes it a major item of costume to this day.

The relation between dreams and fashion—a relation Magritte understood very well—is that they at once hide and reveal something. Just as "dream-work," according to Freud, both hides and reveals the latent "dream-thoughts" by transforming them through a variety of techniques (condensation, displacement, etc.) into the "manifest content" of a dream,[16] so the work of modern fashion both expresses and disguises the desires of the individual through collective means— saying, in effect, these clothes will appeal to you by appealing to many. The formal characteristics of what Freud called the "picture puzzle"[17] provide clues to the meanings that they hide, evoking mystery through the familiar.

One of Magritte's earliest bowler-hat paintings, *The Menaced Assassin* (*L'assassin menacé*, 1926; fig. 39), makes clear in a more narrative way what is to be understood in all of his paintings: that there is a mystery to be solved. However we read this meticulously constructed painting, we are struck by the "exchange" between the respectable and the criminal. The fact that all the men have roughly the same suits and standard, apathetic faces suggests this scene as a drama of the self, a drama acted out in three stages. In the background, looking in the window, are three generic men who look very much like the assassin they seem to be watching. The assassin has turned from his murder (and rape?) of the naked woman to listen to an oversized gramophone. His pose is languorous and fashionable; he seems to be casually modeling his suit, unaware of his crime. In the forestage, two bowler-hatted men wait for him with devices—a fishnet and a crude club—inappropriate to their respectable appearance.

It is interesting that the interior space is foregrounded—the drama opens out to the inside. The two figures waiting for the assassin to don his coat and hat, pick up his briefcase and attempt to leave the scene of the crime, bring the drama forward. Also, there is a hat sequence: the men (eyewitnesses?) at the window are bareheaded, the assassin has taken off his hat (a Stetson?), and the two (police?) who menace him have their bowlers impolitely on. These last two would seem, then, to represent the assassin's inner self as they embody the contradiction be-

*Fig. 38. René Magritte,* The Man in the Bowler Hat, *1964*
*(© 1992, C. Herscovici / ARS, New York)*

tween respectability and primitive violence. Perhaps they are assassins, like him—all of them expressing the passionless detachment of those hired to murder. The eyewitnesses express a similar detachment in their *badaud*-like gazing; perhaps they too menace the assassin, blocking a possible escape, forcing him to move inward, towards us—a move he is temporarily postponing.

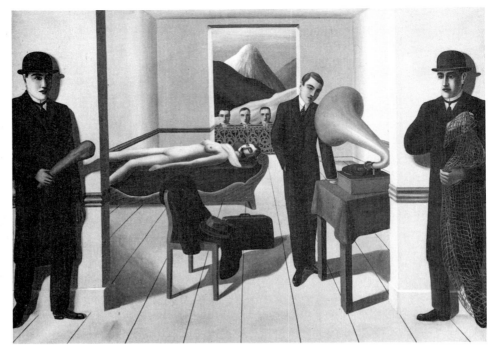

*Fig. 39. René Magritte,* The Menaced Assassin, *1926 (© 1992, C. Herscovici /
ARS, New York; Collection, The Museum of Modern Art, New York. Kay Sage
Tanguy Fund.)*

It was significant for Magritte to conflate the publicly respectable with the interior self. Bowler-hatted men were never simply "outer" or social figures for
him—that is, merely standardized representatives of the world of conventional
appearance. That they *do* represent all this is a given, and Magritte doubtless
drew (in both senses) his figures from a couture world that reflected and elaborated how Western middle-class men had come to regard themselves in their
work: as sober, conventional, respectable people. It is their hiddenness that interests Magritte, their bland reserve. In this aspect they wait for the assassin,
themselves cruder embodiments of his murderous impulses (one holds a club
that resembles a human limb and is juxtaposed to the corpse of the woman).

In all his paintings of bowler-hatted men, Magritte meditates on how the very
outwardness of things—their presenting themselves for being looked at—expresses inwardness precisely by concealing it. Everything in Magritte's world is
literally respectable (good enough to be looked at). His technique of rendering
objects as generic (this *is* a pipe, there's no mistaking it) is itself a concealment,
a set-up for subversion (this is *not* a pipe, it's a representation of one, or it's

an object to which we have conventionally and arbitrarily assigned the word "pipe"). The bowler-hatted men are generic people under which could be written: These are not conventional men. We are to understand that their conventionality masks unconventional impulses, or an outlaw inner life.

In the case of *The Menaced Assassin* these impulses are violent, insofar as the bowler-hatted men can be said to embody the passionless criminality (but not the stylish languor) of the assassin himself. Their bowler hats have enough public weight to make them appropriate for police, but the "weapons" with which they will snare and subdue the assassin compromise this orderly image and fill their bowlers with a darker life. The suggestion seems to be that the anonymously respectable is violent in a particularly bourgeois way—a theme that would soon be struck in Brecht's *Threepenny Opera*. All this makes the painting, despite the mystery of its situation, one of Magritte's most narrative and conventional. His bowler-hatted men will never again be associated with the violent and criminal; their mysteries will be more meditative. But *The Menaced Assassin* points to the image of these figures as a mask rather than as an essence or an empty suit of clothes. What the conventional does for Magritte is conceal, and what it most conceals is its own inner life, which is revealed through the contradictions, displacements, substitutions (that is, the dream-work) that subvert the familiar reality of the objects. The generic and functionally designed bowler conceals, in Magritte's paintings, a magical life: the pigeon is, as it were, pulled out of the hat.

# READY-MADE EXPERIENCE

At times the faces of Magritte's bowler-hatted men are concealed by objects—a pigeon, as we've seen, or an apple, as in *The Great War* (*La Grande Guerre*) and *The Son of Man* (*Le fils de l'homme*), both painted in 1964— or their backs are turned to us. A good example of the latter is *The Ready-Made Bouquet* (*Le bouquet tout fait*, 1957; fig. 40). The man stares at what would seem to be a summer landscape while seemingly appliquéd to his back is a figure from Botticelli's *La Primavera*. Because the man's back is to us, the rest of the painting becomes a psychological landscape once removed. That is, the man becomes the substitute for the viewer. Magritte's figure stands facing something, as we do looking at the painting, and what he sees seems, naturally, alive with his thought. But this thought is obscure to us. The figure is inexpressive and anomalous: a crowd figure without a crowd, a city man without a city, a clerk without an office, a mannequin without a window. All that we can know of him—with one exception, as we shall see—is what he watches. In *The Ready-Made Bouquet* the woods are lit with the intense green of summer. The stone wall at the bottom suggests a balcony or some raised viewpoint, but the woods are at eye level and closer than they should be. There is little spatial perspective. All this gives the woods a slightly fake aspect, and the stone wall seems to frame a mental picture more than a real landscape. Like the man, the woods have a staid immediacy; the trees repeat his figure and loom as his strong idea of summer.

The floral figure of Spring is even more anomalous, being at once inappropriate and borrowed, a "ready-made" Spring from one of The Masters. These qualities make her seem part of the man's mental life, an idea of Spring literally at the *back* of his mind. As summer with its insistent foliage (most of it seemingly elaborated from his bowler) looms for him, he thinks "Spring," something more floral and desirable. Certainly the contrast between her figure and his—the first thing we notice—along with her being a thought or memory of his, enlivens the bowler-hatted man's aspect. Her head is juxtaposed to his, and we think, There's more to this man than meets the eye. But at the same time, if she is an idea or memory she is a borrowed one. He conjures an image, not from his own experience, but from his viewing of paintings. She is, in this sense, as conventional as he is, and both seem out of touch with a landscape that is immediate. His desire (for Spring, for a woman, for both) can only be expressed as part of his cultural baggage.

What we *can* know of this man—which doesn't come through strongly in reproductions of this painting—is that he is rather shabby. His bowler is a little frayed, his haircut is awful, his coat is rumpled and ill-fitting. So his fashion-advertisement aspect is marred by his seeming barely respectable, a "little man" from the lower middle class. This gives the painting an added poignancy. In this ordinary man lives an imagination of beauty unrelated to his experience. He may never visit the Uffizi Gallery, but he has seen reproductions of Botticelli's *Primavera*, and it has become part of his mental life. If his image of Spring is, like him, a facsimile, it nonetheless animates him, and the painting.

Magritte used the phrase "ready-made" in "Lifeline."[18] He describes "ready-made" experience as that which explains and justifies "this contradictory and disorderly world of ours" in order to hang it together—that is, to keep it from seeming contradictory and disorderly. Such "ready-made" life avoids "an analysis of its own real conditions" and any experiences—poetic or clairvoyant or otherwise—that would destabilize its explanations. In the context of the whole of "Lifeline," we may identify the ready-made with the bourgeois. At one point in

*Fig. 40. René Magritte,* The Ready-Made Bouquet, *1957 (© 1992, C. Herscovici / ARS, New York; reproduced from Suzi Gablik,* Magritte *[New York: Thames and Hudson, 1985])*

the essay, Magritte writes of Marx and Engels as influencing him because they wanted, as he did, to act upon "the real" and transform life. He also remarks on the influence of the Surrealists, "who were violently demonstrating their loathing of all bourgeois values, both social and ideological, that have maintained the world in its present ignoble condition. I became certain that I would need to live with danger, so that the world, and life, would correspond more closely to thought and to feeling." Bourgeois values, then, maintain the world as something un-transformable, safe, unfeeling, and lacking in the mystery that Magritte feels puts us in touch with reality. In a word the bourgeois world is staid. It is not to be questioned. It involves the "mediocre tendency to facile self-assurance" of which Magritte's titles are meant to inspire mistrust. It achieves the illusion of stability (and what could be more illusory than any stability in 1940?) at the cost of what makes reality available to the workings of consciousness. These are hard-ly new sentiments in the history of antibourgeois thought, but they were motiva-tions in the development of Magritte's techniques. Like Marx and Engels and the Surrealists (as he understood them), Magritte developed methods of thinking and painting "employed to establishing a contact between consciousness and the external world," a contact which is transforming and "mysterious." Those who want a ready-made experience might, for example, make clear-cut distinctions between what is "outside" and what is "inside" themselves, when, as Magritte points out, we actually see the world as both "simultaneously." The world needs to be "made" by us over and over again.

## THE SUBVERSIVE EVERYDAY

The bowler-hatted man is clearly a "ready-made" figure, all of a piece, so composed as to be frozen: a bourgeois mannequin from the pages of bourgeois couture advertisements. But Magritte, unlike many of his critics, is not interested in using him to satirize the bourgeoisie. Magritte wishes to make con-tact with mystery (that is, with reality), not simply by subverting the bourgeois world that the bowler-hatted man represents, but by creating, through his dream-techniques, a "perfectly natural exchange" between the subversive and the everyday. Magritte not only wants the real world to yield to mystery, but also wants mystery to return to the real world. That is why his bowler-hatted men are almost always represented as wholly what they are: inviolate, untransformed, unanimated. They are depicted in their inexpressive banality, in ironic contrast to whatever else is in the picture frame, so that the mystery evoked in the trans-gressions and contradictions can be returned to this figure without his needing to be anything more than what he is: *un homme du jour le jour*, an everyday man. The "objective" world is not merely exposed and is never judged by Magritte's subversions—as George Melly implied when he said on BBC-TV in 1965 that Magritte's "object is to bring into disrepute the whole apparatus of bourgeois reality."[19] Rather, Magritte imagines the bourgeois world as itself capable of being subversive.

One of the keys to Magritte's method lies in his personal discovery of the "affinity of two objects," a discovery which he discusses in "Lifeline," following his previously noted mention of Marx et al. Before an experience in 1936 in which he mistakenly saw an egg instead of a bird in a cage, he had "used to provoke this shock by bringing together objects that were unrelated." After this experience, he began his researches into the "element to be discovered . . . obscurely attached to each object." The shock of the *un*related gave way to the shock of "affinity." If we can trust his account of the nature of his work before and after this experience, then we can say that the fullest expression of Magritte's dream-work/joke-work had begun.[20] For just as dream-work expresses as well as conceals the latent dream-thoughts, so joke-work expresses an affinity while dramatizing an irony between the terms of a joke.

It is not only that Magritte's bowler-hatted man is surrounded with seemingly unrelated objects—a dove, a floral beauty from Botticelli, a white rose (*Pandora's Box*)—but that relations between him and these objects are suggested, affinities which at once animate him (by evoking his mental landscape) and return the mystery which these displaced objects evoke to the everyday world of the bourgeois sustained and embodied by the sheer imperturbability of the bowler-hatted man. While the dreamscapes of artists like Max Ernst and Yves Tanguy, for example, seem timeless, Magritte's are rooted in the contemporary through the banality of his objects. The tension set up—say, between the respectable and the outlaw, or between the delineation and transgression of boundaries—manufactures both irony and mystery. The modern, as Baudelaire described it in "The Painter of Modern Life," is an expression of the timelessness of what passes, the eternal in the contemporary.[21] The bowler-hatted man is not modern because he was or is as up-to-date as a figure in a fashion magazine; he is modern because his contemporaneity seems timeless as his consciousness is expressed. There is nothing more modern than the acceptance of what is modern.

In *Pandora's Box* (*La boîte de Pandore*, 1951; fig. 41), a bowler-hatted man, his back to us, looks across a bridge to a row of urban dwellings, probably bourgeois apartments. Standing next to him, as if a shorter companion, is a white rose on a stem. In a 1957 letter Magritte wrote about this painting:

> The presence of the rose next to the stroller signifies that wherever man's destiny leads him he is always protected by an element of beauty. The painter hopes that this man is heading for the most sublime place in his life.

*Fig. 41. René Magritte,* Pandora's Box, *1951 (© 1992, C. Herscovici / ARS, New York; Yale University Art Gallery. Gift of Dr. and Mrs. John A. Cook.)*

> The rose's vividness corresponds to its important role (element of beauty). The approach of nightfall suits withdrawal, and the bridge makes us think something will be overcome.[22]

The presence of the rose, then, is meant to transform our sense of where the man is headed, which otherwise would seem very ordinary. As beauty is his companion, so the urban residences toward which he is making his crossing will become, for him, "sublime." For Magritte, the affinity between the rose and the bowler-hatted man's world is more important than the irony of seeing a rose in such a hard setting. If a Pandora's box of subversive beauty will be opened inside the man's bowler, it will be, in an "exchange" of energies, the beauty of the world as it is, which is the world Magritte paints. "I detest," he wrote in a letter in 1959, "this tendency to change the forms of admirable things."[23]

André Breton said, apropos of Magritte, "Are we not foolish to alienate ourselves from familiar, everyday objects by confining them strictly to their utilitarian functions?"[24] The bowler-hatted man is lifted, by Magritte, from the very site and functions which his image projects: city, office, work, conventionality, dull respectability. He is as much alienated from the office as he is from a world in which roses appear as strolling companions, doves are frozen in Zenonian flight, or everything turns to stone. These dream environments liberate the man from his uniformity and fill the hard, unyielding contours of his bowler with mental activity, at the same time that his formality and uniformity root the images in everyday consciousness. "Nous sommes chez nous," Magritte has said: "here is where we really belong."[25] And, we might add, where we belong is much more than it seems, is filled with mystery.

A good example of a "natural exchange" between things through both their contradictions and affinities is seen in *Golconda* (*Golconde*, 1953; fig. 42), in which a multitude of bowler-hatted men rise like souls from, or descend like rain to, their bourgeois row houses. The ambiguity of their movement (a third possibility: are they just frozen in the air?) describes the contradiction between their staid, stereotyped aspect, their being weighted with the workaday, and their apparently buoyant, lawless life. They are as unanchored and airborne as the imagination in flight, yet are as stiff as mannequins and identical as raindrops, very much part of the bourgeois world from which they seem to float. The everyday seems miraculous without being transformed, and the miraculous is given a ballast in the everyday. Like Golconda, the sheer numbers of the stereotyped men are a source of great wealth—the wealth of a familiar world.

This wealth has become a cultural currency. The *Golconda* figures have often been borrowed and adapted. The French television station Antenne Deux used (still uses?) floating bowler-hatted men as its logo. At midnight the logo was animated, and the stiff, unchanging figures *seemed* to fly in outer space as the planet shifted beneath them and eventually became a curved field on which they came to rest. All the while, somber, meditative music played. What seemed to be eerily imparted was that Antenne Deux, as an active part of our everyday life, both lifted and settled us. It was imaginative but regular, on schedule.

Something about this—and I think it is this conflation of the banal and the imaginative, the heavy and the light—has a wide appeal. Only recently (June 1990) the *Golconda* figures were used in an advertising campaign for a New York City clothier. Magritte's fashion mannequins descended/ascended/held still across vast areas of storefront glass. The European row houses were not included, and with this removal of the social context, the design element—strong in any case—became stronger. Magritte's man was returned to his fashion and commercial origins, as though he had no social history, as though, as modern man, he did not have a history of modernity. Modernity is "light" because, like fashion, it

*Fig. 42. René Magritte,* Golconda, *1953 (© 1992, C. Herscovici / ARS, New York; Giraudon / Art Resource, New York)*

remains indefatigably contemporary, au courant; but it is also "heavy" with its history of remaining so. For almost 150 years, the changes of modern life have not changed. The bowler hat, its vestimentary sign, is at once filled with the various fortunes of the middle class and empty of all content but the contours of its immediacy and its ubiquity.

The modernity of the bowler-hatted man is as much a function of his multiple presence as it is of the quality and kind of that presence. It can be said that above all the "modern" is what can be replicated. Fashion describes the modern because it seeks, not only to be au courant, but to replicate an image, to say of one thing that it should be worn in copies by many people. A mannequin is a generic human being; it stands in for those who will wear the clothes it models, which are clothes that are not tailor-made for an individual but are ready-made for minor adjustments (what tailoring has become). Ready-to-wear clothes have

*Fig. 43. René Magritte,* The Time of the Harvest, *1959 (© 1992, C. Herscovici /
ARS, New York; Giraudon / Art Resource, New York)*

produced the ready-made, the fashion(ed) people, and at the same time these
people—with their money to spend but not to spare—have produced, or caused
to be produced, the generic clothes that the generic mannequins display. Is it a
coincidence that the mannequin—literally, "little man"—is an image of the little men of the rising middle class?

In *The Time of the Harvest* (*Le mois des vendanges*, 1959; fig. 43), a crowd of
these mannequins looks in at us through a window like the eyewitnesses of *The
Menaced Assassin.* Only now these *badauds* have bowlers, and the interior drama
is our own. We can only gaze impassively back at them, wondering as much at
what *they* see as at what *we* see. As David Sylvester says, they seem to be "gazing impassively at ourselves . . . accusing or, if not that, at least hostile."[26] Their
perfect replication may make them seem disturbingly alien, but our regarding
them as hostile or accusing or anything else is simply arbitrary. There is no narrative, and no affect, except what we project, and the only mystery is in their
multiple presence. If they seem an invasion (as out of a 1950s science fiction
film), all they are attacking us with is their gaze—the gaze of those who literally
*crowd* the picture frame, which is a window into modernity, theirs and our own.

# MAGRITTE *AU CHAPEAU*

**M**agritte was eager to show that he identified himself with the bowler-hatted men he painted. From the 1930s on he was photographed in a dark suit and bowler, sometimes in imitation of the figures in his art. Duane Michals, in a visit a year and a half before Magritte's death in 1967, photographed him, mostly in a bowler hat, in his home in suburban Brussels. There are shots of him from behind, with his hand in front of his face (fig. 44), superimposed onto a bare canvas on one of his own easels, and in other imaginative poses. As Michals noted, "He was the familiar Magritte man,"[27] an image Magritte modestly promoted and made a part of his personal anti-legend. He evidently never bought a stylish bowler, though Lock's had an agent in Brussels; he preferred standard ones.[28]

Suzi Gablik remarks on Magritte's life as a bowler-hatted man:

> After his return to Brussels [from Paris in 1930] his life became more and more that of an ordinary bourgeois. . . . It was as if he were deliberately trying to obscure himself from worldly success under the protective coloration of conventionality. His desire to live without history (even his own) and without style, was a calculated choice to render himself invisible.[29]

These strange remarks bear pondering. It is true that, by all accounts, Magritte's life was conventionally middle-class: his house resembled the generic suburban houses in his paintings, his habits were regular and meticulous and unpretentious, there was little evidence of his "activity" as an artist in his home,[30] and so on. But what is Gablik's implied connection between life as a bourgeois and "life without history"? The bourgeoisie, even in its most conventional aspect, has a history. The bowler-hatted man, abstract a figure as he may seem, has his history—as we have seen. And how can Magritte's life be said to be "without style"? The bourgeoisie has a style, however colorless or uniform it may be. The very element of calculation in Magritte's choices makes "style" inevitable. What is he calculating? Merely the avoidance of "worldly success"? This indeed seems a conventional, even bourgeois, response, and doesn't account for Magritte's decision to publicize and parody his style of life, to have himself photographed as the artist-as-bourgeois, or the bourgeois-as-artist.

The reason for Magritte's identifying himself with the figures in his paintings may be, in its outline, simple enough: to conflate the images of artist and bowler-hatted man. If Magritte can be the man in his paintings, then that man can be he:

*Fig. 44. Duane Michals, photograph of René Magritte, 1965
(courtesy Duane Michals)*

an artist with an outlaw imagination, someone with a great deal held in reserve. We can see in Michals's photographs what Gablik does not mention: that Magritte's conventional home was filled with his unconventional paintings. So he meant to present himself as embodying, in his style of life, the complex relation between a staid exterior and an active inner life. The latter is made more resonant by the wide appeal of the "admirable forms" of the former. Magritte is not interested in the esoteric. His paintings have the keys to many consciousnesses; they have a *collective* energy. Surely he admired the conventions of popular culture—fashion advertisements, silent film comedy (especially Laurel and Hardy), mystery stories—at least partly because they conceal beneath a stylish or superficial exterior the energies of a democratic imagination.

A photograph of Magritte taken in Brussels in 1934 shows him, in overcoat and bowler, alone in a large, stubbly field (fig. 45). In the distant background are some ugly, run-down structures. Magritte is almost in silhouette, unidentifiable, a bowler-hatted figure on the outskirts of somewhere. The space he occupies, neither city nor country, is—in the literal sense in which the British use the word—a wasteland. It lacks cultivation of any kind. It is neither wilderness nor field nor garden nor park—rather, just a negatively defined, unplanned area be-

*Fig. 45. Photograph of René Magritte, Brussels, 1934 (from Harry Torczyner,*
Magritte: The True Art of Painting *[London: Thames and Hudson, 1979])*

tween things. It is the *banlieue*, that site of modernity, the unattractive place between the ending and beginning of things, in which was "sharpened the dreaming onlooker's sense of what it meant to be bourgeois."[31] We can see here—and
in the shabbiness of the man in *The Ready-Made Bouquet* as well—that Magritte
was aware of the anomalousness of the figure he painted and lived, despite its
uniform dress. If this figure is a businessman or a commercial man, he is a lost
one, strolling and gazing in the vague vicinity of what might be his workplace or
home. If this figure is a bourgeois, then he is a shoddy, barely respectable one.
He inhabits the spaces opened up by modern life. The first and perhaps the
last thing that strikes us about Magritte in this photograph, and about the bowler-
hatted men in his paintings, is that they seem to *contemplate* something: everything apart from them seems to be the theater of their thought.

In *Toward Pleasure (A la recontre du plaisir*, 1950; fig. 46), a bowler-hatted
man contemplates a sleigh bell in a landscape of well-composed trees and ruins,
a landscape which seems to have appeared at the end of a dark curtain. Or has
the curtain parted to reveal this scene? Magritte transgresses the boundaries of
indoors/outdoors, and this transgression, along with the Monet-like landscape,
makes this an interior drama. In this way the other bowler-hatted man—exiting
right, holding a rock—seems an alter ego, the more obscured (curtained) inner
self. Magritte's title is more helpful than most of his: the "outdoor" man looks

*Fig. 46. René Magritte,* Toward Pleasure, *1950 (© 1992, C. Herscovici / ARS, New York; Giraudon / Art Resource, New York; Collection of Harry Torczyner)*

"toward pleasure," embodied in the sleigh bell, a light and festive object that we see in contrast to the rock. He can only stand there and watch it; nevertheless, it's what he wants to do; it is his pleasure. He has begun, perhaps, to move "toward" it, having opened the curtain of his more burdened and interior self. This painting tells us—as much as Magritte's work "tells" us anything, and some of it tells us more than others—that the bowler-hatted man is *not* a figure of pleasure, and that he wants it. He aspires to a more sensuous life, although seemingly one as composed as he is. The sleigh bell, however, being at once familiar and odd (oversized) and displaced, has a kick to it; it seems full of a potential jingling that is already sounding in his head. He will aspire to what he *can* aspire to, something at once provocative and conventional.

The central figure in *Toward Pleasure* stands on a psychological border between an inward life of work and an outward life of pleasure, and in this sense the painting may be said to reflect on the history of the lower middle class, a history the bowler hat signals to us. Like Seurat's bathers at Asnières, he seeks a more leisured life, and it is new to him. More specifically, he may also be said to stand on a social border between the laboring and middle classes. The man in the shadow of the curtain, dressed like him, carries away a rock from a meadow as a farmer might, while he contemplates such landscape as he can find or imagine, as did the newer middle classes whose world the Impressionists painted. Yet he can only regard it. The edge of the curtain is at once a dividing line of the self and the border, the *banlieue*, of class.

In *The Masterpiece or the Mysteries of the Horizon* (*Le chef-d'oeuvre ou Les mystères de l'horizon*, 1955), three bowler-hatted men stand in a field similar to the one in which Magritte was photographed: marked by ugly stubble, structures silhouetted on the horizon below the last of a twilight. One man is in profile, one is three-quarters turned away from us, one's back is to us: fashion mannequins displaying the (questionable) cut of their suits. Above each of their bowlers is a crescent moon, three in all. The moons' positioning makes them seem like thoughts, or interior images; they highlight the bowlers, filling them with a meditative consciousness. And yet nothing is various; the moons are as alike as the men. Each man may be in his own world, but each world is the same. The night is beginning, the moons are beginning (when they have waxed they will be as round as bowlers), and the mannequin figures are becoming as alive in their minds as they are dead in their bodies. Encased in reserve, they begin to raise their consciousnesses above their world, of which they are—physically and mentally—too much a part to leave. This is one reason their world is a borderland.

All of these bowler-hatted men seem to contain their imaginations within the limits of their own circumstances, while dreaming of adventure. In *The Spirit of Adventure* (*L'esprit d'aventure*, 1960), the images of two bowler-hatted figures on the back of the bowler-hatted man's coat are not as animating as the Botticellian figure in *The Ready-Made Bouquet*, nor is it as ready-made, but it also shows poignantly the boundaries of his spirit. The main figure, with a shabby coat and another bad haircut, looks out, away from us, across a stone wall at the sea and sky, while barely visible against his black coat are two other bowler-hatted men in identical black coats, one gesturing toward the other conversationally. The striking contrast is between the familiar longing for "adventure" represented by gazing at the sea (and a dim horizon) and the unadventurous figures that seem to populate an unadventurous man's mind. If we were to compose a narrative from this painting and its title, it might be this: longing for adventure, this man can only conjure images of himself; his version of this spirit, unrelated to the sea or any exotic lands it might beckon him to, is one of companionship. The solitary dreamer dreams of himself in conversation. As in *The Ready-Made Bouquet*, there is a careful balance between irony and sympathy in the expression of contradiction. The conservative businessman with bowler is also the "little man" comedian, aspiring to his own imagination, its very reserve a source of irregular energy. Like Chaplin's, the bowler-hatted man's adventurous spirit is marked by both aspiration and limitation, the unbearable lightness and weight of his bowler.

In *Infinite Gratitude* (*La reconnaissance infinie*, 1963) the same two conversing bowler-hatted men float in a cloudy sky above a "ground" so simply and generically rendered that it seems to function only to suggest where the figures came from. It "grounds" the abstraction of two men floating in an infinite sky, and in this way, the energy of the infinite surrounding these two earthbound/citybound men is composed, reined in. Are they "grateful" for their flotation or for their companionship, which proceeds in a stately way despite their having been lifted free of their world? *Reconnaissance* also suggests recognition and exploration—of a freedom for which they can only don their daily attire and attitude, that is, a freedom that is their own.

# LIBERATED ACCESSORIES

Let us conclude by considering three of Magritte's very late paintings that stress the bowler-hatted man's clothes *as* clothes. In two, *The Road to Damascus* (*Le chemin de Damas*, 1966) and *The Pilgrim* (*Le pèlerin*, 1966), he is detached from his attire. In *The Road to Damascus* (fig. 47), the man stands naked next to his empty suit of clothes, his bowler floating above the suit as though a head were still there, and the man's head is aligned with this empty space. It is as though the man has jumped out of his clothes and stood by them, posing for a double portrait. In *The Pilgrim*, only what would show of the man's head, were he clothed, floats next to his empty dress figure. The remainder of his body still seems inside his clothes and hat, hidden. Here the man is not given a whole self outside his clothes.

Both paintings suggest that the man is (we are) two selves, one naked and one dressed. The latter is external, composed of clothes, which maintain and express his form even when he is absent; the suit is "filled" as though by a headless mannequin, the bowler floating as though still "filled" with his consciousness. Naked, the man is still impassive, still a man without qualities; his nakedness, his escape from his clothes, has not liberated his expression. Is he as empty as his suit of clothes, his hat? Are his clothes still energized with his life? Whatever

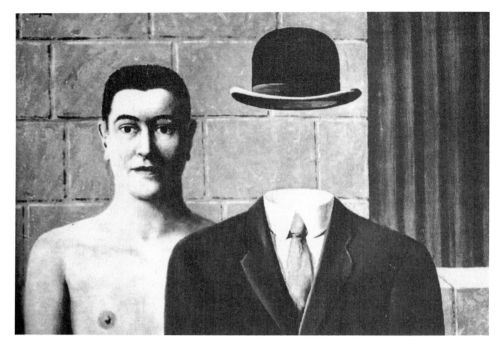

*Fig. 47. René Magritte,* The Road to Damascus, *1966 (© 1992, C. Herscovici /
ARS, New York; reproduced from Suzi Gablik,* Magritte *[New York: Thames and
Hudson, 1985])*

interrogation is started, we are struck by the intimacy between the man and his
apparel: he is removed from it yet it still "contains" him, and he remains posed
with it, as with an alter ego.

The most expressive thing in both paintings is the bowler hat. Where everything else—even the spare backgrounds of brick, curtain, and blank—is heavy
with sobriety, the bowlers have a life of their own. They do not so much float free
as remain in place as accessories to the dress ensemble, weighted with the respectable history of that ensemble. Yet they are buoyant nonetheless. As such—
as something "light," as Kundera would say—it becomes comic: part of a magic
act, *defying gravity* in both senses, or a surreal fashion advertisement, or a cartoon or silent film comedy in which it seems ready to assume an independent life.

In *The Fright Stopper* (*Le bouchon d'épouvante,* 1966; fig. 48), the bowler floats
free of any context other than the swirling lines that give it energy and buoyancy.
It is no longer an accessory to the fact of somebody's being. And yet there is a
label attached to it, warning that it is FOR EXTERNAL USE ONLY. The sense of
this relation to medicine strike us immediately: *of course* a hat is for external use
only. It is an article of protection and warmth, worn to keep body heat from es-

*Fig. 48. René Magritte,* The Fright Stopper, *1966
(© 1992, C. Herscovici / ARS, New York)*

caping—*un bouchon*, a cork. "External," too, carries with it some of the history of the bowler: as a sober, respectable, *public* hat, one whose conforming dimensions express the collective more than the individual, the outer- rather than the inner-directed. In this sense, and in regard to the title as well as the label, the bowler's external use might be said to be to cork, or stopper, whatever is liable to escape as private thought or vision, especially what is disturbing or frightful, *épouvant*, whatever risks disturbing the surface of one's external image. The bowler is a control mechanism, a container of things that would rise and escape, a social medicine. The world it evokes is the settled world of the comfortable middle class. The label, then, would warn against this world's being internalized, becoming more than an external system of signs.

And yet we are left with, and must return to, the bowler's dynamism, its independence from the very world it evokes, its ability to detach itself. It seems to *contain* individual life in two senses: to hold in and be filled with. Whatever outlaw energy it has plugged up is more potent and volatile as a result, able to lift the bowler free. The double sense of "contain" or "hold in"—expressing as it does a contradictory as well as an intimate relation—makes the bowler a comic hat. It contains and sustains the possible subversion of its own meaning—for example, a dreaming, aspiring mind, a mind liberated from the constraints of class even as it belongs to a class. The bowler is at once an item of dress and costume, weighted with social particularity and creatively free-floating. The figure it has topped can do more than both maintain his reserve and express his inner life, the very presence of his mind (one of Magritte's bowler-hatted-man paintings is titled *Presence of Mind* [*La presence d'esprit*, 1960]); he can show how one activity is a function of the other, and so comically forge a link between the mysterious and the banal, the artistic and the bourgeois, the individual and the collective, the volatile and the staid: the very fashion ("making") of modern times.

# BECKETT'S TRAMPS

## KNOCKABOUT

Samuel Beckett did for bowler hats in drama what Magritte did for them in painting: abstract them from the social and cultural milieu that gave them their semantics while drawing on their semantics to ground abstractions in everyday realities. We have noted in the last three chapters that, as the bowler hat emerged from its specific social matrix, as it entered the world of art and entertainment and became a cultural icon as well as a social object, it became more and more abstract in its semantics, a sign of "the modern" as much as an accessory of modern life. Magritte and Beckett carried on this tendency, the former drawing on fashion, the latter on music hall, vaudeville, and silent film comedy. Despite this divergence in their immediate allusions, both artists knew very well the Victorian, middle-class world of business and respectability that lay behind, and was the resonating chamber of, these more popular references. If Magritte embraced this world ironically as the bourgeois artiste, and Beckett rejected it sympathetically as the bohemian artiste, both men understood the world of their fathers, and the semantic rivers in their bowlers run deep.

In a review of Sean O'Casey's *Windfalls* in 1934, Beckett touched on the nature of the particular comedy he was drawn to. He wrote that O'Casey (whose plays he had been seeing for many years), is a master of knockabout in this very serious and honourable sense—that he discerns the principle of disintegration in even the most complacent of solidities, and activates it to their explosion. This is the energy of his theatre, the triumph of the principle of knockabout in situation, in all its elements and in all its planes, from the furniture to the higher centres.

He went on to say that O'Casey's *Juno and the Paycock* seems his best play "because it communicates most fully this dramatic dehiscence, mind and body come asunder in irreparable dissociation."[1] For physical comedy to be serious, then, the same principle must be operating from the props to the planes of abstraction. What works on the level of "furniture" must shape and suggest what can be said about the relation of "mind and body." It is well known that Beckett loved the knockabout comedy of music hall, vaudeville, and silent film. What is less well known and less understood is how important this material was in shaping his ideas, and how much the social world out of which came music hall, etc., affected him.

Fourteen years after his remarks on O'Casey, Beckett would write his own knockabout comedy, *Waiting for Godot* (written, 1948–49; first performed, 1953), and require that all four major characters wear bowler hats. As we shall note further on, Beckett thought of this requirement as crucial; Roger Blin, the director of the first production of *Godot*, remembers that Beckett "couldn't tell me exactly how he saw the characters. All he knew was that they wore bowler hats."[2] Why they are made to and how the hats function in the play are, of course, concerns that we are in a position to address. The bowlers are, in the first place, pieces of dramatic "furniture," and so what they signify should tell us something about the "higher centres" of the play. In the middle of a famously abstract play, with its generic mise-en-scène ("A country road. A tree. Evening.") and the epic and biblical scope of its meditations, float these props (fig. 49), reminding us that whatever we say about humankind, or Western man in this play, we must first say about men in bowler hats—about whom there's a good deal to say. We can begin by noting the bowlers as part of the social *gestus* of the play, the material expression of the social world beyond it.

*Fig. 49. Gogo and Didi in the 1964 London revival of Samuel Beckett's*
Waiting for Godot *(Zoë Dominic, London)*

# HATS OF OUR FATHERS

**N**o writer has given more thought to hats than Beckett. All of his vagrant and often solitary characters are highly conscious of their hats: where they came from, or how to keep them attached to their person, or what condition they're in, and so on. When a hat is specified, it is usually a bowler, a natural choice given Beckett's interests. We learn from Deirdre Bair's biography of Beckett that when the director Roger Blin began to costume the actors for the first production of *Godot*, "Beckett insisted that the actors wear bowler hats, similar to those his father had always worn. It is the one point on which he was absolutely adamant and would not budge."[3] Indeed, Beckett's father liked to wear bowlers.[4] Bill Beckett was the image of a prosperous, bourgeois businessman: round- and ruddy-faced, vigorous and hearty, interested in food and drink, sports and hard work, a man of simple tastes and affections,[5] a more sympathetic version of Lautrec's Monsieur Boileau. Beckett's fullest (and funniest) portrayal of a bourgeois, Jacques Moran in the novel *Molloy*, he of the methodical mind and the huge bunch of keys, is a father with a sullen and resistant son who embarrasses him. Moran wears a straw boater, the summer version of a bowler. (Perhaps, by having Moran lose his middle-class identity in his search for the tramp Molloy, in effect by having Moran *become* Molloy, Beckett is bringing his father closer to his relatively bohemian and artistic self, and in the process is realizing his father inside himself. Although having lost everything, Moran returns to his empty house to write his report on the search for Molloy, to do his own hard work and get the job done. His son has returned, and some night he too will "get up and go to his desk"[6] to write. Father and son will have become one in their tasks.)

So the bowler hat as a sign of the bourgeois was familiar enough to Beckett. In one of his *nouvelles*, "The Expelled," the nameless narrator recalls his father's buying him a hat, in proper middle-class fashion, when he became a man—that is, when his head had reached its "definitive . . . dimensions": "Come, son, we are going to buy your hat, as though it had pre-existed from time immemorial in a pre-established place. He went straight to the hat. I personally had no say in the matter, nor had the hatter."[7] The hat is something timelessly patriarchal, passed on from father to son as the symbol of a kind of preestablished adulthood. The son has no say in the matter of what is supposed to be *his* hat; the hat preexists him; he only inherits it. And yet, having been inherited by him, the hat becomes his. He says, "When my father died I could have got rid of this hat, there was nothing more to prevent me, but not I" (34). And in another *nouvelle*, "First

Love," this same narrator says, "I have always had my own hat, the one my father gave me, and I have never had any other hat than that hat" (19), thereby identifying what is his own with what he inherited from his father. In "The End," this hat is identified as a bowler, and he says, "At first this hat was too small, then it got used to me" (71)—or he to it, and the pain it causes him (75). We shall return to the nature and resonance of what is "inherited" by an individual, but suffice it to say here that the bowler hat is for Beckett bound up with a sense of bourgeois and patriarchal property: it is an item that gives you pain but which you don't want to do without, or cannot avoid. The narrator of the *nouvelles* did not want his hat—he would have preferred to go bareheaded, his "pretty brown hair blowing in the wind" (35)—but once he has it, he wants to keep it. He ties it by a bootlace to his buttonhole, an attached identity that it would be perilous to lose. "My hat flew off, but did not get far thanks to the string" (59).

When, in "The Calmative," a man in a bowler asks the narrator for *his* hat, in exchange for something, the narrator refuses. "What vehemence! he said. I haven't a thing, I said" (64). The hat is no longer a thing, a piece of property, but something essential. The man in the bowler is less interested in a swap of objects than in an emotional exchange. He seems to be a salesman of sorts, with his hearty manner and his black bag full of phials, one of which he offers for the narrator's hat. He is curious about the narrator ("Where did you spring from? . . . What's the matter with you?"); he wants to know the "main drift" of his life, though he himself offers only "facts, without comment" as the sum total of his life (62–63). When refused the hat, and the lace dangling from it, he settles for a kiss, and doffs his bowler so that the narrator can place one on his bald head. Then he puts his bowler back on and leaves. He clearly wants something the narrator has and settles for a brief intimacy, a gesture beyond his bowler-hatted, commercial-seeming identity. In the context of Beckett's work, and of what we can know about his life, this man seems a father figure, making what gesture he can toward the "I," the Beckett narrator, even though he cannot understand him. But in "The End," the narrator one day sees his son, "bald as a coot," striding along with a briefcase, "bowing and scraping and flourishing his hat left and right. The insufferable son of a bitch" (80). The narrator seems in turn to have passed something on—a servile involvement in the "outer world" (the world outside solipsism), signaled by hat-flourishing, and is not happy about it.

Hats, then, for Beckett signify an inherited social identity at once necessary and irritating ("There is something about this strict sit of hats and caps that never fails to exasperate me," says Moran [130]). Bowler hats in particular represent this identity as bourgeois, commercial, businesslike, pointedly male. The most prominent bowler-hatted man in Beckett's fiction is Gaber, the "agent" from an unnamed and obscure "organization" who interrupts Moran's complacent bourgeois life with instructions to find Molloy. Gaber appears in Moran's garden in "his heavy, sombre Sunday best" with bowler, the respectable *petit bourgeois* as "go-between" (93–95), bringing businesslike instructions from the chief ("Youdi"). Moran is an "agent" as well, one who knows his "business" (94). Later, when Moran becomes Molloy as a way of finding him (the chief plot of the novel), in the process losing his son, his health, his keys, his bicycle, even his boater for a time (while thinking he had it on!), Gaber appears again, notebook in hand, instructing him to return home (164). Later he visits Moran to get his "report" (175).

So Gaber represents a side of Moran—and of Molloy, all of them hat-wearers —connecting him to the business of living: getting out into the world and using the world's words, which we also inherit. Beckett has said that "art has always been bourgeois" in the sense in which the artist has been "obsessed with his expressive vocation," with regarding "the relation between the artist and his occasion" as an arena of achievement and success. The artist is bourgeois to the extent that he regards the expressive act as a marking-off of personal property, an expansion and validation of the self into and over "the domain of the feasible": art as "good housekeeping." This property and success ethic avoids the recognition that "to be an artist is to fail" because it excludes what the failed artist knows: that there is no suitable relation between the artist and his occasion, that there is too much of the irrational in the world to be admitted into, much less expressed by, the boundaries of the artist-as-bourgeois. Beckett describes the desire to escape from this failure by "more ample, less exclusive relations" between artist and occasion as "estheticised automatism,"[8] thereby connecting the bourgeois with mechanism, with an organization interested in duties and reports. The artist becomes an "agent" of the larger system of language, the words that are not ours but are passed on to us as if they were ours. ("We start from scratch and words don't; which is the thing that matters—matters over and over again," says Eudora Welty,[9] though Beckett would either argue that we can't start with anything but words, or would substitute "silence" for "scratch.")

This, then, is the broader patriarchy in question, the inheritance for which the transactions between fathers and sons are, in large measure, a metaphor. Hats, for Beckett, are signs of consciousness as an energetic but empty inheritance, something both familiar and impersonal, something through which you try to express yourself, only to have your expression issue in the old heritage of words, soft with use and misuse. Molloy identifies his suddenly remembering his name for the police with their letting him keep his hat on (23), and later describes his awareness of his ego ("I") and his name, and indeed all the phrases that flow from this awareness ("Don't do it Molloy"), as "a kind of consciousness" arising within him (88). Consciousness, for Beckett, is the self composing itself in language, and in doing so connecting itself to the world outside the self, the system of other language-users. It is at one, then, with social identity, any other identity being autistic, enclosed in silence, inexpressible, perhaps only an imagined and imaginary state.

After affirming that his hat has always been attached to the same buttonhole by a long lace, Molloy drily notes, "I am still alive then" (14). With this emblem of consciousness on and attached to him, he can live and breathe in the world into which he has been expelled. His existential majority has been "capped" at last, and he can begin the business of expressing himself automatically. No wonder the hats of Beckett's characters are often bowlers, consciousness itself being patriarchal and bourgeois for Beckett. When Moran has returned to his empty house and property, and has sold all there was to sell, he says, "I have been a man long enough" (175). In this state of relative freedom he will try not to use the words he was taught as a boy—but of course he will use them, even as he tries to subvert them. The hat—full of words, thoughts, vague imperatives, all *handed on*—is with us to the end. What could we do without it? When Molloy takes off his hat in a ditch, he presses his face to the earth in a kind of blind swoon and thinks of his mother (27). Soon, however, he will get up and try to go to her, don his hat and continue his narrative—the "wordy-gurdy," as the Unnamable calls it (399)—continue the words that make up the life of consciousness, its replicated music contained in the easily replicated bowler.

This aspect of the bowler Beckett would have drawn from the somber Victorian male bourgeois world of dense facts, organization, respectability: knowing your business, doing your job—the world of his father. Consciousness for Beckett was bourgeois in nature, and so bowlers were the appropriate signs of consciousness. But before we turn our attention to *Waiting for Godot*, we need to understand something of the psychology of hats in general.

# THE PSYCHOLOGY OF HATS

It does not take much reflection to understand hats as signs of consciousness, or of the personality in its nonbodily life. Hats are, quite simply, extensions of the head. Alison Lurie states this plainly when she says, "Traditionally, whatever is worn on the head . . . is a sign of the mind beneath it."[10] Freud says, reasonably enough, that "the symbolic meaning of the hat is derived from that of the head, though detachable." Unfortunately, he found the hat, like the head, to be "a symbol of the genital organ, most frequently the male," and detachment of it to be related to the castration complex.[11] In Chapter 1, I cast some doubt on this symbolism in relation to top hats, and no amount of study of the way people use or think about hats has convinced me that thinking about them as genitalia has any more use than to get us through what has become a Freudian Victorian parlor charade without being accused of repression.

Jung, though like Freud sketchy about hats (in general, the psychology of hats is a nascent science), is more helpful. For Jung the hat is an image of the self— or, more precisely, one of the many images of the self "as it comes into consciousness."[12] In response to a subject's dreaming that he puts on a stranger's hat instead of his own, Jung remarks: "The hat, as a covering for the head, has the general sense of something that epitomizes the head. Just as in summing up we bring ideas 'under one head' (*unter einen Hut*), so the hat, as a sort of leading idea, covers the whole personality and imparts its own significance to it. . . . A stranger's hat imparts a strange personality" (121–22). In response to a later dream, Jung makes it clear that "the 'strange' hat was the self, which at the time . . . seemed like a stranger to him" (259). So the hat symbolizes for him the totality of the self, and the exchange of hats signals "an emergence of the unconscious" (122)—that is, the emergence of an aspect of the self hitherto unacknowledged.

In this analysis the question arises, How can this detachable and exchangeable thing, a hat, be considered a symbol of what Jung called "the process of individuation" (115), the development of the individual self? We have come across a contradiction that we may discuss outside the terms of Jung's psychology. A hat is at once something we regard as our own, and something manufactured for anyone with our head size. Of course we can say the same for all possessions that we do not make for ourselves, but the hat makes this contradiction especially poignant. It is the most immediately expressive part of our apparel, in terms of both style and social usage, and yet it is the most immediately detachable. In conforming itself to our head, and extending it (or epitomizing it, as Jung says), it is peculiarly close to us, to our seat of consciousness, our very ego. Yet how tenuous is its hold! As Flügel says in *The Psychology of Clothes*, a hat in the wind becomes "a troublesome foreign body rather than an agreeable extension of the self."[13] What makes so venerably comic a hat's being suddenly whisked off a head is precisely the contradiction between what is so intimate and what is so removable. A windblown hat is an abruptly absent mind.

Now if the hat is a sign of consciousness (emergent or otherwise), and if there is a comic contradiction between the intimacy and abstractiveness of hats, then the comically used hat expresses a peculiar idea about consciousness—that is, as something our own and yet not our own. And it is not difficult to see, in this regard, how the bowler hat became the major comic headgear of this century. The bowler, more than any other hat, conforms to the shape of the head as an extension of the head (as it does dramatically in Elie Nadelman's *The Man in the Open Air* [see Chapter 1]), and it is relatively difficult to dislodge, if it fits. At the same time, by virtue of its firmness, its resistance to being shaped by the wearer, its relative lack of variation, and its popularity (cutting across social boundaries), it is the most stereotyping hat. The bowler expresses a modern consciousness: the intimate self as something endlessly reproducible, Jung's epitome of the individual personality become an archetype, a collective phenomenon.

## PASSING THE TIME PROFITABLY

**W**ith this social and psychological background we can turn to the use of the bowler hats in *Waiting for Godot*. Beckett drew their immediate signification from the comedies of "little men" he loved. In his youth, he often saw vaudeville at the Olympia and the Theatre Royal in Dublin and "never missed" a Chaplin or Laurel and Hardy film. In Paris in the 1950s, he went regularly to a music hall, to which he always took visitors from Ireland.[14] He pays tribute to "the pantomime/The circus The music-hall" in *Godot*, when Didi and Gogo compare the events onstage with these entertainments.[15] There is a story that he had Laurel and Hardy in mind for the parts of Didi and Gogo,[16] and Chaplinesque gestures are everywhere in his fiction: "I perfected a method of doffing my hat at once courteous and discreet, neither servile nor insolent. I slipped it slightly forward, held it a second poised in such a way that the person addressed could not see my skull, then slipped it back."[17] Indeed, "very Chaplinesque" is the phrase Beckett once used to describe the kind of performance he wanted for *Godot*.[18] Like Chaplin, Didi and Gogo are vagrants with baggy pants and bowlers, and the play is, of course, full of music-hall and vaudeville staples (cross-talk, slapstick, penis jokes, a round song, not to mention pants-dropping[19]) and touches from Chaplin and Laurel and Hardy, most prominently—as we shall examine—a lot of business with bowler hats.

In the first place, the bowlers express a *petit bourgeois* aspiration not unlike Chaplin's. Didi and Gogo used to be "respectable" (7)—"presentable" in the Faber edition[20]—and are "not in form" (49) any more, but they are appalled at being taken for beggars or "highwaymen" (54). They will try everything, resume the struggle to better themselves by waiting for Godot, whom they imagine as having agents, correspondents, and a bank account (13). Scraps of self-bettering language fill their minds/hats, some of it ill-remembered: "It might be better to strike the iron before it freezes," says Gogo in reference to their knowing "exactly how [they] stand" with Godot. Didi responds with all the acumen he can muster: "I'm curious to hear what he has to offer. Then we'll take it or leave it" (12). They wonder what truth there will be in their experience, how to "make the most" of opportunities to help mankind (51), how to "beguile" the long hours with habitual "proceedings" (51) and "pass the time" by occupying themselves with relaxation and recreation (49). They have a task, and they reason about it; they go on with their business, keeping up appearances as best they can, reminding themselves to make notes of things (10, 21).

When authority comes, in the person of Pozzo, they are deferential but opportunistic. If Didi and Gogo aspire to "save" themselves from their desolate situation, Pozzo is a darkly comic image of the form their aspiration takes. He is a parody of a snobbish landowner (the two vagrants are on his "land" [16]). Beckett imagined him, despite his Italian name, as a member of the British gentry,[21] and his bowler brings that social history with it; it is a good and not uncommon idea to costume Pozzo in a Norfolk jacket and knickerbockers, to go with his Kapp and Peterson pipe. Like Didi and Gogo, only more clearly and anxiously, Pozzo is full of canned wisdom ("From the meanest creature one departs wiser, richer, more conscious of one's blessings" [20]) and has "Professional worries!" (22) and a "schedule" he is concerned to observe (24). He is anxious about faltering (19) and fears the stoppage of time: "Whatever you like, but not that" (24). Better Godot's not arriving, better the endless waiting, than the periodic arrival of this image of gentility and his slave, both of whom falter badly, especially in Act 2.

Pozzo is in the process of losing his props throughout. When he misplaces his watch, an inheritance from his grandfather, he turns over Lucky's fallen hat with his foot to look for it (30), thereby relating, unconsciously, an image of chronological time with that of automatic thinking, both of them evoking the middle-class milieu of Victorian England, in which appointments were kept by standardized time and language was acquired as a commodity of self-improvement.

Of course, none of this business works, even though how things "work" is of primary importance. It has become comic business. Pozzo concludes that he has left his watch "at the manor" (31), when we have observed him consulting it, cuddling it to his ear, returning it to his pocket, etc., not minutes before. In evoking a way of ordering one's life that no longer works, Beckett locates his bowler-hatted men in a music-hall environment in which their middle-class anxieties are exposed and analyzed. To be bourgeois is to be comic—that is, not to get things quite right when having them be right is a source of anxiety. Aspirations are tripped up by realities: "Charming spot . . . Inspiring prospects" (10), says Didi of their bleak surroundings, as though he had settled down near the Seine riverbank at Asnières for an intake of nature; "muckheap!" Gogo calls it, challenging Didi with "You and your landscapes!" (39), as if smelling the river sewage.

The bowler hats in this play are at once filled with the vestiges of a solid, "presentable" way of life and knocked aslant by the inappropriateness of this way of life as a model of reality. Music hall made the lower middle class comic by exposing the contradiction between its aspirations and its roots. Chaplin and Stan Laurel refined and adapted music-hall techniques and subjects, only alluding to a social matrix while tending to "universalize" its energies—that is, make a troubled middle-class experience a general one, expressed in a medium (film) with general appeal. As the bowler-hatted clerk in his Sunday best left the city streets for the music-hall stage, then stepped into a celluloid world with vaguer social references, then onto the barren stage of *Godot*, he found himself at each step refined from an image of Victorian man to modern man, his bowler hat filled with more and more abstract aspirations and defeats. Yet the bowler would always be filled with the semantics of its origins.

# BOWLER BUSINESS

**W**hen, in the first act of *Waiting for Godot*, at the point where Pozzo commands Lucky to take off his hat and reveal his white hair and then takes off his own hat to reveal his baldness (and, presumably, his relative youth), Beckett appends the footnote, "All four wear bowlers" (22), it is a way of insisting that, no matter the differences between these men, all are alike in possessing this most stereotyping of headgear. This leads us to wonder what the four have in common, a way of wondering what their bowlers signify. And the primary thing that all four have in common is that they *think* in circumstances in which thinking is futile. As in silent comic films, the physical activity of these characters is constantly contradicted by a misplaced attention to the decorum of mental life.

In the considerable comic business of the play, the bowlers are signs (not symbols, as in Freud and Jung, not fixed in their reference) of consciousness as it expresses itself in reasoned language. Near the beginning Didi (Vladimir, his name in the text) muses about not losing heart, about feeling hope even if it is deferred:

> *Vladimir: (musingly).* The last moment . . . *(He meditates.)* Hope deferred maketh the something sick, who said that? . . . Sometimes I feel it coming all the same. Then I go all queer. *(He takes off his hat, peers inside it, shakes it, puts it on again.)* How shall I say? Relieved and at the same time . . . *(he searches for the word)* . . . appalled. *(With emphasis.)* AP-PALLED. *(He takes off his hat again, peers inside it.)* Funny. *(He knocks on the crown as though to dislodge a foreign body, peers into it again, puts it on again.)* Nothing to be done. (8)

The "it" that he feels may refer to "the last moment" or to "hope." Didi and Gogo hope for the last moment—for Godot, salvation, death, an end to their waiting—and this hope is always deferred. Didi's bowler seems at once to contain thought (hence hope) and to be empty (hope being always deferred; hence nothing is to be done). Thought is there, inside the hat, but it is futile. Didi's attempt to dislodge a foreign body from his bowler suggests that thinking, like a hat, is not native to us, is something *worn*, an *accessory*. At the same time Gogo has pulled off an ill-fitting boot, looked inside it, felt about inside it, shook it to dislodge something, and so on. He doesn't try to put it on again, as Didi does with his hat, because the fit is so obviously bad. Didi responds:

*Vladimir:* There's man all over for you, blaming on his boots the faults of
his feet. *(He takes off his hat again, peers inside it, feels about
inside it, knocks on the crown, blows into it, puts it on again.)*
This is getting alarming. (8)

This parallel irritation suggests at once that thought is anchored in the life of the
body and that it is far more detachable than feet. Hats often don't fit us any better than boots do, but they are easier to remove, especially if they don't fit. Perhaps what is "alarming" about what is under—or what is not under—Didi's bowler is the idea, implied by the parallel, that we blame the faults of our thinking
on our hats. There's nothing *in* Didi's bowler, just phrases (about "hope deferred," about "there's man all over for you") that nevertheless seem lodged
there, irritants. Later Didi says, ambiguously, "Thinking is not the worst. . . .
What is terrible is to *have* thought" (41). He means it is terrible to have thought
in the past, and to have acquired thought, like a possession. Didi and Gogo (Es-
tragon) have had thoughts, which came to nothing, and now these dead thoughts
are theirs. They look for these thoughts, peering into their hats, in order to keep
their act going, to pass the time so that, paradoxically, the last moment of that
time can arrive.

> *Estragon*: That wasn't such a bad little canter.
> *Vladimir*: Yes, but now we'll have to find something else.
> *Estragon*: Let me see.
> *He takes off his hat, concentrates.*
> *Vladimir*: Let me see.
> *(He takes off his hat, concentrates. Long silence.)* Ah!
> *They put on their hats, relax.*
> *Estragon*: Well?
> *Vladimir*: What was I saying. we could go on from there. (42)

This fooling with hats is the most consistent comic business in the play. The
characters take off their bowlers to concentrate, to recover the gist of their conversation, to feel inside for something more, then don them again to keep the dialogue going. It is as though thought, and the consciousness that produces it,
were something constantly to be discovered, then kept, in any case never *assumed*, as part of one's natural makeup. Pozzo puts it directly when he says that
Lucky "can't think without his hat" (27).

Lucky's mad speech is the climactic expression, in this play, of Beckett's view
of thought. Lucky carries thought as if in a cassette tape that is switched on

by the combination of having his bowler on and receiving the order, "Think!" His speech is a wildly telescoped review of the most unresolved and unresolvable problems in Western thought, combined with obscure, private references —thought being at once abstract and personal, given to us and used by us. The other three suffer this performance until Pozzo cries, "His hat!" and Didi seizes it.

> *Vladimir examines the hat, peers inside it.*
> *Pozzo*: Give me that! *(He snatches the hat from Vladimir, throws it on the ground, tramples on it.)* There's an end to his thinking! (30)

Lucky's thought, automatic and unfinished, has come to naught, or to the relative naught of an unsuccessful "number" on the stage—all it can do is replicate itself. Like his bowler, it seems full but is empty. He is stopped from thinking, his bowler trampled, but neither is destroyed. His bowler remains onstage after Pozzo and he exit in Act 1, and it is still there in Act 2: "Lucky's hat at same place," Beckett specifies. Didi, usually more thoughtful and hopeful than Gogo, is very pleased to spot it: "I knew it was the right place. Now our troubles are over. *(He picks up the hat, contemplates it, straightens it.)* Must have been a very fine hat" (46). The hat marks the spot where they will wait for Godot, which gives Didi more hope that they will be there when Godot arrives. Beyond that, Lucky's bowler is the sign that thinking (about Godot, or about anything to pass the time while waiting for him) *is* the site for waiting for Godot: the world created by the dialogue (language) is where his arrival will not take place; their wait is interminable, as thinking is "unfinished" (Lucky's last word). Didi admires Lucky's hat because he admires thinking, no doubt remembering what Pozzo told them in Act 1: that but for Lucky all his thoughts and feelings "would have been of common things"; instead, Lucky taught him "Beauty, grace, truth of the first water" (22). So much for that; now Lucky is a slave, and Gogo, once a poet, is in rags (9).

As soon as Didi straightens out Lucky's newly discovered hat, he puts it on in place of his own, then hands his own hat to Gogo, who puts it on in place of his own and hands his own to Didi, who puts it on in place of Lucky's, and so on and on. Thus begins a "'three hats for two heads' routine," an exchange out of music hall through Laurel and Hardy and the Marx Brothers.[22] It would have driven Jung himself into analysis. (Such exchanges tap into a general anxiety about losing or mistakenly identifying one's hat, an anxiety obviously increased by the mass manufacture of headgear. A glance at a book on Edwardian inventions turns up many hat-securing devices, far more elaborate than those contrived by Beckett's tramps, and also "Wacker's Improved Device for Preventing Mistakes in Taking Hats and other Head Gear,"[23] which prevents any unconscious exchange of hats—or, as Jung would have it, any exchange of the unconscious self.) But no new personality is imparted in the hat exchange in *Godot*. The bowlers are interchangeable, and so, by implication, are the thought processes interchangeable, each as futile as Lucky's. Didi breaks the chain by keeping Lucky's hat on ("How does it fit me?"—often, in productions of the play, Lucky's bowler is more dusty and battered than the others, to help distinguish it at this moment) and throwing his own down ("Mine irked me"). He goes through the business of taking it off, peering into it, shaking it, and putting it back on, and when Gogo, sensing the significance of this, says "I'm going," Didi asks, bright with newly acquired thought, "Will you not play?" (46–47). He then proceeds to imitate Lucky, sagging with the weight of imaginary baggage.

So Lucky's unfinished thought is passed on in the sign of his bowler, and the play, and the waiting, goes on unfinished. When Lucky turns up in Act 2, he has a "different" hat on (49). And at the end, Didi does his ritual business with his (i.e., Lucky's) hat after saying "We'll be saved" (60) when Godot comes. It doesn't matter that Lucky's speech was a torture to them. Perhaps Didi wants the advancement and refinement of Lucky's discourse. Or perhaps he thinks the discourse will become hopeful in *his* head—as though Lucky, faltering, had passed the baton of cognition on to him, for him to carry forward the saving virtues of beauty, grace, and truth.

Near the end, reviewing the events of their waiting, Didi wonders what he should say of their day, and after reviewing its events, asks rhetorically, "But in all that what truth will there be?" (58). The point to be made is that whatever truth was there will be lost in the saying. There is nothing to be done but "find something" and then "go on from there" (42), taking off their hats, concentrating, putting them on again and continuing to utter words too tired ("We should turn resolutely towards Nature," says Gogo, offering an example of the "charnel-house" [41] of their thinking), too repetitive, too bourgeois, to bring them anywhere near mystery (the absent Godot). Whatever they say and do will be as unfinished as Lucky's speech, and as their own waiting. They are the "little men," the clerks of reason, who have fallen on harder times than they could have imagined. The note-takers and cliché-manglers and appointment-keepers have been placed in an abstract site—a sort of music-hall stage as mystery play—in which their rituals of consciousness can only be comic. Didi and Gogo (and Pozzo and Lucky) are, in a sense at once literal and profound ("from the furniture to the higher centres"), bourgeois people out of work. Their bowler hats are the signs of the middle-class aspirations and failures that they have inherited, expressed in

163

Beckett's

Tramps

a collective consciousness with a history deep and pervasive enough (though ill-remembered) to seem to speak for all of us—or, rather, to *hope* to speak for all of us, such universalizing being an example of their own consciousness: "At this place, at this moment of time," says Didi in high form, "all mankind is us, whether we like it or not. Let us make the most of it, before it is too late!" (51). Calling themselves mankind *is* making the most of it, which is very little, and their bowler hats signify their collective, replicable, and comic aspiration.

# POSTSCRIPT: THE POSTWAR BOWLER

## ODDJOB

n the James Bond film *Goldfinger* (1964) there is a villain named Oddjob with a lethal bowler hat. Its rim is fitted with an edge so sharp that, when flung by Oddjob—as one would fling a Frisbee —it can decapitate a statue. Oddjob is played by a Japanese actor in a black business suit, which gives a peculiar resonance to his weapon. (In the fiction of the film Oddjob is North Korean —and so is a more politically suitable thug—but he is clearly a Japanese presence.) In the so-called "opening" of Japan, which by 1867 had rapidly Westernized Japanese life and institutions, the bowler became a sign of the West, appropriate to the commercial and financial ties being made. The Japanese adopted it and began to wear it along with the Western business suit, as they do to this day. Stephen Sondheim's musical *Pacific Overtures* (1976) includes a song about this Westernization called "Bowler Hat." The Japanese had joined the legions of the modern.

Oddjob's bowler carries this semantics. A villain in the aggressively occidental world of Ian Fleming, Oddjob flings back at his Western adversaries the murderousness of their own culture. The bowler, a sign of commercial energy and solidity, becomes in his hands a sign of power that hurts—colonialism, exploitation, imposition, etc.—and is returned to the West for what it is, a lethal weapon. The filmmakers allow us to regard Oddjob as a dangerous Other who has perverted the bowler's uses, but its semantics, rooted in history, suggest something more reflexive and provocative.

The roundness and hardness of the bowler serve it amusingly well as such a weapon. What other hat would do? Its semantics shift from hard-headed practicality to hard-hearted capitalist cruelty, from respectability to criminality, to be inflicted now on those who have inflicted it.

# DRESS AND COSTUME

Oddjob's hat is an extreme sign of the bowler's having the weight of its own history, the history of the modern industrial West. It returns to this West, anti-levitational, spinning fatally, as colonialism—particularly Britain's—has declined. The British bowler has indeed become what Lawrence's Gudrun in 1920 already recognized as "old bowler hat!" in 1920. It is not so much a sign of power or commercial élan as an advertising symbol, something to lend a sort of Lloyds-of-London solidity to Schweppes tonic water. And as the West in general has had to realize the peaking and slowing of its ascendancy, the bowler, as its vestimentary sign, has declined as an item of dress.

"Dress" is, loosely defined, the fashion of everyday life; it is what you wear, however frequently or rarely, in your domestic, occupational, or sabbatical arenas. After the Second World War, the bowler was worn for dress almost exclusively by men in the City of London, or by London men who wished others to think they were in banking or trade, that is, at the heart of things British. In the Fifties this unflappably uniform bowler-hatted man was the subject of many *New Yorker* cartoons. In 1962 Anthony Sampson wrote that in the inner square of the City nearly everyone wore a dark suit and bowler and carried an umbrella,[1] and as late as 1986, an article in the *New York Times* (of July 7), describing the opening of the new Lloyds Building in the City, noted pin stripes and bowlers as common wear among the underwriters.

It is interesting to reflect on the persistence of this dress during the time when the bowler-hatted man, whether painted by Magritte or mocked in cartoons, had become a comic stereotype of respectability shrunk to conformity. City of London dress no longer had the energy of the modern; it had already become the sign of something past, almost a parody dress. The revival of the bowler, after a wartime shellac shortage threatened its existence, was part of an Edwardian revival in men's clothes; the Duke of Edinburgh wore one in 1949 at the opening of the

Ideal Home Exhibition, and bowlers were made part of civilian dress for Guards Officers.[2] By 1950, the Edwardian look "had evolved completely: curly bowlers and single-breasted coats with velvet collars and ticket pockets, trousers narrowed almost to drainpipes, and a rolled-up umbrella."[3] However, this evolution was not to fulfill itself at the level of peacetime nostalgia for the Belle Epoque. By 1954, this retro style had been taken over by the urban delinquent Teddy boys (after "Edwardians"), who revealed it as costume by caricaturing it and revitalized it as costume by adding amusingly downmarket elements (string ties, white socks, crepe-soled shoes).[4] The Teds seemed to recognize, and then to exploit, the Edwardian revival as a parody of what British respectability had become. As little men—of the same class as Chaplin—turned threatening, they instinctively understood the bowler as a sign of the modern, of the energetic ongoing, no matter in what dark direction. Anthony Burgess's novel *A Clockwork Orange* (1963) projected the Teddy phenomenon into a ghastly and violent future, and in Stanley Kubrick's film version (1971) of the novel, the teenage thugs wear bowler hats. It is more natural, more historically inevitable, for the bowler to allude to the past while floating into the future than it is for it to be an accessory to a fixed idea. Bowlers were part of a rearguard sartorial action during a time when men's hats were disappearing altogether. In the *New York Times* article already mentioned, the radical design of the new Lloyds Building is contrasted with the bowlers of the men who worked there: emblems of tradition rather than modernism. The bowler was on its way out as an item of dress.

A London *Times* editorial of August 23, 1986, laments "The Fall of the Bowler Hat." The bowler is now, so the anonymous writer says, worn only as part of hunting costume and army mufti. "The bowler hat made Britain great, the Empire was won by men in bowler hats, the Industrial Revolution would never have happened without the bowler hat." It was clearly a sign of hegemony, "a focus of pride, dignity, rectitude and, ultimately, power." While this rhetoric is tongue-in-cheek, it is not empty. The shrinkage of the bowler's dress usage to London from its ubiquity in the Western world and Japan represented a postcolonial, perhaps even a postindustrial, situation. Having lost the torque that spun it through modern times, the bowler could only settle on the heads of conservatives.

In a chapter of his 1946 book *The English Way* titled "Class Feeling and Bowler Hats," Pierre Maillaud reflects on Sean O'Faolain's remark that "between England and Revolution there will always stand an army of bowler hats." Maillaud's general and rather smug argument is that England has had no real class warfare and little class hatred. In this context he regards bowler hats as connecting links between social classes: "To the workman the bowler hat of the foreman of old was more desirable than a brand new social order." To put it more bluntly, a large and healthy middle class kept English social boundaries more fluid and social aspirations more possible. Maillaud's bowler hat is not so much a sign of conservatism as it is of the progressively modern as an antirevolutionary force. His reflections on English politics of the 1930s can serve as a thumbnail analysis of the politics of Weimar Germany: liberalism without sufficient initiative was crushed in a vise between the Right, which identified individuality with "personal privilege," and the Left, which attacked personal privilege on behalf of mass privilege. A revolution, Nazi rather than Bolshevik, overthrew Weimar in 1933, and the bowler hat more or less disappeared from Germany. Maillaud wonders whether the present—that is, the immediate postwar—disappearance of the bowler from the heads of the lower middle classes might not presage class warfare.

This may be carrying symbolism too far, but the point is not idle. English conservatism "is made up of daily habits, understandings, attachments, and practical rather than theoretical ambitions. It is also colored with a marked potentiality for a modern degree of social climbing."[5] We may wish to intervene and claim that English conservatism can also be described as marked by an antimodern obsession with personal privilege. Nevertheless, Maillaud's reading is right for the bowler: it is staid only in being unflamboyantly practical in the maintenance of modern mobility.

Writing in the Thirties, the American humorist Robert Benchley would have agreed with Maillaud's reading. In his sketch "Johnny-on-the-Spot" he imagined men in derby hats as always oblivious to cataclysmic or revolutionary events taking place, as always blithely absorbed in daily activities while bullets are flying: "Are these men in derby hats really men of iron, who take revolutions and assassins in their stride as all part of the day's work, or are they hard of hearing, or near-sighted, or, possibly, are they just men who go through life missing things?"[6] Benchley likes to think the last analysis is the most accurate, that the men in derbies are, in effect, little people concerned with their *petites histoires* while wars and elections are won and lost, theories proved and disproved.

All this is background to saying that the bowler is not an effectively *retrospective* sign. Although it signifies the practical and respectable, those are among the qualities of a dynamic industrial life; and although the bowler is staid and reserved, those are qualities more middle-class than feudal. But of course, as we have often had occasion to note, modern life has created its own traditions, and the use of the bowler to signify some deeply settled state in a world of flux, something timelessly British, as it seemed to do in the postwar years, is an indication that it was becoming an item of costume more than dress.

Dress becomes "costume" when the arena into which it is worn is marked off as somehow theatrical and presentational. Even though our generic clerk in his Sunday bowler and sack suit is dressing up, what he wears is still an expression of his ongoing life—that is, life that does not involve a different role definition for himself. Even if what he engages in is distinct from the everyday—for example, taking his family to the circus or to Asnières—he is a spectator at some event. Whereas the peasant who unpacks his clothes from the trunk for wear in a yearly village folk ritual is preparing to costume himself. By participating rather than, or as well as, spectating, he enters the realm of theater, whether it be an actual stage or the stage of life, whether the performance be ritual or spontaneous and the audience specific or at large. Obviously, in these terms costume and dress are not clearly distinct. The City man in bowler and pin stripes in the 1960s is at once dressing for work and costuming for a part in a cultural drama. Indeed, the very stylish modernity of the bowler, worn in the opened-up urban spaces of the late nineteenth century, made it presentational enough to be easily worn as costume on the music-hall stage. And if the music-hall audience thought of itself as on display, as performers in their own leisure time—a night at the theater become theater itself—then its dress shaded into costume.

Still, costume is definable, having the qualities of panache, humor, self-consciousness and detachment from the urgencies of current fashion that we associate with theatrical clothes. What is striking about the bowler in this regard is that it was a signal item in a fashion revolution (itself part of the Industrial Revolution) that tried to separate male dress from the qualities of costume mentioned above. Yet it was to become a major costume accessory, floating apart from the weight of its occupational and recreational ensembles to be worn in any number of dramatic circumstances inappropriate to its use as dress. It was as if its ability to cross social boundaries made it easier for it to cross other boundaries as well. Its modernity always won out.

An interesting conflation of the dress and costume uses of the bowler has been made by Andean *cholas*, native women from Ecuador to Chile who have moved to the towns. They have been wearing bowler hats since the 1920s,[7] when, presumably, British workers arrived in Bolivia to build the railroads that transformed much of the tribal life of the Indian peoples.[8] Bowlers are ubiquitous among the *cholas* of the Aymara and Quechua Indians (see fig. 50). Andean women wear hats as signs of wealth and position, and traditionally wore round "pudding hats" (one traveler reported their wearing men's hats of white felt in 1830), so bowlers must have been suitable for aesthetic as well as social purposes: they were at once Andean-like (durable, for one thing) and modern, that is, signs of a new commercial status and wealth.

Although the Andean bowlers have their conventional dress associations (urbanity, commerce), they have a costume aspect as well. Factory-made locally, they come in many colors,[10] are sometimes beribboned, and often are perched precariously on coiffures. It is as if the *cholas*, in a complex cultural statement of their own, wish to express their detachment from the very influence of the West that the bowlers express; they wish to make the power of the West their own. Describing with ethnocentric distaste the *chola* combination of bowlers and colorful skirts, one Western traveler wrote,

> It was all an extraordinary miscarriage of Western dress. The hats were not in the least practical: they were not warm, they were always several sizes too small, and they weren't even intended for women. Though they were once obligatory [?], now they are worn only through habit. Yet they seem like a deliberate effort to dress up, to assert a cultural identity; even to mock the foreigners who introduced the hats in the first place.[11]

Clearly the cultural identity asserted is confusing to this observer, yet through his confusion he is able to suggest its complexity. The Andean *cholas* seem to realize that bowler hats signify a power that they can wear very lightly, not take too seriously, adapt for their own purposes, and so use to achieve what the underwriters at Lloyds could not: a successful expression of the modern.

## BOWLER DRAG

**T**he *cholas* of the Andes are not the only women to demonstrate that the bowler hat can easily cross gender as well as social boundaries. The bowler has always looked good on women, perhaps because it is at once evocative of the Victorian male world and yet round and small enough, like the boater, to be easily adaptable to the female physique. That is, the bowler helped free women from the constraints of their own fashions (crinolines, bustles) without making them feel like parody males in the process. This is to overstate the effect; the bowler never played a major role in female dress—as trousers and sports jackets did, for example—but its occasional appearance is suggestive.

*Fig. 50. Aymara Indian women (reprinted by permission of the publishers from Harold Osborne,* Indians of the Andes: Aymaras and Quechuas *[Cambridge: Harvard University Press, 1952] © 1952 by Harold Osborne)*

The first females to wear bowlers were undoubtedly horsewomen, who needed protection as much as men, and who must have liked—as women have traditionally liked—some item of male dress as a sign that they were engaged in an activity usually reserved for men. The bowler was only one such item: late nineteenth-century women riders were called "Amazons" and wore masculine trousers under long skirts, along with boots, and top hats with veils.[12] And riding was only one such activity: the number of sports in which women could respectably participate, including lawn tennis and cycling,[13] increased quickly, especially in the 1890s. "Strong-minded females" (a common phrase in the 1880s)[14] were discovering what middle-class men were discovering in modern life: increased mobility and independence.

Cycling—and only a little later, motoring—expressed mobility literally as well as figuratively. This was especially true when bicycles and automobiles became means of transport as well as sporting activities. Bicycles became transport for the working and lower middle classes in the 1890s, "a factor which helped to expedite the growing freedom gradually being accorded to young women."[15] By 1896, motoring had become fashionable. Of course this mobility had a signal effect on women's clothing, resurrecting bloomers and requiring knickerbockers, Norfolk jackets, and small felt hats,[16] often bowlers. Women were also, like men, walking in the urban streets more often and so demanding more protective clothing. It would not be long before trousers would make their mainstream appearance on women in the twentieth century. The point is no less true for being obvious: like men, women wore the bowler hat as a sign that they were participating in the boundary-crossing of modern life.

However, wearing bowlers as a sign of participating in modern male activities cannot account for their later popularity as items of performance and costume drag, from music hall and cabaret to Broadway musicals and tomboy dress. In performance and costume drag, the bowler was and is often used to contrast with items of obviously female dress, including net stockings and even lingerie. The masculine bowler brings to these ensembles a touch of hard-edged allure. Elizabeth Wilson reflects on this when she says there is erotic appeal in "a sexual presence tinged with ambiguity . . . a hint of manliness at the very heart of [the] feminine presence"[17]—the appeal of Garbo and Dietrich, for example. The bowler in these cabaret-style costumes has a brassy assertiveness that makes the revealing sexuality of the rest of the costume more aggressive. At the same time the skimpy costume accentuates the jaunty stylishness of the bowler. A trademark of the Broadway choreographer-director Bob Fosse was his use of bowlers in this way, on men and women alike (fig. 51), always with some historical resonance (Chaplin and machines in *The Pajama Game* [1954], music hall in *Redhead* [1959], Weimar Germany in his film version of *Cabaret* [1972]) played off against the more abstract modernity of unisex costuming.[18]

The interplay, then, between the bowler hat as a sign of the "public" world (male, official, businesslike, vigorous) and the "private" signs of the rest of the costume (female, erotic, languid) involves a blurring of the very definitions of public and private. The male is no longer repressed, the female no longer merely passive. The bowler is a useful accessory to an androgynous presentation because it signifies a strictly masculine world as demarcated by the Industrial Revolution, and also the aspirations to a more stylish life of leisure and sport, aspirations that were affecting women by the 1880s, as more careers were opening up to them[19] and more activities were created for them.

Women's appropriation of the bowler hat, then, points to its tendency to become an item of costume as well as dress. For women, as for men, the bowler signified, among other things, that modern life was a spectacle, an urban theater where people have just enough leisure to perform their lives in public or to watch the lives of others as performance. This was as true for women wearing bowlers while motoring at the turn of the century as it was for women cabaret performers in Germany in the 1920s. They could at once liberate the bowler from

*Fig. 51. Gwen Verdon in Bob Fosse's production of* Redhead, *1959, photographed by Fred Fehl (Hoblitzelle Theatre Arts Library, Harry Ransom Humanities Research Center, University of Texas at Austin)*

the staid world of male dress, thereby carrying on its history of crossing social boundaries, and use its male, occupational resonance to indicate that women meant business. For them it was a vestimentary sign in what was becoming their own living theater.

## THE SIGN OF THE MODERN

A recent advertisement for children's clothes made by Nannette Manufacturing Company (fig. 52) shows two little girls in appropriately girlish outfits but wearing adult, hence outsized, bowler hats. One of them holds a man's briefcase. The copy reads, "Nannette: because they'll never be this age again." The bowler, of course, along with the briefcase (allusions to our Man in the Bowler Hat) is a sign of the adult world of work, responsibility, severity, and so on. The clash with the girls in their dresses makes the girls seem even younger and cuter (may they never grow up!), which casts a more ironic reflection on the effects of bowler drag: that it confirms the girlish, "feminine" status of the woman through contrast with the masculine, that is adult, hat. This may well be so, though the bowlers in the Nannette ad, which match the girls' ensembles, do not look grotesque on them—just a little big.

What makes the bowler hat such an ideal item of costume is, to use Kundera's term, its very "lightness," its ability to free itself from all but the most vestigial of its references, to become a design object with little or no social and fashion history. Of course this is itself an aspect of its history, as we have noted. When Kundera's naked Sabina puts on her grandfather's bowler, she makes it an accessory to nothing but herself. She liberates it from a past that is painful to both her and Tomas. And yet that past must still be signified, so that it may be overcome; the nostalgia that the bowler invokes in Tomas is part of the eroticism of Sabina's wearing it naked.

"Dress" is bound to fashion, which is in turn bound to social history. "Costume" is created when something inappropriate to the weight of the present is worn, whether something "historical" (as in costume drama) or spontaneously and wittily thrown together. Whatever history costume suggests becomes theater. While Barthes is right that theatrical costume has a social *gestus*, it is also true that a theatrical *gestus* emerges from and transcends the social and historical. The bowler hats on the characters in *Waiting for Godot* evoke a middle-class milieu, but also theatrical traditions that were a part of that milieu: music hall and

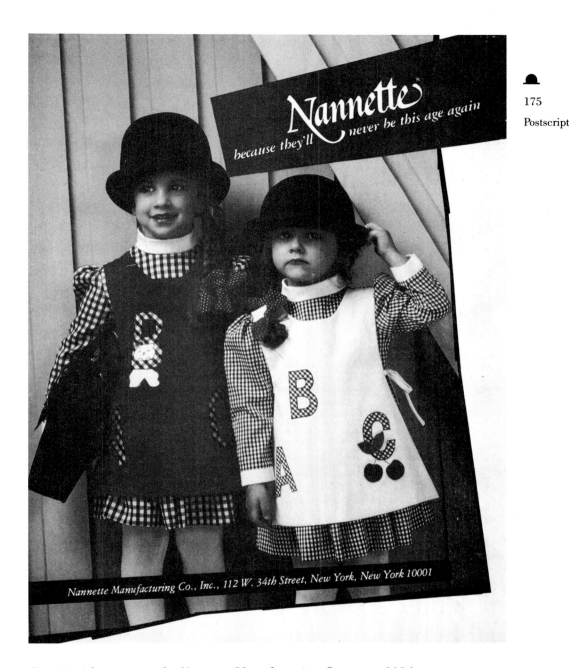

*Fig. 52. Advertisement for Nannette Manufacturing Company, 1986
(courtesy Eric Miller, Nannette Manufacturing Company)*

silent film. Didi and Gogo are "modern" characters in the sense that they express aspects of Victorian bourgeois social history and at the same time are Everymen, existential characters stripped of all but some barely remembered sociohistorical references. The bowler is "modern" because it can transcend continually its own history, and so can function as costume and dress at once.

The survival of the bowler as purely costume, which has been a long time developing and has only very recently been the case, is at once the end and the fulfillment of it as a sign of the modern. It still appears, most often in advertising, as a sign of the British (especially the horsy British) and/or of the business and financial world, and/or of that most recent symbol of the latest phase of the Industrial Revolution, the computer. In regard to the last of these, IBM employs a Chaplin figure to show how user-friendly its computers are to the technologically innocent, and Northeast Computer Stores shows a Sherlock Holmes and a bowler-hatted Watson trying to solve the mysteries of the PC. In both cases, the bowler invokes a more innocent past and also identifies the figures as modern people who can learn to adapt to technology (having done so for 150 years!).

The bowler expresses its history precisely as it floats past it, and on into a world in which what it signifies becomes more and more vestigial until, in some distant and possibly Utopian/Dystopian future, it becomes a pure design object, invoking nothing and admired only for its stylish, minimalist shape. "It can go with anything, adapt to anything!" people will say, and the dream of the modern will be realized, in at least one small object, at the end of the modern age.

# NOTES

INTRODUCTION

1. Kundera, *The Unbearable Lightness of Being*, p. 87. Hereafter cited in parentheses in the text.
2. Barthes, "Diseases of Costume," in *Critical Essays*, p. 46. Hereafter cited in parentheses in the text.
3. Barthes, "Imagination of the Sign," in *Critical Essays*, p. 207.
4. See de Saussure, "On the Nature of Language," pp. 46, 50. This is a collection of extracts from de Saussure's *Course in General Linguistics*, trans. Wade Baskin (New York: Philosophical Library, 1959). Barthes's writing on the nature of the sign reflects de Saussure's.
5. Baur, *Sculpture and Drawings of Elie Nadelman*, p. 9. Lincoln Kirstein, in *Elie Nadelman*, discusses Nadelman's "inclination toward dandaical outlines" (p. 161). Kirstein's essential book will hereafter be cited in parentheses in the text.
6. Baudelaire, *Painter of Modern Life*, p. 29.
7. Baur, *Sculpture and Drawings of Elie Nadelman*, p. 10.
8. Quoted in Kirstein, *Elie Nadelman*, p. 26.
9. Baudelaire, *Painter of Modern Life*, p. 13.
10. Ibid., p. 12.
11. See Ola d'Aulaire and Ola d'Aulaire, "Mannequins," p. 70: "Most experts agree that the succession of stages set in motion during the Industrial Revolution—the manufacture of large, steel-framed, plate-glass windows, the invention of the sewing machine, the electrification of cities—cleared the way for its [the mannequin's] arrival. The men and women who strolled the boulevards were the audience; all that was needed were players. Enter, stage left: the mannequin."
12. A "comic" contradiction is one that expresses both an irony and an affinity between its terms. See Fred Miller Robinson, *Comic Moments*.
13. See Baur, *Sculpture and Drawings of Elie Nadelman*, p. 8.


CHAPTER ONE

1. Whitbourn, *Mr Lock of St James's Street*. Hereafter cited in parentheses in the text.
2. Lurie, *Language of Clothes*, p. 176; Brummell, *Male and Female Costume*, p. 104.
3. Notestein, *English Folk*, p. 94.
4. Cunnington, *The Art of English Costume*, p. 73.
5. Wilcox, *The Mode in Costume*, p. 298.
6. Miller, *Textiles*, p. 16.
7. Cunnington and Cunnington, *Handbook of English Costume in the Nineteenth Century*, p. 341.

8. Levitt, *Victorians Unbuttoned*, p. 111.

9. Hendrickson, *Dictionary of Eponyms*, c.v. "Bowler, Billycock."

10. Ginsburg, *Victorian Dress in Photographs*, pp. 106, 128.

11. See Lambert, *Victorian and Edwardian Country-House Life.*

12. From *Clothes* (1953), quoted in Pear, *English Social Differences*, p. 174.

13. Quoted in Wiener, *English Culture*, p. 13.

14. Best, *Mid-Victorian Britain*, p. 252.

15. Harrison, *The Early Victorians*, p. 99.

16. Best, p. 256; see also p. 47.

17. James Laver, *Victorian Vista*, p. 26.

18. DeMarly, *Working Dress*, p. 123.

19. Roebuck, *Making of Modern English Society*, p. 4.

20. Flügel, *Psychology of Clothes*, pp. 27, 30.

21. "J.S.," "Natural History of Dress," p. 565.

22. Nevill, *Fancies Fashions and Fads*, p. 195.

23. Levitt, *Victorians Unbuttoned*, pp. 106–8.

24. Cunnington and Lucas, *Occupational Costume in England*, p. 227.

25. Nevill, *Fancies, Fashions and Fads*, p. 194.

26. DeMarly, *Working Dress*, p. 149.

27. Fiona Clark, *Hats*, p. 42.

28. DeMarly, *Working Dress*, p. 149.

29. Brander, *Victorian Gentleman*, p. 101.

30. Perrugini, *Victorian Days and Ways*, p. 105.

31. From *Letters to the Duke of Richmond*, 1772, quoted in Bedarida, *Social History of England, 1851–1975*, p. 41.

32. Laver, *Victorian Vista*, p. 216.

33. "Costume and Character," pp. 568–69.

34. Nevill, *Mayfair and Montmartre*, pp. 65, 122.

35. Binder, *Peacock's Tail*, p. 20.

36. Nevill, *Mayfair and Montmartre*, p. 65.

37. "Costume and Character," p. 569.

38. Ibid.

39. Quoted in Mansfield and Cunnington, *Handbook of English Costume in the Twentieth Century*, p. 290.

40. Nevill, *Mayfair and Montmartre*, p. 49.

41. Walkley and Foster, *Crinolines and Crimping Irons*, p. 127.

42. Waugh, *Cut of Men's Clothes*, p. 112.

43. Walkley and Foster, *Crinolines and Crimping Irons*, p. 128.

44. Ibid., p. 131.

45. Ibid., p. 128.

46. Pear, *English Social Differences*, p. 176.

47. Mottram, "Town Life and London," p. 177.

48. Ibid., p. 186.

49. Ibid., p. 183.

50. Brummell, *Male and Female Costume*, pp. xviii, 126.

51. Ibid., p. xviii.

52. See the comments of Eleanor Parker in the Introduction to ibid., pp. ix–x.
53. Mottram, "Town Life and London," p. 182.
54. Baudelaire, *Painter of Modern Life*, plates 12, 14–15, 22–24.
55. Perrugini, *Victorian Days and Ways*, p. 102.
56. Quoted in ibid., p. 103.
57. Tozer and Levitt, *Fabric of Society*, p. 100. They are paraphrasing Albert Smith in his *Natural History of the Gent* (1847).

CHAPTER TWO

1. Simmel, "Fashion," in *On Individuality and Social Forms*, p. 303. Hereafter cited in parentheses in the text.
2. DeMarly, *Working Dress*, p. 116.
3. Cunningham, *Leisure in the Industrial Revolution*, p. 116.
4. Crossick, "Petite Bourgeoisie in Nineteenth-Century Britain," p. 74.
5. Cunningham, *Leisure in the Industrial Revolution*, pp. 148, 150.
6. See Haupt, "Petite Bourgeoisie in France," pp. 95–119.
7. See Rearick, *Pleasures of the Belle Epoque*, p. 24.
8. T. J. Clark, *Painting of Modern Life*, pp. 212, 214, 154. Hereafter cited in parentheses in the text. The last phrase is from an 1872 speech by Léon Gambetta.
9. Cooper, Introduction to *Georges Seurat: Une Baignade, Asnières*, p. 12.
10. A phrase from a satirical verse by Jean Ajalbert. See T. J. Clark, *Painting of Modern Life*, pp. 156, 299–300.
11. Weber, *France, Fin de Siècle*, p. 204. Hereafter cited in parentheses in the text.
12. Seigel, *Bohemian Paris*, pp. 279–80.
13. Wilson, *Adorned in Dreams*, pp. 3, 15.
14. Cooper, Introduction to *Georges Seurat: Une Baignade, Asnières*, p. 4.
15. Simmel, "Fashion," pp. 311, 312.
16. Whiteing, *Paris of To-day*, p. 151.
17. Ibid., p. 53.
18. Ibid., pp. 182–83.
19. Quoted in Benjamin, *Charles Baudelaire*, p. 62.
20. Quoted in ibid., p. 58 (the English translation is from Karl Marx and Friedrich Engels, *On Britain* [Moscow, 1962], pp. 56–57).
21. Ibid.
22. Ibid., p. 69 (from Victor Fournel, *Ce qu'on voit dans les rues de Paris* [Paris, 1888], p. 263).
23. Ibid.
24. Rearick, *Pleasure of the Belle Epoque*, p. 181. This quote is part of a useful section on flâneurs and *badauds*, pp. 176–81.
25. Whiteing, *Paris of To-day*, p. 154.
26. Eliot, *Collected Poems, 1909–1962*, p. 55.
27. T. J. Clark, *Painting of Modern Life*, p. 258.
28. Coxe, *A Seat at the Circus*, p. 41.
29. Moffett, *Impressionist and Post-Impressionist Paintings*, p. 227.

30. Ibid.

31. Weber, *France, Fin de Siècle*, p. 231. Weber borrows this trope from Pierre de Coubertin, who wrote of sports as *parades* against industrial civilization.

32. Fry, "Seurat's *La Parade*," p. 63.

33. Rimbaud, "*Parade*," in *Illuminations and Other Prose Poems*, p. 20.

34. Coxe, *A Seat at the Circus*, p. 225.

35. Fry, "Seurat's *La Parade*," p. 64.

36. Whiteing, *Paris of To-day*, p. 61.

37. J. C. Squires, Introduction to Grossmith and Grossmith, *Diary of a Nobody*, p. 8.

38. Crossick, "Petite Bourgeoisie in Nineteenth-Century Britain," pp. 78–79.

39. Grossmith and Grossmith, *Diary of a Nobody*, p. 67. Hereafter cited in parentheses in the text.


CHAPTER THREE

1. Traies, "Jones and the Working Girl," pp. 31, 47.

2. Beerbohm, *More*, pp. 120–21.

3. Titterton, *From Theatre to Music Hall*, pp. 116, 224, 117.

4. Jules Lemaître, "Les Café-Concerts 1885," *Impressions du Theatre* (Paris: Ancienne Librairie de France, 1930), 2:290, quoted in Harris "'A Great Bath of Stupidity,'" p. 32 (Harris's translation).

5. Beerbohm, "At the Tivoli" (December 3, 1898), in *Around Theatres*, 1:16–17.

6. Bailey, "Custom, Capital and Culture in the Victorian Music Hall," p. 200.

7. J. K. Cook, "The Labourer's Leisure," *Dublin University Magazine* 40 (1871), quoted in Bailey, "Champagne Charlie," p. 68.

8. Rutherford, "'Harmless Nonsense,'" p. 147.

9. See Cheshire, *Music Hall in Britain*, pp. 86–88.

10. Bailey, "Custom, Capital and Culture in the Victorian Music Hall," p. 199.

11. Beerbohm, "The Older and Better Music Hall" (November 14, 1903), in *Around Theatres*, 2:383.

12. Titterton, *From Theatre to Music Hall*, p. 129.

13. Ibid., p. 143.

14. Bailey, "Champagne Charlie," p. 64.

15. Quoted in Vicinus, *The Industrial Muse*, p. 262.

16. See Simmel, "Fashion," in *On Individuality and Social Forms*, p. 296.

17. See Naomi E. Maurer's catalogue notes in Stuckey, *Toulouse-Lautrec: Paintings*, p. 95.

18. Baudelaire, *Painter of Modern Life*, p. 13.

19. Perruchot, *Toulouse-Lautrec*, pp. 142–43.

20. Davis, *About Paris*, pp. 75, 79.

21. Frey, "Henri de Toulouse-Lautrec," p. 27.

22. See Huisman and Dortu, *Lautrec by Lautrec*, p. 69.

23. Perruchot, *Toulouse-Lautrec*, p. 115; see also p. 161.

24. Ibid., p. 126.

25. Seigel, *Bohemian Paris*, p. 240.

26. Ibid., p. 10.

27. Ibid., p. 11.

28. Perruchot, *Toulouse-Lautrec*, p. 169.

29. See Huisman and Dortu, *Lautrec by Lautrec*, p. 45.

30. Loftus, *Toulouse-Lautrec*, p. 16.

31. See ibid., p. 42.

32. Barthes, "At the Music Hall," in *The Eiffel Tower and Other Mythologies*, pp. 123–26.

33. Nabokov, *Lolita*, p. 249.

34. David Robinson, in *Chaplin*, p. 13ff., argues convincingly that Chaplin made his first trademark appearance in this film rather than in *Kid Auto Races in Venice, California*, which was released first but probably shot later. See also Manvell, *Chaplin*, pp. 78–79. The most recent update on this controversy is in Geduld, *Chapliniana*, 1:14–17. Unlike Robinson (and Chaplin in his autobiography), Geduld agrees with "most scholars" that *Kid Auto Races* was shot before *Mabel's Strange Predicament*.

35. Chaplin, *My Autobiography*, p. 144.

36. Sobel and Francis, *Chaplin*, pp. 164–65; this is an essential book on Chaplin.

37. Ibid., p. 162.

38. David Robinson, *Chaplin*, p. 115.

39. Quoted in McCabe, *Mr. Laurel and Mr. Hardy*, p. 100.

40. Quoted in Sobel and Francis, *Chaplin*, p. 170. They cite the source as *Women's Home Companion*, November 1933.

41. Churchill, "Everybody's Language," p. 74 (excerpted from *Colliers* 96 [October 26, 1935]: 24, 37–38).

42. Payne, *The Great God Pan*, p. 13; Gehring, *Charles Chaplin*, p. 15.

43. Chaplin, *My Autobiography*, pp. 14–15.

44. Manvell, *Chaplin*, p. 82.

45. Ibid., p. 78.

46. McCabe, *Comedy World of Stan Laurel*, p. 143.

47. McCabe, *Mr. Laurel and Mr. Hardy*, p. 134.

48. See Gehring, *Laurel and Hardy*, pp. 29–34; and Skretvedt, *Laurel and Hardy*, p. 97.

49. Guiles, *Stan*, p. 99.

50. Brecht, "On the Use of Music in an Epic Theatre" (1935), in *Brecht on Theatre*, p. 86; Brecht, "A Short Organum for the Theatre" (1948), in *Brecht on Theatre*, p. 198.

51. Quoted in McCabe, *Mr. Laurel and Mr. Hardy*, p. 135.

52. McCabe, *Comedy World of Stan Laurel*, pp. 64–65.

53. McCabe, *Mr. Laurel and Mr. Hardy*, p. 176.

54. Nollen, *The Boys*, p. 51.

55. Geduld, *Chapliniana*, 1:24.

56. Quoted in McCabe, *Mr. Laurel and Mr. Hardy*, p. 46.

57. Skretvedt, *Laurel and Hardy*, p. 55.

58. Nollen, *The Boys*, p. 38.

59. From "Dessau Bauhaus—principles of Bauhaus production," a sheet published by the Bauhaus in March 1926, quoted in Whitford, *Bauhaus*, p. 206.

60. Rutherford, "'Harmless Nonsense,'" p. 146.

61. Priestley, *The Edwardians*, p. 173.

62. See Wilmut, *Kindly Leave the Stage!*, p. 44; Mander and Mitchenson, *British Music Hall*, illus. 166.

63. For a fine elaboration of this comic theme, see Hugh Kenner, "The Man of Sense as Buster Keaton," in *The Counterfeiters*, pp. 31–55.

64. I am relying on John McCabe's description and photographs in *Laurel and Hardy*, pp. 38–41.

65. Kerr, *Silent Clowns*, p. 334.

66. Hugh Kenner, in *A Reader's Guide to Samuel Beckett*, pp. 23–26, discusses the relation between Laurel and Hardy and *Godot*, claiming that the two comedians are "the immediate model" for Didi and Gogo. See also Gehring, *Laurel and Hardy*, pp. 137–38.


## CHAPTER FOUR

1. *The Gentleman's Tailor* 40, no. 7, July 1911.

2. Lawrence, *Women in Love*, p. 407. Hereafter cited in parentheses in the text.

3. Fallada, *Little Man, What Now?*, p. 14. Hereafter cited in parentheses in the text.

4. Alfred Döblin, *Berlin Alexanderplatz*, p. 47. Hereafter cited in parentheses in the text.

5. Willett, *Art and Politics in the Weimar Period*, p. 150.

6. Ibid. pp. 110, 150.

7. Laqueur, *Weimar*, p. 43.

8. Quoted in Willett, *Art and Politics in the Weimar Period*, p. 65.

9. See Maland, *Chaplin and American Culture*, pp. 64–67.

10. Chaplin, *My Trip Abroad*, p. 114.

11. Chaplin, *My Autobiography*, p. 248.

12. Chaplin, *My Autobiography*, pp. 216, 350.

13. See Willett, *Art and Politics in the Weimar Period*, pp. 33, 144.

14. Lawder, *Cubist Cinema*, p. 167. Lawder devotes a whole chapter to *Ballet mécanique*.

15. Originally published in *The Little Review* (Paris) 11, no. 2 (Winter 1926): 7–8, Léger's essay is excerpted in Chipp, *Theories of Modern Art*, pp. 279–80.

16. See also Léger's "The Aesthetics of the Machine" in Chipp, *Theories of Modern Art*, pp. 277–79. This essay was originally published in *Bulletin de l'Effort Moderne* (Paris) 1, nos. 1 and 2 (January/February 1924): 5–9.

17. Kracauer, *From Caligari to Hitler*, p. 193.

18. Willett, *Art and Politics in the Weimar Period*, p. 19.

19. Willett, *The Weimar Years*, p. 57.

20. Kolb, *The Weimar Republic*, p. 85.

21. Eberle, *World War I and the Weimar Artists*, p. 16.

22. The lines are from a comedy, *Palme oder der Gekrankte* (1924), quoted in Kolb, *The Weimar Republic*, p. 85.

23. See Whitford, *Bauhaus*, p. 20; and Willett, *Art and Politics in the Weimar Period*, p. 19.

24. Whitford, *Bauhaus*, pp. 23, 121.

25. Ibid., p. 198.

26. Eberle, *World War I and the Weimar Artists*, p. 16.

27. Pachter, *Weimar Etudes*, p. 303.

28. Ibid., p. 305.

29. See Laqueur, *Weimar*, p. 9.

30. Quoted in Pachter, *Weimar Etudes*, p. 112.

31. Laqueur, *Weimar*, p. 19.

32. Quoted in Eberle, *World War I and the Weimar Artists*, p. 65 (Eberle's translation). The original is in Grosz, *Ein kleines Ja und ein groszes Nein* (Reinbeck, 1974), p. 101.

33. Quoted in ibid., p. 65 (Eberle's translation); original from *Ein kleines Ja*, pp. 219, 220.

34. See ibid., chap. 3, esp. pp. 64–65.

35. Pachter, *Weimar Etudes*, p. 72. Pachter is especially articulate about the unity of intellectuals Right and Left against the bourgeoisie.

36. See ibid., p. 16, and Gay, *Weimar Culture*, p. 80. The terms are from Ferdinand Tönnies's pioneering work in sociology, *Gemeinschaft und Gesellschaft* (1887), which was very influential in Weimar culture.

37. Pachter, *Weimar Etudes*, p. 277.

38. Tucholsky, *Deutschland, Deutschland über Alles*, pp. 48, 191.

39. Ibid., p. 153.

40. Ibid., p. 191.

41. Ibid., p. 60.

42. Pachter, *Weimar Etudes*, p. 277.

43. Ibid., p. 306.

44. *Menswear*'s "75 Years of Fashion" (unpaginated).

45. See Niewyk, *Jews in Weimar Germany*, pp. 12–13.

46. Mosse, *Jews in the German Economy*, p. 398.

47. Laqueur, *Weimar*, p. 72.

48. Conversation with Willy Shumann, professor of German at Smith College, Northampton, Massachusetts, fall 1987.

49. See Pachter, *Weimar Etudes*, p. 219. See also Laqueur, *Weimar*, p. 32.

50. See Mosse, *Jews in the German Economy*, p. 401.

51. Tucholsky, *Deutschland, Deutschland über Alles*, p. 48.

52. Quoted in Pachter, *Weimar Etudes*, p. 112. The phrase is from Ludwig Marcuse.

53. Heartfield, *Photomontages of the Nazi Period*, fig. 31.

54. Sombart, *Jews and Modern Capitalism*, p. 275.

55. Pachter, *Weimar Etudes*, p. 177.

56. Herf, *Reactionary Modernism*, pp. 226–27.

57. Reprinted from *Impact* 1 (March/April 1955) in Smith and Barrier, *A Smithsonian Book of Comic-Book Comics*, pp. 326–33.

58. Niewyk, *Jews in Weimar Germany*, pp. 28, 41.

59. Brecht, "Notes to *The Threepenny Opera*," in *The Threepenny Opera*, pp. 92, 96. The text of the play is hereafter cited in parentheses in the text.

60. Brecht, "On the Use of Music in an Epic Theatre" (1935), in *Brecht on Theatre*, p. 85.

61. Brecht, "Notes to *The Threepenny Opera*," p. 90.

62. Ibid., p. 96.

63. Ibid., pp. 92, 93.

64. From a fragmentary essay reconstituted in Brecht's *Schriften zum Theater*, 1:129ff., and quoted in *Brecht on Theatre*, p. 17n.

65. Brecht, "The Street Scene: A Basic Model for an Epic Theatre" (1950), in *Brecht on Theatre*, pp. 121, 126.

66. See Brecht, "Notes to *The Threepenny Opera*," p. 90.

67. Brecht, "Street Scene," p. 125.

68. Brecht, "The Film, the Novel and Epic Theatre" (from *The Threepenny Lawsuit*, 1931), in *Brecht on Theatre*, p. 50.

69. "Conversation with Bert Brecht" (1926), in *Brecht on Theatre*, p. 14.

70. Brecht, "The Modern Theatre is the Epic Theatre" (1930), in *Brecht on Theatre*, pp. 38, 42.

71. Brecht, "Interview with an Exile" (1934), in *Brecht on Theatre*, p. 68.

72. From an early fragment on "the theatre of the big cities," quoted in an editorial note in *Brecht on Theatre*, p. 51.

73. "Conversation with Bert Brecht" in *Brecht on Theatre*, pp. 14, 16.

74. Brecht, "On the Use of Music," p. 86.

75. Brecht, "On Experimental Theatre" (1959), in *Brecht on Theatre*, p. 132.

76. Brecht, "The Popular and the Realistic" (1958), in *Brecht on Theatre*, p. 112.

CHAPTER FIVE

1. Hammacher, *René Magritte*, pp. 37–38.

2. Ibid., p. 62.

3. Calvocoressi, *Magritte*, p. 11.

4. For example, Alexandrian and Waldberg, *René Magritte*, p. 75.

5. Roberts-Jones, *Magritte*, p. 48.

6. Calvocoressi, *Magritte*, p. 7.

7. Soby, *René Magritte*, p. 11.

8. Gimferrer, *Magritte*, p. 7.

9. Ibid.

10. Hammacher, *René Magritte*, p. 7.

11. Ibid., p. 156.

12. Quoted in Gablik, *Magritte*, p. 184 (Gablik's translation). "Lifeline" is the revision of a lecture, "La ligne de vie," delivered at the Musée des Beaux-Arts in Antwerp, November 20, 1938.

13. Hammacher, *René Magritte*, p. 156.

14. Noel, *Magritte*, p. 24.

15. Simmel, "Fashion," in *On Individuality and Social Forms*, pp. 311–12.

16. Freud, *Interpretation of Dreams*, chap. 6.

17. Ibid., p. 312.

18. Gablik, *Magritte*, p. 187; all of the quotations from "Lifeline" cited in this and later paragraphs are taken from the essay as it appears in Appendix II of Gablik's book.

19. From his script for *René Magritte—Middle Class Magician*, BBC-TV, 1965, quoted in Soby, *René Magritte*, p. 7.

20. Freud, *Jokes and Their Relation to the Unconscious*, pp. 130–31.

21. Baudelaire, *Painter of Modern Life*, p. 12.

22. Letter from Magritte to Mr. and Mrs. Barnet Hodes, undated, 1957, quoted in Torczyner, *Magritte*, p. 72 (Torczyner's translation).

23. Letter from Magritte to André Bosmans, August 22, 1952, quoted in ibid., p. 26 (Torczyner's translation).

24. Breton, "Magritte's Breadth of Vision," p. 72.

25. Quoted in Gablik, *Magritte*, p. 101 (no source given).
26. Sylvester, *Magritte*, p. 14.
27. Duane Michals, *A Visit with Magritte* (unpaginated).
28. See Sylvester, *Magritte*, p. 14.
29. Gablik, *Magritte*, p. 154.
30. Ibid.
31. T. J. Clark, *Painting of Modern Life*, p. 26.

CHAPTER SIX

1. In Beckett, *Disjecta*; originally published in *The Bookman* (Christmas 1934).
2. Blin, "Blin on Beckett," p. 228.
3. Bair, *Samuel Beckett*, p. 388.
4. Ibid., p. 371.
5. See ibid., pp. 5–6, 162.
6. Beckett, *Three Novels*, p. 92. Hereafter cited in parentheses in the text.
7. Beckett, *The Expelled and Other Novellas*, pp. 34–35. Hereafter cited in parentheses in the text.
8. These quotations are all from "Three Dialogues" (with Georges Duthuit), in *Disjecta*, pp. 138–45; originally published in *transition* (December 1949).
9. Welty, *Eye of the Story*, p. 134.
10. Lurie, *Language of Clothes*, p. 176.
11. Freud, "Connection between a Symbol and a Symptom," pp. 143–44. See also his *Interpretation of Dreams*, pp. 391, 395–97.
12. Jung, *Dreams*, p. 115. Hereafter cited in parentheses in the text.
13. Flügel, *Psychology of Clothes*, p. 105.
14. Bair, *Samuel Beckett*, pp. 48, 417.
15. Beckett, *Waiting for Godot* (New York: Grove Press, 1982), p. 23. Hereafter cited in parentheses in the text; unless otherwise noted, all citations are to this edition.
16. For a discussion of the Beckett–Laurel and Hardy connection, see Gehring, *Laurel and Hardy*, pp. 137–38.
17. The passage is from "The End" (Beckett, *The Expelled and Other Novellas*, p. 76). See also Fred Miller Robinson, "Stumbling on a Smooth Road."
18. Bair, *Samuel Beckett*, p. 55.
19. See Fred Miller Robinson, "Tray Bong! *Godot* and Music Hall."
20. Beckett, *Waiting for Godot* (London: Faber and Faber, 1981), p. 10.
21. Bair, *Samuel Beckett*, p. 422: "With Pozzo, both men [Beckett and Roger Blin, who directed the first production] were in agreement from the beginning. They saw him as an English gentleman farmer, carrying a case of wine bottles, wearing a MacFarlane jacket, a beautiful necktie, bowler hat and gleaming leather riding boots."
22. Knowlson, *Samuel Beckett: An Exhibition*, p. 70.
23. Dale and Gray, *Edwardian Inventions*, p. 85.

1. Sampson, *Anatomy of Britain*, p. 346.

2. Fiona Clark, *Hats*, p. 66.

3. Howell, *Vogue*, p. 205.

4. See Baines, *Fashion Revivals*, pp. 142–43; Wilson and Taylor, *Through the Looking Glass*, pp. 163–65.

5. Maillaud, *The English Way*, pp. 78–81.

6. Benchley, *From Bed to Worse*, p. 256.

7. Osborne, *Indians of the Andes*, p. 223.

8. Morrison, *Indians of the Andes*, p. 26.

9. Osborne, *Indians of the Andes*, p. 222.

10. Ibid.

11. Shukman, *Sons of the Moon*, p. 25.

12. Kybalova et al., *Pictorial Encyclopedia of Fashion*, p. 535.

13. Gernsheim, *Victorian and Edwardian Fashion*, p. 81. See also Wilson, *Adorned in Dreams*, p. 160.

14. Gernsheim, *Victorian and Edwardian Fashion*, p. 73.

15. Ibid., p. 81.

16. Cunnington, *Feminine Attitudes in the Nineteenth Century*, p. 292.

17. Wilson, *Adorned in Dreams*, p. 120.

18. See Gottfried, *Broadway Musicals*, pp. 111–20.

19. Gernsheim, *Victorian and Edwardian Fashion*, p. 73.

# BIBLIOGRAPHY

Alexandrian, S., and P. Waldberg. *René Magritte*. Translated by Elisabeth Abbot. New York: Filipacchi Books, 1980.

Bailey, Peter. "Champagne Charlie: Performance and Ideology in the Music Hall Swell Song." In *Music Hall: Performance and Style*, edited by J. S. Bratton, pp. 49–69. Milton Keynes: Open University Press, 1986.

————. "Custom, Capital and Culture in the Victorian Music Hall." In *Popular Culture and Custom in Nineteenth-Century England*, edited by Robert D. Storch, pp. 180–208. London: Croom Helm, 1982.

Baines, Barbara Burman. *Fashion Revivals, from the Elizabethan Age to the Present Day*. London: B. T. Batsford, 1981.

Bair, Deirdre. *Samuel Beckett: A Biography*. New York: Harcourt Brace, 1978.

Barthes, Roland. *Critical Essays*. Translated by Richard Howard. Evanston, Ill.: Northwestern University Press, 1972.

————. *The Eiffel Tower and Other Mythologies*. Translated by Richard Howard. New York: Hill and Wang, 1979.

Baudelaire, Charles. *The Painter of Modern Life and Other Essays*. Edited and translated by Jonathan Mayne. London: Phaidon Press, 1964.

Baur, John I. H. *The Sculpture and Drawings of Elie Nadelman, 1882–1946*. New York: Whitney Museum, 1975.

Beckett, Samuel. *Disjecta: Miscellaneous Writings and a Dramatic Fragment*. New York: Grove Press, 1984.

————. *The Expelled and Other Novellas*. Harmondsworth: Penguin Books, 1973.

————. *Three Novels: Molloy, Malone Dies, The Unnamable*. New York: Grove Press, 1965.

————. *Waiting for Godot*. London: Faber and Faber, 1981.

————. *Waiting for Godot*. New York: Grove Press, 1982.

Bedarida, François. *A Social History of England, 1851–1975*. Translated by A. S. Forster. London: Methuen, 1979.

Beerbohm, Max. *Around Theatres*. 2 vols. New York: Knopf, 1930.

————. *More*. London: John Lane, 1899.

Benchley, Robert. *From Bed to Worse*. New York: Harper & Bros., 1934.

Benjamin, Walter. *Charles Baudelaire: A Lyric Poet in the Era of High Capitalism*. Translated by Harry Zohn. London: NLB, 1973.

Best, Geoffrey. *Mid-Victorian Britain, 1851–1875*. New York: Schocken Books, 1972.

Binder, Pearl. *The Peacock's Tail*. London: George G. Harrap, 1958.

Blin, Roger. "Blin on Beckett." An interview by Tom Bishop. Translated by James Knowlson. In *On Beckett: Essays and Criticism*, edited by S. E. Gontarski, pp. 226–35. New York: Grove Press, 1986.

Brander, Michael. *The Victorian Gentleman*. London: Gordon Cremonesi, 1975.

Brecht, Bertolt. *Brecht on Theatre: The Development of an Aesthetic*. Edited and translated by John Willett. New York: Hill and Wang, 1964.

———. *The Threepenny Opera*. Translated by Ralph Manheim and John Willett. Vol. 2, pt. 2, of *Bertolt Brecht: The Complete Plays*. London: Eyre Methuen, 1979.

Breton, André. "Magritte's Breadth of Vision." Translated by Simon Watson Taylor. *Studio International* 177, no. 908 (February 1969): 72–73.

Brummell, Beau. *Male and Female Costume*. Edited by Eleanor Parker. New York: Benjamin Blom, 1972.

Calvocoressi, Richard. *Magritte*. Oxford: Phaidon Press, 1979.

Chaplin, Charles. *My Autobiography*. New York: Simon and Schuster, 1964.

———. *My Trip Abroad*. New York: Harper & Bros., 1922.

Cheshire, D. F. *Music Hall in Britain*. Newton Abbot: David & Charles, 1974.

Churchill, Winston. "Everybody's Language." In *Focus on Chaplin*, edited by Donald W. McCaffrey, pp. 74–81. Englewood Cliffs, N.J.: Prentice Hall, 1971.

Clark, Fiona. *Hats*. London: Anchor Press, 1982.

Clark, T. J. *The Painting of Modern Life: Paris in the Art of Manet and His Followers*. Princeton: Princeton University Press, 1984.

Cooper, Douglas. Introduction to *Georges Seurat: Une Baignade, Asnières*. London: Percy Lund Humphries, n.d.

"Costume and Character." *The Cornhill Magazine* 9 (November 1865): 568–69.

Coxe, Antony Hippisley. *A Seat at the Circus*. 1951. Reprint. Hamden, Conn.: Archon Books, 1980.

Crossick, Geoffrey. "The Petite Bourgeoisie in Nineteenth-Century Britain: The Urban and Liberal Case." In *Shopkeepers and Master Artisans in Nineteenth-Century Europe*, edited by Geoffrey Crossick and Heinz-Gerhard Haupt, pp. 62–94. London: Methuen, 1984.

Cunningham, Hugh. *Leisure in the Industrial Revolution, c. 1780–c. 1880*. New York: St. Martin's Press, 1980.

Cunnington, C. Willett. *The Art of English Costume*. London: Collins, 1948.

———. *Feminine Attitudes in the Nineteenth Century*. London: William Heinemann, 1935.

Cunnington, C. Willett, and Phillis Cunnington. *Handbook of English Costume in the Nineteenth Century*. London: Faber, 1966.

Cunnington, Phillis, and Catherine Lucas. *Occupational Costume in England*. London: Adam & Charles Black, 1967.

Dale, Rodney, and Joan Gray. *Edwardian Inventions, 1901–1905*. London: W. H. Allen & Co., 1979.

Davis, Richard Harding. *About Paris*. New York: Harper & Bros., 1895.

DeMarly, Diana. *Working Dress: A History of Occupational Clothing*. New York: Holmes & Meier, 1986.

De Saussure, Ferdinand. "On the Nature of Language." In *Structuralism: A Reader*, edited by Michael Lane, pp. 43–56. London: Jonathan Cape, 1970.

Döblin, Alfred. *Berlin Alexanderplatz: The Story of Franz Biberkopf*. Translated by Eugene Jolas. New York: Frederick Ungar, 1983.

Eberle, Matthias. *World War I and the Weimar Artists: Dix, Grosz, Beckmann, Schlemmer*. New Haven: Yale University Press, 1985.

Eliot, T. S. *Collected Poems, 1909–1962*. New York: Harcourt, Brace & World, 1963.

Fallada, Hans. *Little Man, What Now?* 1933. Reprint. Chicago: Academy Chicago, 1983.

Flügel, J. C. *The Psychology of Clothes*. London: Hogarth Press, 1930.

Freud, Sigmund. "A Connection between a Symbol and a Symptom." In *Delusion and Dream and Other Essays*, edited by Philip Rieff and translated by Douglas Bryan, pp. 143–44. Boston: Beacon Press, 1956.

———. *The Interpretation of Dreams*. Translated by James Strachey. New York: Avon Books, 1965.

———. *Jokes and Their Relation to the Unconscious*. Translated by James Strachey. Harmondsworth: Penguin Books, 1981.

Frey, Julia. "Henri de Toulouse-Lautrec: A Biography of the Artist." In *Henri de Toulouse-Lautrec: Images of the 1890s*, edited by Riva Castleman and Wolfgang Wittrock, pp. 19–35. New York: Museum of Modern Art, 1985.

Fry, Roger. "Seurat's *La Parade*." In *Seurat in Perspective*, edited by Norma Broude, pp. 62–64. Englewood Cliffs, N.J.: Prentice Hall, 1978.

Gablik, Suzi. *Magritte*. New York: Thames and Hudson, 1985.

Gaines, William M. "Master Race." In *A Smithsonian Book of Comic-Book Comics*, edited by Michael Barrier and Martin Williams, pp. 326–33. Washington, D.C.: Smithsonian Institution Press, 1981. Reprinted from *Impact* 1 (March/April 1955).

Gay, Peter. *Weimar Culture: The Outsider as Insider*. New York: Harper & Row, 1970.

Geduld, Harry M. *Chapliniana: A Commentary on Charlie Chaplin's 81 Movies*. Volume 1: *The Keystone Films*. Bloomington: Indiana University Press, 1987.

Gehring, Wes D. *Charles Chaplin: A Bio-Bibliography*. Westport, Conn.: Greenwood Press, 1983.

———. *Laurel and Hardy: A Bio-Bibliography*. New York: Greenwood Press, 1990.

*The Gentleman's Tailor* 46, no. 7, July 1911.

Gernsheim, Alison. *Victorian and Edwardian Fashion: A Photographic Survey*. New York: Dover Publications, 1981.

Gimferrer, Pere. *Magritte*. New York: Rizzoli, 1987.

Ginsburg, Madeleine. *Victorian Dress in Photographs*. New York: Holmes & Meier, 1982.

Gottfried, Martin. *Broadway Musicals*. New York: Harry N. Abrams, 1979.

Grossmith, George, and Weedon Grossmith. *Diary of a Nobody*. 1892. Reprint. London: J. W. Arrowsmith, 1924.

Guiles, Fred Lawrence. *Stan: The Life of Stan Laurel*. New York: Stein & Day, 1980.

Hammacher, A. M. *René Magritte*. Translated by James Brockway. New York: Harry N. Abrams, n.d.

Harris, Gerry. "'A Great Bath of Stupidity': Audience and Class in the Cafe-Concert." *Theatrephile* 2, no. 6 (Spring 1985): 29–32.

Harrison, J. F. C. *The Early Victorians, 1832–1851*. London: Weidenfeld and Nicolson, 1971.

Haupt, Heinz-Gerhard. "The Petite Bourgeoisie in France, 1850–1914: In Search of the *juste milieu?*" In *Shopkeepers and Master Artisans in Nineteenth-Century Europe*, edited by Geoffrey Crossick and Heinz-Gerhard Haupt, pp. 95–119. London: Methuen, 1984.

Heartfield, John. *Photomontages of the Nazi Period*. New York: Universe Books, 1977.

Hendrickson, Robert. *The Dictionary of Eponyms*. New York: Stein & Day, 1985.

Herf, Jeffrey. *Reactionary Modernism: Technology, Culture and Politics in Weimar and the Third Reich*. Cambridge: Cambridge University Press, 1986.

Howell, Georgina. *Vogue: Six Decades of Fashion*. London: Allen Lane, 1976.

Huisman, P., and M. G. Dortu. *Lautrec by Lautrec*. New York: Viking Press, 1964.

"J.S." "The Natural History of Dress." *The Cornhill Magazine* 42 (November 1880): 560–72.

Jung, C. G. *Dreams*. Translated by R. F. C. Hull. London: Routledge & Kegan Paul, 1974.

Kenner, Hugh. *The Counterfeiters*. Garden City, N.Y.: Anchor Press, 1973.

———. *A Reader's Guide to Samuel Beckett*. New York: Farrar, Straus, 1973.

Kerr, Walter. *The Silent Clowns*. New York: Alfred Knopf, 1975.

Kirstein, Lincoln. *Elie Nadelman*. New York: The Eakins Press, 1973.

Kolb, Edward. *The Weimar Republic*. Translated by P. S. Falla. London: Unwin Hyman, 1988.

Knowlson, James. *Samuel Beckett: An Exhibition*. London: Turret Books, 1971.

Kracauer, Siegfried. *From Caligari to Hitler: A Psychological History of the German Film*. Princeton: Princeton University Press, 1974.

Kundera, Milan. *The Unbearable Lightness of Being*. Translated by Michael Henry Heim. New York: Harper & Row, 1984.

Kybalova, Ludmila, Olga Herbenova, Milena Lamarova, eds. *The Pictorial Encyclopedia of Fashion*. Translated by Claudia Rosoux. Feltham: Hamlyn, 1968.

Lambert, Anthony J. *Victorian and Edwardian Country-House Life*. New York: Holmes & Meier, 1981.

Laqueur, Walter. *Weimar: A Cultural History, 1918–1933*. New York: Perigee Book, 1980.

Laver, James. *Victorian Vista*. London: Hulton Press, 1954.

Lawder, Standish D. *The Cubist Cinema*. New York: New York University Press, 1975.

Lawrence, D. H. *Women in Love*. New York: Viking Press, 1960.

Léger, Fernand. "The Aesthetics of the Machine." In *Theories of Modern Art: A Source Book by Artists and Critics*, edited by Herschel B. Chipp, pp. 277–79. Berkeley: University of California Press, 1968.

———. "A New Realism—the Object." In *Theories of Modern Art: A Source Book by Artists and Critics*, edited by Herschel B. Chipp, pp. 279–80. Berkeley: University of California Press, 1968.

Levitt, Sarah. *Victorians Unbuttoned: Registered Designs for Clothing, Their Makers and Wearers, 1839–1900*. London: George Allen & Unwin, 1986.

Loftus, John. *Toulouse-Lautrec*. New York: McGraw-Hill, 1969.

Lurie, Alison. *The Language of Clothes*. New York: Random House, 1983.

McCabe, John. *The Comedy World of Stan Laurel*. Garden City, N.Y.: Doubleday, 1974.

———. *Laurel and Hardy*. New York: Bonanza Books, 1983.

———. *Mr. Laurel and Mr. Hardy*. New York: Doubleday, 1961.

Maillaud, Pierre. *The English Way*. New York: Oxford University Press, 1946.

Maland, Charles J. *Chaplin and American Culture: The Evolution of a Star Image*. Princeton: Princeton University Press, 1989.

Mander, Raymond, and Joe Mitchenson. *British Music Hall*. London: Gentry Books, 1965.

Mansfield, Alan, and Phillis Cunnington. *Handbook of English Costume in the Twentieth Century, 1900–1950*. Boston: Plays, Inc., 1973.

Manvell, Roger. *Chaplin*. Boston: Little, Brown, 1974.

Michals, Duane. *A Visit with Magritte*. Providence: Matrix Publications, 1981.

Miller, Edward. *Textiles: Properties and Behaviour*. New York: Theatre Arts Books, 1968.

Moffett, Charles S. *Impressionist and Post-Impressionist Paintings in the Metropolitan Museum of Art*. New York: Harry N. Abrams, n.d.

Morrison, Marion. *Indians of the Andes*. Vero Beach, Fla.: Rourke Publications, 1987.

Mosse, W. E. *Jews in the German Economy: The German-Jewish Economic Elite, 1820–1935*. Oxford: Clarendon Press, 1987.

Mottram, R. H. "Town Life and London." In *Early Victorian England, 1830–1865*, 2 vols., edited by G. M. Young, 1:155–223. London: Oxford University Press, 1934.

Nabokov, Vladimir. *Lolita*. New York: Vintage International, 1989.

Nevill, Ralph. *Fancies, Fashions and Fads*. London: Methuen, 1913.

———. *Mayfair and Montmartre*. London: Methuen, 1921.

Niewyk, Donald L. *The Jews in Weimar Germany*. Baton Rouge: Louisiana State University Press, 1980.

Noel, Bernard. *Magritte*. New York: Crown Publishers, 1977.

Nollen, Scott Allen. *The Boys: The Cinematic World of Laurel and Hardy*. Jefferson, N.C.: McFarland & Co., 1989.

Notestein, Wallace. *English Folk: A Book of Characters*. London: Jonathan Cape, 1938.

Ola d'Aulaire, Emily, and Per Ola d'Aulaire. "Mannequins: Our Fantasy Figures of High Fashion." *Smithsonian* 22, no. 1 (April 1991): 67–78.

Osborne, Harold. *Indians of the Andes: Aymaras and Quechuas*. Cambridge: Harvard University Press, 1952.

Pachter, Henry. *Weimar Etudes*. New York: Columbia University Press, 1982.

Payne, Robert. *The Great God Pan*. New York: Hermitage House, 1952.

Pear, T. H. *English Social Differences*. London: George Allen & Unwin, 1955.

Perruchot, Henri. *Toulouse-Lautrec*. Translated by Humphrey Ware. New York: Collier Books, 1962.

Perrugini, Mark Edward. *Victorian Days and Ways*. London: Jarrolds, 1932.

Priestley, J. B. *The Edwardians*. London: Heinemann, 1970.

Rearick, Charles. *Pleasures of the Belle Epoque: Entertainment and Festivity in Turn-of-the-Century France*. New Haven: Yale University Press, 1985.

Rimbaud, Arthur. *Illuminations and Other Prose Poems*. Translated by Louis Varese. New York: New Directions, 1957.

Roberts-Jones, Philippe. *Magritte: poète visible*. Brussels: Laconti, 1972.

Robinson, David. *Chaplin: His Life and Art*. London: Collins, 1985.

Robinson, Fred Miller. *Comic Moments*. Athens: University of Georgia Press, 1992.

———. "The History and Significance of the Bowler Hat: Chaplin, Laurel and Hardy, Beckett, Magritte and Kundera." *TriQuarterly* 66 (Spring/Summer 1986): 173–200.

———. "Stumbling on a Smooth Road: Silent Film Comedy and Beckett's *Nouvelles*." *Bucknell Review* 24 (Fall 1978): 107–19.

———. "Tray Bong! *Godot* and Music Hall." In *Approaches to Teaching Beckett's Waiting for Godot*, edited by June Schlueter and Enoch Brater, pp. 64–70. New York: Modern Language Association, 1991.

Roebuck, Janet. *The Making of Modern English Society from 1850*. London: Routledge & Kegan Paul, 1982.

Rutherford, Lois. "'Harmless Nonsense': The Comic Sketch and the Development of Music-Hall Entertainment." In *Music Hall: Performance and Style*, edited by J. S. Bratton, pp. 131–51. Milton Keynes: Open University Press, 1986.

Sampson, Anthony. *Anatomy of Britain*. London: Hodder and Stoughton, 1962.

Seigel, Jerrold. *Bohemian Paris: Culture, Politics, and the Boundaries of Bourgeois Life, 1830–1930*. New York: Viking Penguin, 1987.

Shukman, Henry. *Sons of the Moon*. London: Weidenfeld and Nicolson, 1990.

Simmel, Georg. *On Individuality and Social Forms: Selected Writings*. Edited by Donald N. Levine. Chicago: University of Chicago Press, 1971.

Skretvedt, Randy. *Laurel and Hardy: The Magic Behind the Movies*. Beverly Hills: Moonstone Press, 1987.

Sobel, Raoul, and David Francis. *Chaplin: Genesis of a Clown*. London: Quartet Books, 1977.

Soby, James Thrall. *René Magritte*. New York: Museum of Modern Art, 1965.

Sombart, Werner. *The Jews and Modern Capitalism*. Translated by M. Epstein. 1951. Reprint. New Brunswick, N.J.: Transaction Books, 1982.

Stuckey, Charles F., ed. *Toulouse-Lautrec: Paintings*. Chicago: Art Institute, n.d.

Sylvester, David. *Magritte*. London: Lund Humphries, 1969.

Titterton, W. R. *From Theatre to Music Hall*. London: Stephen Swift, 1912.

Torczyner, Harry. *Magritte: The True Art of Painting*. London: Thames and Hudson, 1979.

Tozer, Jane, and Sarah Levitt. *Fabric of Society: A Century of People and Their Clothes, 1770–1870*. Carno: Laura Ashley, 1983.

Traies, Jane. "Jones and the Working Girl: Class Marginality in Music-Hall Song, 1860–1900." In *Music Hall: Performance and Style*, edited by J. S. Bratton, pp. 23–48. Milton Keynes: Open University Press, 1986.

Tucholsky, Kurt. *Deutschland, Deutschland über Alles*. Photographs assembled by John Heartfield. Translated by Anne Halley. Amherst: University of Massachusetts Press, 1972.

Vicinus, Martha. *The Industrial Muse: A Study of Nineteenth Century British Working-Class Literature*. New York: Barnes & Noble, 1974.

Walkley, Christine, and Vanda Foster. *Crinolines and Crimping Irons. Victorian Clothes: How They Were Cleaned and Cared For*. London: Peter Owen, 1985.

Waugh, Nora. *The Cut of Men's Clothes, 1600–1900*. London: Faber, 1964.

Weber, Eugen. *France, Fin de Siècle*. Cambridge, Mass.: Belknap Press, 1986.

Welty, Eudora. *The Eye of the Story: Selected Essays and Reviews*. New York: Random House, 1977.

Whitbourn, Frank. *Mr Lock of St James's Street*. London: Heinemann, 1971.

Whiteing, Richard. *Paris of To-day*. New York: The Century Co., 1900.

Whitford, Frank. *Bauhaus*. London: Thames and Hudson, 1985.

Wiener, Martin J. *English Culture and the Decline of the Industrial Spirit, 1850–1980*. Cambridge: Cambridge University Press, 1981.

Wilcox, R. Turner. *The Mode in Costume*. New York: Scribner's, 1958.

Willett, John. *Art and Politics in the Weimar Period: The New Sobriety, 1917–1933*. New York: Pantheon Books, 1978.

———. *The Weimar Years: A Culture Cut Short*. New York: Abbeville Press, 1984.

Wilmut, Roger. *Kindly Leave the Stage! The Story of Variety, 1919–1960*. London: Methuen, 1985.

Wilson, Elizabeth. *Adorned in Dreams: Fashion and Modernity*. London: Virago Press, 1985.

Wilson, Elizabeth, and Lou Taylor. *Through the Looking Glass: A History of Dress from 1860 to the Present Day*. London: BBC Books, 1989.

# INDEX

Library of Congress Cataloging-in-Publication Data

Robinson, Fred, 1942–

   The man in the bowler hat : his history and iconography /

by Fred Miller Robinson.

      p.   cm.

   Includes bibliographical references and index.

   ISBN 0-8078-2073-3

   1. Hats—History.   2. Hats—Europe—History.   3. Europe—Social

life and customs.   4. Costume—Symbolic aspects.   I. Title.

GT2110.R63    1993

391'.43—dc20                                   92-37188

                                        CIP